ASA STUDIES

General Editor: Edwin Ardener

2

Marxist Analyses and
Social Anthropology

ASA STUDIES

Marxist Analyses and Social Anthropology

Edited by
Maurice Bloch

MALABY PRESS LONDON

First published in 1975
by Malaby Press Limited
Aldine House, 26 Albemarle Street, London W1X 4QY

This book has been set in 11 on 12 point Times New Roman
and was printed by The Aldine Press,
Letchworth, Herts

ISBN 0 460 14003 5

Contents

General Editor's Note

ASA Studies is a new series largely based upon selected sessions of the special Decennial Conference of the Association of Social Anthropologists of the Commonwealth, entitled, 'New Directions in Social Anthropology', and held at St John's College, Oxford, 4–11 July 1973.

The last special conference had taken place at Jesus College, Cambridge, in 1963, and a preliminary word should be said about it, to provide a suitable perspective. Those who convened it had, as they later wrote, two main purposes in mind: to provide a 'joint, organized stock-taking' between British and American social anthropologists, and to reflect 'the problems and views of a younger generation of anthropologists'. It was pointed out that between 1946 and 1962 the Association of Social Anthropologists had increased its membership from under a score to over one hundred and fifty. In retrospect, the 1963 Cambridge Conference can be seen to represent on the one hand a kind of coming-of-age of the ASA as an organization (in its rather awkward seventeenth year) and, on the other, an awareness of changes to come in the aims, interests, and personnel of the formerly close-knit British branch of the subject. The four volumes that emerged from that Conference were entitled *The Relevance of Models for Social Anthropology, Political Systems and the Distribution of Power, Anthropological Approaches to the Study of Religion*, and *The Social Anthropology of Complex Societies* (published by Tavistock, 1964–6) each with a general Introduction by Max Gluckman and Fred Eggan, from which my quotations here and later come.

It was that occasion which provided the base-line for the 1973 Decennial Conference. The ASA committee, under the Chairmanship of Professor Meyer Fortes, wished the 1973 Conference to play the same kind of role in its period as the previous one had done in its own time. The task was, however, quite complicated. The membership of one hundred and fifty or so of ten years before had now risen to several hundreds, while the Conference was this time to be international, not merely Anglo-American. Furthermore, although 'new directions' were to be emphasized as far as possible, subjects which had in recent years been covered by the regular annual ASA conferences (and thus published), or were already scheduled for the future, were to be excluded. Eventually the Committee chose eleven topics, each to be covered in a half-day session, and invited a convener to organize each of them.

Finally, the Conference was placed by the Committee under my general convenership. This, I should emphasize, was seen as largely an organizational task, which I have been invited to continue here as General Editor of these volumes. The session-conveners had a free hand in the choice of contributors on their topics, within certain limits of numbers and finance, and each session-convener decided the structure of his own half-day session.

An immediate difference between this conference and the 1963 one lies in this much looser 'federal' structure. The Committee were of the opinion that all sessions should be consecutive, so that all could be attended by the participants despite the wide range of topics covered. These were: Social Anthropology and Ethology (Robin Fox), Social Anthropology and Psychology (Esther Goody), Social Anthropology and Development (Peter Lloyd), Social Anthropology and Oral and Literary Sources (Ravindra Jain), Structuralism (Nur Yalman), Marxist Analysis (Maurice Bloch), Mathematical Analysis (Clyde Mitchell), Transactions (Bruce Kapferer), Systems of Thought (Edwin Ardener), The Analysis of Symbolism (Roy Willis), and Problems of Fieldwork (Julian Pitt-Rivers). The Conference ended with general statements from the Chairman (Professor Meyer Fortes), Professor Raymond Firth, Professor R. F. Salisbury, and Dr Ralph Grillo. There were daily attendances of two hundred and fifty or more, including a large international group of guests and observers from, for example, France, Germany, the United States, Sweden, South America, Denmark, Holland, Israel, and Japan, as well as very many from the countries of Commonwealth tradition from which the Association draws its main membership. Most senior members in the British profession were able to attend part, at least, of the sessions, and many made contributions from the floor. In addition, it was frequently pointed out that there were present on this occasion more generations of British social anthropologists than at any Association meeting in the past: from recent graduates to founding members of the modern subject. The uniqueness of this occasion was underlined by the fact that this turned out, sadly, to be the last public appearance before his colleagues of the Life President, Professor Sir Edward Evans-Pritchard, who opened the sessions of the second day.

No one can make an easy assessment of the intellectual impact of this conference. A look back on the 1963 gathering may offer us some lessons. While that ASA conference does in retrospect seem to mark the close of one period of social anthropology, its 'new approaches' turned out to hint only remotely at the kinds of controversies that were actually to fill the next decade. All that can be safely said without adding fresh controversy is that controversy did become commonplace, while France, hardly mentioned by the 1963 conveners, frequently supplanted Britain or the United States as a source of new or fashionable theory. On the whole, the topics and styles of the 1963 contributors did not necessarily or entirely prefigure the immediate future, although a number of them were important in it. The joint conveners wrote 'that the essays . . . reflect the feeling of their younger colleagues', and that they favoured 'clarification, the breaking down, and the refinement, of standard concepts, together with the closer specification of narrower social contexts . . .' That remained in part true, but the very process of clarification was changing the view that social anthropologists had of their subject, in ways that 1963 did not directly express. Things in fact moved more quickly, some thought more interestingly, other though more hastily (many doubted less surely) than they had been doing.

It is certainly doubtful then whether the 1973 Conference will turn out to be more predictive of 'new directions' than the last was of 'new approaches'. It should best be regarded as the record of a particular moment, with no exaggerated aims. In this respect the Conference was of its age. Its structure and its topics were approached perhaps with a little more reserve, even scepticism, than greeted 1963. For some the range of topics and their 'interdisciplinary' appearance seemed to represent a dispersal of academic energy. For some the balance appeared to have moved in the direction of various 'ideological' or 'transactional' analyses, and away from more tried methods. For others, on the contrary, the chosen topics were already ageing or old and did not reflect the most promising lines for the future. For still others the occasion appeared merely as a useful tribal rite of little intellectual significance. A women's session met amicably outside the official programme. Some radical leaflets were circulated. The third world now figured as a political as well as an academic subject. The historical period at least (it may well be thought in 1983) was unmistakable.

But, taking as neutral a view as possible, it is quite reasonable to say that, by contingency as well as by design, the volumes published in this series, which are based on a selection of the sessions, represent a number of subjects developed in social anthropology either relatively newly, or in greater depth, or with greater insight, over the last decade. This is certainly true of the first three titles: *Biosocial Anthropology, Marxist Analyses and Social Anthropology*, and *The Interpretation of Symbolism*; which will be followed shortly by *Text and Context, Transaction and Meaning, Numerical Techniques*, and *Structuralism*. All these titles represent recognized and authoritative developments in the current repertoire of social anthropology, which have grown from deep roots in the subject over more than one generation. Although not every social anthropologist in this more specialized age will be competent in or even sympathetic to all of them (they incidentally straddle several theoretical divides), they reflect a number of characteristic concerns in the subject today which, taken together with the regular annual series of ASA publications, suggest that social anthropology still retains its traditional curiosity and adventurousness—a feature emphasized by the number of younger contributors represented. Even a 'Decennial Conference' can do no more than that.

The present volume is based on a session convened on 7 July 1973. Editors have been free to seek amendments or additions to the papers in the sessions they convened, and to shape their volumes as they saw fit.

The ASA would like to thank warmly the President and Fellows of St John's College, Oxford, and the Warden of Rhodes House, Oxford, for providing the home for the Conference, and the staff of both for their willing assistance. It records its deep gratitude to the Wenner-Gren and H. F. Guggenheim Foundations for their welcome financial help. The major convening task was shared with me by Shirley Ardener, who found smooth solutions to many problems. In addition, the practical arrangements would have been impossibly complicated without the help of Nigel Barley, Martin Cantor, Christine Cooper, Robert Heath, Joy Hendry, John Mathias, David Price, Matt Schaffer, and Drid Williams, all then mostly graduate students of the Oxford University Institute of Social Anthropology.

As General Editor, I should like to acknowledge the role of the present chairman of the ASA, Dr Jean La Fontaine, and her Committee, in establishing this series.

© Edwin Ardener 1975

E. W. A.

Introduction

The committee set up by the Association of Social Anthropologists to organize the decennial conference in Oxford on New Directions in Social Anthropology decided that one of the topics it should consider was the place and the influence of marxist theories in anthropology. The reason for this decision was the renewed interest in fundamental marxist concerns on the part of many British anthropologists and especially among their students. This renewal of interest can be directly traced to the influence of two tendencies in French anthropology which caused much interest and even enthusiasm in Britain. The first of these tendencies goes back to the reanalysis of the basic tenets of marxist thought in the work of Althusser. Of special relevance was the fact that Althusser insisted on the relevance of marxism for societies other than those dominated by the capitalist mode of production. As a result several writers, such as Pierre-Philippe Rey and E. Balibar, began to reconsider some of the data traditionally studied by social anthropologists in the light of this revivified marxism. Among this group of writers the best known to the English-speaking anthropologists is Emmanuel Terray, partly because of the interest aroused by the translation of his book *Marxism and 'Primitive' Societies*, and partly because his studies concern a part of the world, West Africa, where so much of the work of British anthropology has been concentrated. The Association was therefore extremely fortunate when he agreed to accept an invitation and present the paper translated here. In it Terray not only outlines his position and the evolution of his position since *Marxism and 'Primitive' Societies* but also gives a remarkable study of the light his point of view throws on the social history of a particular example. The clarity and consistency of his analysis seem to me admirable; not only is his paper a major contribution to the science of history but also, and unlike so many anthropologists, he leaves us in no doubt where he stands. He offers us tools for other analyses, the implications of which he is fully aware of, and it is because of this that they can be accepted or rejected by others with complete knowledge of what they are doing. This is a pleasant change in a subject where the ideological implications of so many theories and concepts are unclear, both to their inventors and to those who use them.

The other French influence which gave new strength to British marxist studies in anthropology is closely allied to the development of the theories of culture of Claude Lévi-Strauss, but in other hands than his. Foremost among the scientists who have combined Marx with the theories of the French structuralists is Maurice Godelier. It was therefore essential for him to be willing to attend our conference. He not only came but made an essential contribution concerning what it meant to be a marxist anthropologist in 1973. The article presented in this volume makes most of the points he stressed then, concerning the similar functions different institutions can perform in the mode of production in different societies, the political meaning of the task of reconstructing intellectually the causal relations in various pre-capitalist systems, and generally the question of what is ideology in classless societies. The article we have here discusses these points in more detail than was possible during the short time at our disposal during the conference. It is particularly valuable in that it illustrates Godelier's position applied to a set of problems with which anthropologists have been much concerned: the kinship systems of the Australian Aborigines. This particular example enables him to suggest the lines of analysis he has used and intends to use for other studies on other societies such as the Inca state and the pygmies of the Ituri forest.

Godelier's paper also contains a vigorous attack on what he calls empiricism: unconsciously attaching functional labels to the phenomena studied as though these functional attributions came from the data themselves. It is clear that Godelier is directing his criticism at work which includes many aspects of the studies of British social anthropologists. A defence of this position is found in the paper by Professor Sir Raymond Firth, which we were very fortunate to be able to reprint here. In a way Godelier and he represent two sides of a dialogue which both are anxious to maintain.

Firth's paper originally consisted of a lecture delivered at the British Academy to honour the memory of A. R. Radcliffe-Brown and was sponsored by the Association. It was delivered before the conference took place but its content was present in the minds of several of the contributors. As the title indicates, Firth is sympathetic to Marx's theories, though not unsceptical. His lecture explains well why Marx's work had been so little referred to by social anthropologists. Some of his criticism of Marx, especially that relating to the specific aspects of the evolutionary scheme inherited from Morgan, would be endorsed by the most 'marxist' of the contributors, though this is not necessarily true of all these criticisms. (For example, I have argued that some aspects of Marx's notion of property are analytically more fruitful than the concept of rights.) The difference between Firth and the marxist is more at the level of the relationship between theory, data, and practice. Firth is arguing for a science where new data will in the end direct theory; Godelier and the other contributors are starting from certain postulates about the notion of society whose purpose is to 'show up', so to speak, exploitative social systems. The study of other societies will modify the view of how basic relationships can manifest themselves, but will not challenge the postulates, since they are seen as preceding subjective perception. Put in this way, the contrast between the two views is stark but in practice the contrast is much less marked. This is so for two reasons. The criticism which marxists and others would make of empiricism is not so much that it is wrong but that it is impossible; this means that there are theoretical postulates present in the work of all social anthropologists and that these have political significance. For example, Evans-Pritchard's denial of the legitimacy of the pursuit of laws in social science implies *laissez-faire* politics and support for the *status quo*. Now, most social anthropologists do not take this view, and, consciously or unconsciously, they have absorbed much of marxism and materialism. For example, Terray notes 'marxist' elements in the work of Gluckman and Fortes, while Godelier comments on them in the work of Firth himself. The difference seems, therefore, to stem from the theoretical eclecticism underlying empiricism rather than reflecting a total break.

The other reason why there is less of a break between the empiricists and the marxists than would at first appear is that the monolithic form which has until recently characterized marxism, whether in science or in world politics, has clearly broken down. The essays in this book are proof enough of this, since several 'marxist' contributors criticize each other, either directly or by implication. This has meant, as Firth notes, that we are much less sure of ourselves. The marxist history of mankind still needs writing; it was not given ready-made once and for all. I think the spirit of inquiry and the willingness to be found wrong by the facts which Firth wishes for will be seen to be present in many of the contributions to this volume.

The same fundamental issue is raised in the paper by Stephan Feuchtwang, but specifically applied to the problems of the study of religion. Feuchtwang applies critically Althusser's development of the notion of ideology. In doing this, he contrasts his attitude with that of other anthropologists who, because they do not draw a sharp distinction between two unlike and incompatible types of data, the material and the ideal, see the investigation of religion as being placed uncomfortably and illogically somewhere between them. This position is the result of the reluctance of many anthropologists to treat religious beliefs as illusions, albeit socially powerful illusions, and they consequently allow these illusions a volition of their own. The intermediary position taken by the anthropologist who is willing neither to say that he believes in the reality of the supernatural nor to accept the implications of dis-belief leads to the ironical result that he finds himself giving credence not only to the precepts of one religion, as does the believer, but of all religions. Feuchtwang applies his more rigorous approach to aspects of the religion of late imperial China, closely relating it to the structures of domination in that period, of which he gives us a fascinating and thought-provoking sketch.

Introduction

The papers by Jonathan Friedman and myself are concerned with similar problems centred on the relationship between economic base and other aspects of culture and society. Both the papers, especially the one by Friedman, consider this relationship in a historical context, stressing how different social systems are transformations of one another. These transformations are driven by changes in the economic base, but no *direct* relationship is seen between base and superstructure. Friedman studies the historical transformation of a group of societies on the southern Chinese cultural boundary and considers them all as a set of transformations in varying ecological conditions. He pays special attention to the anthropologically famous Kachin of Highland Burma, explaining the changes in their political structure within a general marxist theory. Of particular interest is Friedman's integration of changes in the religious system into his overall scheme. This work illustrates some of the points made both by Feuchtwang and by Godelier, especially the latter's insistence that the dominant structure in a society cannot be known simply by its form.

A concern of Friedman is the mystification of the real nature of production, the result of human work, in particular cultural systems. This is also a central theme in my own paper, which illustrates the difference in this respect of two Malagasy societies: one which misrepresents production as though this process was due simply to ancestral lands, and another which, because of different technical and ecological conditions and the absence of slavery, represents production accurately in terms of labour. The effect of these different ways of representing production for the historical transformations of kinship is explained.

Joel Kahn's paper deals with a technologically more advanced type of production. He considers the production of metal goods by small-scale blacksmiths in West Sumatra in a similar theoretical framework to that used in other parts of this book, but the involvement of these blacksmiths in world capitalism makes him consider their mode of production as caught in the contradiction between capitalism and traditional organization. This contradiction is, of course, of foremost importance for the understanding of much of the Third World today. It is here extremely well documented in a specific instance. What is particularly striking in this paper is how well it reveals the full significance of the combination of a genuine historical and materialist method. Not only are the facts accounted for unambiguously but he shows how such an analysis implies inescapably an exposure of a system of exploitation.

MAURICE BLOCH

© Maurice Bloch 1975

Note on References

Numerous editions and impressions of the various English translations of the works of Marx and Engels (particularly the first volume of *Capital*) have appeared at different dates under the imprint of Russian, British, and American publishers. Since even some of those which are textually identical have been found to show differences in pagination, an attempt to standardize the references given by contributors to the present volume had to be abandoned, but as far as possible fuller bibliographical information has been supplied (e.g. dates of first German and/or English publication, names of editors and translators) to assist the reader in identifying and locating the passages cited.

EMPIRICISM AND
HISTORICAL MATERIALISM

Maurice Godelier

Modes of Production, Kinship, and Demographic Structures

Translated by Kate Young and Felicity Edholm

This chapter [1] is intended to present with as much clarity and brevity as possible some theoretical considerations of the problem on the relationship between mode of production, kinship relations, family organization, and demographic structures. The aim is above all methodological, and its basic source is the recent work of Aram Yengoyan (1968a, b; 1970; 1972a, b) concerning the section and subsection systems of the Australian Aborigines. A complete analysis of these societies is not attempted here, still less a comparison, statistical or otherwise, of the various forms of economic and social organization found among hunting and gathering peoples about which we have valid information. What is attempted is a contribution to the study of the problem of the 'structural causality' of the economy: the effect of relations of production at a given level of development of the productive forces, that is to say the mode of production, on other levels of social organization (see Godelier 1973: foreword and Ch. 1).

Two preliminary points should be made. The family is not, contrary to what some demographers and sociologists still think, the basic unit, or the cell of society, nor is it, as the evolutionary anthropologist Julian Steward (1951) argues,[2] the first step in the evolution of human society, nor even the first 'level of integration' of society. A family cannot exist and reproduce itself through the generations independently of other families (Lévi-Strauss 1960: 278). This interdependence is imposed, in the first place, by the universal existence of the incest prohibition and the rule of exogamy which accompanies it, whatever its forms or the range of its application may be. The internal structure of a family presupposes from the first the existence of social rules regulating forms of marriage, filiation, and residence, which are required for the legitimate existence of any family and which determine some aspects of the 'developmental cycle' (Goody 1972: 22, 28; Fortes 1958). These social rules, together with the terms which describe relations of consanguinity, alliance, etc., make up the tangible aspect of what, in an empirical and unrigorous fashion, is called kinship.

3

In order, however, to explain why, within a given society, a type of family organization functions as part of the organization of production and/or consumption, or why it does not function in this way, or why it does so only partially, we must go beyond these tangible aspects of kinship relationships and also examine the social conditions of production, the material means of social existence. It is these social conditions which determine the role of the domestic group in the social process of production, the presence or absence of a social division of labour existing beyond the limits of the domestic group and of local communities (see Kula 1972). It is these social conditions which also determine the presence or absence of slaves or other types of dependants within the domestic groups. These aspects of the function of family groups depend on the nature of the social relations of production. In other words, the internal structure of the type of family 'appears' to depend on at least two sets of prerequisite social conditions: kinship relations and relations of production. This is never more than an empirical and provisional formulation which will be untenable or will at least present insoluble problems when we come to analyse societies in which kinship relations take on directly, from within, the function of relations of production. In this case it is difficult to contrast economy and kinship as though they were two 'institutions' with different functions. One can already see here some of the dangerous assumptions of the empiricist method. On the one hand, institutions are defined by their apparent functions, and, on the other, it is presumed that distinct institutions are necessary to carry out distinct functions. The epistemological consequences of such assumptions are critical because, as we shall see in greater detail, they preclude the construction of a rigorous theory of 'structural causality' of the infrastructure.

Our second preliminary point is concerned with demographic structures. These structures are not a *primum movens* but rather the combined result of the action of several 'deeper' structural levels, of a hierarchy of causes, the most important of which is again the mode of production; that is to say the productive forces and the nature of the social relations of production which make up the infrastructure of the society. Having noted this, the significance of the fact that demography is the 'synthetic' result of the action of several structural levels, of a combination of causes of varying importance, must be analysed further. It means (and it is in this that the complexity of the analysis of the demographic structures lies) that every type of social relations, each structural level, is subject to the functioning and reproduction over time of specific demographic conditions. The population of a society is the synthetic result of the combined action of these specific demographic constraints which affect it differently at each level.[3] The combined effect of these constraints is that every demographic structure has a causal effect on the functioning and the evolution of societies. The work of Aram Yengoyan on the demographic conditions necessary for the working of the Australian kinship systems serves as an example which shows how demography is, at one and the same time, cause and effect; i.e. the condition of the functioning and of the reproduction through time of economic and social structures. By way of example we may take the case of the Kamilaroi of New South Wales as described by Elkin (1967: 162).[4] They have a section system and each section has a different name.

Diagram of the Kamilaroi Marriage System

= links the sections which practise marriage exchange

⌐ arrows link the sections of mother and child

This diagram tells us that a man from Kambu section will marry a woman from Mari section and that their children will be Kabi. A Kabi man will marry an Ipai woman and their child will be Kambu. If the wife of a Mari man is Kambu, their child is Ipai, and this child then marries a Kabi woman and their child will be Mari. It will be seen that all Kamilaroi belong to a number of kinship categories. If I am Kambu, my wife is Mari, my son is Kabi; his wife is Ipai and my grandson belongs to my section. Equally, since I am Kambu, my mother is Ipai and my father Kabi; my mother's brother, like my mother, is Ipai and his children are Mari since he married a Kabi. My father's sister is Kabi and her children are also Mari. In the Mari section are all my patrilateral and matrilateral cross-cousins and this is the section to which my potential wives belong.

The same principles that apply to section systems also apply to sub-section systems but in their case Ego's kinsmen are divided into 8 groups instead of 4. This produces a division between the category cross-cousins and their children. Marriage with a first-degree cross-cousin is prohibited but it is prescribed with a second-degree cross-cousin, i.e. MMBD or FFZSD. The diagram below, following Elkin (1967: 168), shows the working of a subsection system of a tribe from East Kimberley.

Diagram of a Subsection System in East Kimberley

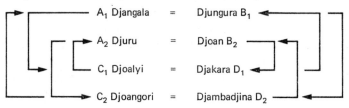

The arrows link the subsections of a mother and her child

5

If I am A_1, my cross-cousin is B_2 but the daughter of the cross-cousin of my mother belongs to B_1, that is the subsection into which I can marry, etc. Here we have the characteristics of the so-called Aranda system which were extensively analysed by Claude Lévi-Strauss in *The Elementary Structures of Kinship*. Aram Yengoyan tried to determine mathematically what the total population of a tribe which is divided into 10 local groups (hordes or bands), each occupying a defined territory, has to be to enable a kinship system of subsections to function so that all men of 25, the marriageable age, can find a wife of about 15 or more within the subsection prescribed for him. Each man should have a choice of about 25 women who satisfy these conditions. Yengoyan (1968a: 194–8) shows that the total population has to be 1,070 individuals equally divided between the two sexes.[5] He also shows that if the total population were to fall much lower than this, new types of marriage, including marriage alliances normally forbidden, would either appear or develop in an exceptional way and produce new contradictions and social conflicts within society. Such a population decrease might be caused by epidemics, famines following an exceptional drought, the worsening of ecological and economic conditions after European conquest, and the introduction, for example, of extensive stock grazing which changes the animal and vegetable environment and upsets the balance of the resources of hunters and gatherers. The 'action' on kinship relations of the change in the material base of the societies thus leads first to a modification of marriage practices, but this modification takes place only if the transformations of the material base result in a lowering of the total population below the level compatible with the normal reproduction of the kinship system.

Two theoretical conclusions not considered by Yengoyan may be drawn from this analysis. First, it shows clearly that changes in the material base do not uniformly affect kinship relations—either the diverse elements which compose them or the discrete spheres of action which they organize. Marriage practices are the first part of the system that is modified. This may produce changes in residence, but in the two cases above rules of filiation remained intact. This confirms Morgan's findings: relationships of consanguinity change less quickly than those of alliance[6] and, since modifications in the system of alliance are immediately reflected in the family, new types of family appear at the same time as do new alliance rules.

Second, the action of a change in the conditions of production on the most dynamic element of kinship relations, alliance, is only possible if these changes have previously upset the demographic conditions necessary for the reproduction of the kinship system. The demographic constraints internal to kinship relations thus constitute a necessary mediation for transformations of the material base to affect alliance relations.

These two analyses reveal 'relations of order' existing among diverse structural elements of society. These relations of order ensure that the determination by the material base is mediated by unintentional objective properties of the other levels, and produce differentiated, heterogeneous effects in the conditions of reproduction of these levels. It could be said that before reaching such general, theoretical conclusions we should at first ensure that Yengoyan's findings are correct. They have, in fact, been shown to be right on two occasions. His findings have been tested against demographic data collected by anthropologists working in subsection systems, and not only were they proved correct but they have removed an apparent contradiction or at least severe disagreements concerning the data. Among the Walbiri, a central desert group studied by Meggitt in 1954, the whole population was then approximately 1,400, that is to say more than the 1,070 necessary for the normal functioning of the system. As could be expected from Yengoyan's calculations, 91·6 per cent of marriages followed the rule of preferential marriage with the second-degree matrilateral cross-cousin (Meggitt 1962, 1965, 1968). By contrast, among the Angula of the Gulf of Carpentaria, studied by Mary Reay in 1958–9, only 57·95 per cent of marriages followed the rules, and this was in a group which, as a result of the drastic effects of contact with Europeans, numbered only 288 individuals (Reay 1962).

In a more recent work, Yengoyan (1972a) has given supplementary proof of the accuracy of his analyses by showing the effect of the reversal since 1950 of the constant decline in aboriginal population which started in 1788 following the first contact with Europeans and continued right through until the 1930s. Since then, as a result of sedenterization in reservations (due to more or less disguised compulsion on the part of missions and government—see Jones 1965, 1970), where they have had to rely on government hand-outs, change of diet, increase in birth frequency (due to settlement), and the drop in infant mortality (due to increasing control of epidemics and diseases), the population has begun to rise sharply, so that today the birth rate is almost 3·5 per cent per annum. This has resulted in the groups that have not lost their essential tribal structure, such as the Pitjandjara, gradually reactivating their former marriage rules and intensifying ceremonial practices (Yengoyan 1970). This politico-religious phenomenon expresses of course the desire of these groups to reaffirm their cultural identity and to resist the destructive pressures of the process of domination and acculturation they have undergone, which has deprived them of their land and subjected their ancient religious and political practices to a systematic process of erosion and destruction.

We should not forget, however, that this reactivation of the traditional kinship system in its formal aspect only occurred when the demographic conditions permitted it, at a time when the traditional economic infrastructure was not just gravely dislocated and in the process of rapid collapse (as it had been during the first stages of contact), but had

7

already been largely replaced by a new system in which the subsistence of the group was assured more and more by the men's wage-labour, and when hunting and gathering had become marginal activities restricted to 'high days and holidays'.[7] The economic importance of women is considerably reduced and this results in a reduction in the number of polygamous marriages, since additional wives, instead of being a source of supplementary resources, simply represent increased outlay (Rose 1965). These new economic relations now provide the material resources necessary for an intensification of ritual life beyond the limits which the old aboriginal way of life had permitted. The ceremonies are now more numerous and the number of participants is greater. Before the arrival of the Europeans it was very rarely that hunting and gathering groups had food resources sufficient for 200 or more people for two or three weeks at their disposal.

Thus at the very moment when the new economic system provides the material and demographic conditions for a return to formal rules of kinship and to religious and ritual practices, and encourages an intensification of these practices as a reaction to economic, political, and cultural oppression and alienation, the function of these relations, as relations of production implicit in the old system, is progressively disappearing. Although the old system starts up again and retains its form, it changes in its functions. It no longer functions as a system of relations of production, and at the same time its other political and religious functions also change in meaning and importance. Henceforth the aborigines have another form of division of labour and are subject to relations of production which have nothing to do with their sections and subsections and which are distinct from them. In order fully to understand the significance of this transformation we must go backwards to discover and explain the 'internal' link which existed in aboriginal society between the social conditions of production and the presence and functioning of sections and subsections. Here again we turn to the work of Yengoyan as well as to that of Meggitt, Hiatt, Gould, Rose, and others.

Yengoyan, basing himself on the work of Davidson (1928), Radcliffe-Brown (1930–1), Tindale (1940, 1953), Elkin (1964), and others has tried to discover whether a statistical correlation exists that would express a functional relationship between the demographic composition of the various Australian tribes, the size of their territory, their population density, and, above all, the presence or absence of moieties, sections, and subsections. His starting-point is the fact that they are hunters and gatherers, that is to say that their economy corresponds to a level of development of the productive forces which does not transform nature and where productivity depends above all on variations in ecological conditions. By 1940 Tindale had already noted that the size of tribal territories varied in inverse proportion to the amount of rain remaining on the ground after evaporation. In 1952 Birdsell established for a sample of 123 tribes a positive correlation (0·8) between rainfall and population density. The rain determines the amount of vegetation and, since vegetation is the first link in the trophic chain, it also regulates the abundance of animal life (Birdsell 1953, 1958, 1970). Man, as a hunter and gatherer, is at the top of the trophic chain and exploiting, as he does, all the available vegetable and animal resources, is dependent on their ecological conditions of reproduction.

Yengoyan goes further than Birdsell and attempts to account for the distribution of the various kinship systems. He has been able to show the existence of a triple correlation between the increasing aridity of the environment as one goes from the humid coasts of Australia to the desert interior and the accompanying scarcity and increasing dispersion of resources and:

1 an increasing size of tribal territories;
2 a progressive increase in the size of tribal groups and a growing necessity for the local bands of which they are composed to increase their mobility, their nomadism, and hence their separation in time and space;
3 a progressive increase in the number of social divisions, moieties (2), sections (4), subsections (8).

How can we account for the presence of more and more internally diversified and complex kinship systems as we go further into the desert interior of Australia? To do this satisfactorily we must bear in mind an essential property of these complex systems; that multiplication of social divisions makes the network of rights and duties among groups and the individuals of which they consist more complex, thus intensifying and extending social reciprocity and ensuring greater flexibility in social organization.

Given the level of productive forces and the nature of the techniques of production in the widest sense of the term, the more arid the ecological environment, the more the local groups, the hordes, consisting of several related nuclear families, must move over an ever wider area, leaving the individuals separated one from another by ever greater distances for ever longer periods of time. In these areas the risk of a catastrophic failure of available vegetable and animal resources due to drought is also greater, making it essential for the short- or long-term survival of groups that they have a guaranteed right of reciprocal access to more favoured neighbouring lands occupied by adjacent local groups. A right which guarantees reciprocal access by each local group to the territory of other groups implies reciprocal social relations, individual or collective, and implies access to the material conditions of production. For hunters and gatherers these are the land, which following Marx's phrase is a 'primitive larder' as well as 'the primitive tool-house of their means of labour' (1970, Vol. I: 179). Now, we see section and subsection systems functioning internally as social relations of production and responding to the constraints of flexibility and reciprocity

9

which the very conditions of production impose on them. This is precisely the conclusion that Yengoyan reached in his analysis, although he does not use the term relations of production:

> It is thus suggested that the ability of local populations to survive under rigorous environmental conditions requires a certain flexibility in local organisation which allows for maximum mobility of exploiting groups and a means of linking vast numbers of individuals and groups through sections and subsections into a network which permits small mobile units to expand and contract under varying experimental conditions. Consequently one of the functions of sections and subsections may have been an economic factor in allowing populations to 'insure' a vast territorial domain from non-tribal groups, as well as 'insuring' each local group's future against economic hardship by permitting access into more favorable environments (Yengoyan 1968a).

We are here clearly dealing with kinship relations that function simultaneously as infrastructure and superstructure. In effect they control the access of groups and individuals to the conditions of production and to resources, they regulate marriages (when demographic conditions permit), they provide the social framework of politico-ritual activity but they also function as an ideology, as a symbolic code for expressing relations between men, and between men and nature.

This last aspect of the function of sections should be described in more detail since it provides evidence of great importance for the elaboration of a scientific theory of ideology. It will also enable us to evaluate critically the contribution of Lévi-Strauss's work on totemism, on mythology, and more generally on the evidence for and the workings of what he has called 'the savage mind'. To clarify this aspect we shall use the findings of the linguist G. C. von Brandenstein (1970) concerning the names of the four sections of the Kariera of Western Australia, who provide the classic example of a section system.

The Kariera are divided into named sections:

Pannaga   : Purungu
Karimarra : Palt'arri

The analysis of the etymology of these terms and their semantic field, together with that of the totemic affiliations associated with each of these sections, shows that all the creatures of nature, man included, are divided according to the double opposition:

horizontal	cold-blooded (temperament) or abstract (element)
	hot-blooded (temperament) or concrete (element)
vertical	active | passive

If we superimpose these two oppositions, we obtain four divisions:

active / cold-blooded / abstract	passive / cold-blooded / abstract
active / hot-blooded / concrete	passive / hot-blooded / concrete

To illustrate how these oppositions work in practice for classifying all creatures in nature, including man, we will put together in the table overleaf some of Von Brandenstein's material. This diagram clearly shows how the division into sections provides an organizing scheme for the Australians' symbolic representation of the world and of its immanent order. The same principles and the same divisions order nature and society, dividing human beings and all natural creatures into the same categories; nature appears as an enlarged image of society, as its continuation.

A corresponding practice is based on this ideology. If certain natural species, objects, and so on belong to the same section as certain men, it is because they all have something in common, because they are 'like each other', because they identify themselves in opposition to other men and other beings who belong to other sections. It is here that the problem of totemism arises, but this would take us beyond the scope of this article. The essential point to note is that because human beings share something in common with all the other real or imaginary beings who belong their section, they have certain special duties towards them and special rights over them. For example, only the men of Palt'arri can perform the rites which allow a person to 'make a baby' or to multiply kangaroos, because they 'belong' to the same section as sperm in general and kangaroo sperm in particular. The Karimarra, who are rainmakers, can make themselves heard by the thunder, the sun, and so on, which belong to the same section as they do. In this way the function and importance of each section in daily ritual practice or in ceremonial practice are established. It is most noteworthy that all these ritual activities constitute a true form of *symbolic labour* working on the contradictions of social practice and on the imaginary beings who control the conditions of reproduction of both nature and society and therefore of the world.[8] However, and this is fundamental, for the world-order to reproduce itself and for the symbolic labour of each section to be fully efficacious, all the sections must fulfil their own allotted tasks. In this way the survival of each and every one depends not only on his own efforts but on those of all others. The symbolic reproduction of the world-order depends on the reciprocal and generalized cooperation of all individuals within the framework of the section system. This cooperation is thus formally identical to the generalized and reciprocal cooperation which exists between sections within the relations of production. It reproduces in the field of symbolic and ideological practice the cooperation of the social process of production. Here one could start a critical and fruitful discussion of Lévi-Strauss's thesis concerning mythical thought because, while it is clear that there is no symbolic practice without the activity of the human mind, it is also

11

System of Sections and Totemic Affiliations of the Kariera

cold-blooded / with scales / abstract

	Active / with clear and fluid blood / Sun — PANNAGA	Passive / with dark, thick blood / lazy / Shade — PURUNGU
Man	tall wild quick, busy, slim, nervous, muscular tough, dry cough	big, massive amiable, sweet slow, lazy, fat, plump flaccid, liquid sweat, vomit, mucus, saliva
Animals	wild iguana	lazy iguana wild turkey
Plants		fruits seeds of wild plants
Elements & Objects	cold moon	dew, sea, salt water damp heat daylight

hot-blooded / furry / concrete

	Active / with clear and fluid blood / Sun — KARIMARRA	Passive / with dark, thick blood / lazy / Shade — PALT'ARRI
Man	bringer of discord, bad character wild, ferocious rainmaker	pliant, amiable, pleasant baby child sperm
Animals	kangaroo of the plains	kangaroo of the hills kangaroo sperm
Plants		
Elements & Objects	fire, drought, lightning, thunder, cyclone sun, hot	calm air calm water, clear pool, drinkable water moon / temperate

equally clear that the myth-producing mind is not concerned simply with thinking about itself and producing a fantastic representation of its own internal architecture. Beyond the structural analysis of the form of mythical discourse and the question 'how do myths speak?' lies the question 'what do myths speak about?' The answer to this is neither 'nothing' nor 'reflections' of speculations about reality (cf. Godelier 1971a).

In these Australian societies we find kinship systems that function as both infra- and superstructure. This plurality of functions has always been clearly understood by all the specialists in this area, whether Spencer, Radcliffe-Brown, Elkin, or Yengoyan, who writes:

> Thus, the section system is a shorthand index for combining kin relations into categories for multiple purposes, be it possible marriage rates, ritual, or economic activity. Finer distinctions within each section category are left to genealogical connections and locality (Yengoyan 1968a: 188).

The majority of anthropologists, when faced by a multifunctional institution—whether it be kinship, as in the case of Australian section systems or of acephalous segmentary societies like the Nuer or the Tiv; or religion, as in the case of the Indian caste system; or a politico-religious system such as might be reconstructed for the Inca before the Spanish conquest; or, again, a Polynesian chiefship such as that of Tikopia [9]—infer that it is because of its multifunctional character that this institution dominates the structure of the whole society and the logic of its reproduction. The analysis, however, stops there, in the blind alley of a tautological empirical 'explanation'. If one should then ask 'why is it kinship or any other institution that is multifunctional in this society?' the answer is 'because it is dominant'. An institution is dominant because it is multifunctional and it is multifunctional because it is dominant. This type of explanation can take us no further but continues in an abstract vein creating phantom explanations, pseudo-analyses, which do nothing but reproduce the empirical appearances of the facts in the abstract language of social science. This is how general theories proliferate that do no more than generalize the specific facts which have been studied by their particular authors. For some it is kinship, for others politics, for still others religion, which is the determinant instance of the working of the whole of the society, the ultimate cause of its internal logic. At this point, and at this level, all these theoretical opinions find themselves in opposition to Marx's hypothesis that it is the economic infrastructure of society which in the last analysis determines the inner logic of its working and of the evolution of the various types of society. These various empirical theories are bound to be in disagreement with Marx and to reject his hypothesis in 'the name of the facts'.

Yengoyan, in contrast, is explicitly looking for the causes that determine the dominant role of kinship and is trying to discover the existence of a hierarchy of causes, a hierarchy that actually points in the last analysis towards the economy. He confirms the hypothesis outlined in my article 'Système, Structure, et Contradiction dans *Le Capital*' (1966) that it is not enough for an institution such as kinship to assume several functions for it to be dominant within a society and to integrate all levels of social organization, all the parts of society, as the functionalists would say. Over and above this, kinship (or whatever the type of social relations for the society concerned) must also function as the system of relations of production regulating the rights of groups and of individuals in respect to the means of production and their access to the products of their labour. It is because the institution functions as the system of relations of production that it regulates the politico-religious activities and serves as the ideological schema for symbolic practice.[10] However, for a society such as the Inca where relations of politico-religious dependence functioned as the relations of production, the reverse would have been true, as was made evident each time that the subject Indian tribes and local communities dedicated, whether of their own free will or not, a significant part of their labour to maintaining the gods, the dead and the living members of the dominant class personified and directed by the Inca Shinti, the son of the Sun (Godelier 1971b).

A common error of many 'positivist' specialists in the human sciences, whether they be demographers, economists, anthropologists or historians (an error which causes them to neglect or reject the marxist hypothesis of the determinant role in the last instance of the economic infrastructure) is to confuse the visible hierarchy of institutions with the real invisible hierarchy of functions assumed by these institutions.[11] This is the direct effect of the insurmountable subjectivism and ethnocentricism of the empirical approach, which cannot accept that identical functions may have different institutional forms in other societies from the form they take in societies characterized by the capitalist or the socialist mode of production. The empiricist error is twofold and it occurs again and again. It is a misunderstanding about what the economic infrastructure is—whether it consists of one or more modes of production—and it is a misunderstanding about what is meant by the determinant role in the last instance of this infrastructure.

By economic infrastructure is simply meant the totality of the productive forces and of the social relations of human beings with each other and with nature that depend on the level of development of those forces, and that program and control the social process of production of the material conditions of existence. On this definition, there is no theoretical reason for prejudging the nature of the social relations that in any particular society will assure this programming and control, nor for prejudging the number of functions a social structure can assume. As I have already stated in *Horizon, trajets marxistes en anthropologie* (in opposition to many students of Marx who, whether they agree or disagree with him, all make him out to be a vulgar materialist), when Marx distinguished between infra- and superstructure and proposed that the deep logic of evolution and history depends in the last analysis on the properties of their infrastructure, he did no more than to point out, for the first time, that there is a hierarchy of functions and structural causalities, without in any way prejudging the type of social relations which take on these functions, nor the number of functions that any structure can assume (Godelier 1973: ii—iii). Therefore to discover the deep logic of the history of societies it is necessary to go beyond the structural analysis of 'forms' of social relations or of thought, and to try to detect the effects of the various 'structures' on each other, and their hierarchical arrangement and articulation resting on the base of their particular modes of production. This is why Yengoyan's analysis is so interesting since, at the same time as confirming the conclusions of Lévi-Strauss in *The Elementary Structures of Kinship*, he has gone beyond the limits of a structural morphology of Australian kinship systems to take into consideration the social functions which these forms assume as well as their hierarchical arrangement.

Lévi-Strauss's structural analysis explains the logic of forms but ignores the logic of functions. This is why it can never explain societies, that is to say, account for them as concrete totalities capable or not of reproducing themselves under certain specific conditions. It cannot understand *history*.[12] A marxist methodology in anthropology or in the social sciences demands an analysis that traces a hidden network of causes linking forms, functions, mode of articulation, hierarchy, and the appearance and disappearance of specific social structures. This methodology should lead to the disappearance of the oppositions between anthropology and history; it should make it no longer possible to treat economic relations or any other type of social relations, as autonomous domains, in other words to fetishize them; that is, to achieve something beyond the capacities of functionalist empiricism and structuralism. But in order to arrive at this position—for building a science of history and developing historical materialism—an entirely new field of investigations must be tackled which will answer the following question: *Under what conditions and for what reasons do certain social relations take on the functions of relations of production and thereby control the reproduction of these relations, as well as the reproduction of all social relations?*

To answer this question it is not enough again to fall back on concepts of kinship, economy, production, society, causality, structure, transformation, etc., in the old way and to use them as a ready-made analytical framework in order to categorize facts and eventually to subject them to statistical and mathematical analysis in the search for correlations showing causal relationships. It is for this reason that an uncritical use of the statistical data supplied by Murdock and his team in the *World Ethnographic Atlas* seems doomed to failure and sterility.

15

However, the most serious obstacle to answering the question of how the infrastructure determines the dominant role of a particular field of social relationships does not come from this quarter. It originates with marxists themselves, in their essentially positivist and empiricist confusion between the labour process and the social process of production. To clarify the distinction, let us return to the Australian Aborigines. What is called the labour process is the concrete process of production which takes place daily within the framework of the horde, that is the local group composed of several related families, who wander in search of sustenance over the territory normally received from the ancestors. The horde functions as the direct unit of production and consumption, and within this framework all its individual members occupy distinct positions according to sex and age. Their cooperative efforts constitute the concrete process of labour. At this level everything occurs as though production relations were merged, on the one hand, with the division of labour within each band, which is identical for all of them, and, on the other, with the rights held by the members of each band over certain territories and over the product of their labour.

This, however, is not all: we also know that each band does not possess *exclusive* rights over its own territory and its products (Hiatt 1968: 94–102; also Hiatt 1966 and Rose 1968). Members of other bands living near by are linked to it through overlapping section membership and therefore have the right to use each other's territory, for periods of varying length. This right is exercised on numerous occasions, particularly in difficult times, such as prolonged droughts, famines, or epidemics. A cooperation more deep-rooted than the reciprocity involved in daily production is manifested on such occasions. This cooperation does not in any way affect the form taken by the concrete labour process. What happens is simply that two hordes instead of one exploit the same territory with the same techniques and the same division of labour. However, this reciprocal guarantee of access to the conditions of production reveals more than the fact that the means of production are not the exclusive property of each local group. It shows that the division into sections, and the complementarity of these sections, constitute the very basis of the relations of individuals and groups in relation to the means of production; in other words it is the basis itself of the relations of production: the appropriation by the whole tribal community of the 'primitive larder and the primitive tool-house of their means of labour . . .' (Marx 1970, Vol. I: 179).

It is not an accident that the basis of the relations of production, usually invisible at the level of the daily process of labour, suddenly becomes overt when the material and social reproduction of the whole community is threatened. It is this reproduction over time which the cooperation and reciprocity between sections guarantee. The social process of production is clearly distinguishable from the technical process of labour, and the social division of labour is not reducible to the technical division of labour. The social process of labour, over and above the division of labour by age and sex, relates all individuals and groups to the conditions of production on the basis of their section membership, and of the relations of reciprocity and complementarity this implies with all the others. At this point the analysis must be pursued in order to show that if the sections never function directly as the unit of production, they function as social units in matrimonial exchanges and political and ritual practices. We cannot do this within the limits of this article, but an essential question remains to be answered: why the tribe must, in the first place, be divided into local groups for direct production and then subdivided into cross-cutting sections to guarantee reciprocal access to the means of production.

The answer to this question is to be found in the level of the development of the productive forces and in the nature of the constraints they exert and the possibilities they allow. It is the nature of the productive forces which, on the one hand, imposes limitations on the size of the unit of production and consumption, hence the division of the tribe into distinct local groups which must also be nomadic and living far apart one from another, and, on the other hand, imposes cooperation and complementarity for all groups and individuals. The marxist method does not take as its starting-point the technical division of labour found in the various concrete processes of production: hunting, gathering, fishing, the manufacture of tools and handicrafts, or the preparation and cooking of food, but rather the 'means of labour', that is to say the productive forces of the society, the constraints they impose and the possibilities they offer, for extracting from nature the material conditions of existence.

> It is not the articles made, but how they are made, and by what instruments, that enables us to distinguish different economic epochs. Instruments of labour not only supply a standard of the degree of development to which human labour has attained but they are also indicators of the social conditions under which that labour is carried on (Marx 1970, vol. I: 180).

Now, these social conditions are simultaneously relations of individuals and groups among themselves in the technical division of labour and also the relation of the means of production and the product of labour. If one tries to look for the origins of the rights of access to the means of production in the division of labour within the various concrete processes of labour, and to deduce the former from the latter, one replaces marxism by a vulgar economism and ends in the same position as Emmanuel Terray, who, relying on his knowledge of the 'real' Marx of Althusser and Balibar, 're-reads' Meillassoux and discovers that the Guro of the Ivory Coast have as many modes of production as forms of labour processes: an agricultural mode of production, a hunting mode of production, etc. (Terray 1972).[13] In this way several

17

other 'revolutionary' marxist anthropologists have already invented a mode of production for men, another for women, and one for youths, etc. It then becomes possible to call all these social categories classes and to 'generalize the class theory' to all epochs and all social formations in the history of humanity. To put it in another way, we can say that the order of necessary connections is:

$$
\begin{matrix} \text{nature} \\ \text{and} \\ \text{level} \end{matrix} \begin{matrix} \text{of the productive} \\ \text{forces} \end{matrix} \left\{ \begin{matrix} \text{technical division of} \\ \text{labour} \\ \text{forms of appropriation,} \\ \text{means of production} \\ \text{and product; social} \\ \text{relations of production} \end{matrix} \right\} \begin{matrix} \text{social process} \\ \text{of production} \end{matrix}
$$

and not:

technical division of labour → social relations of production → superstructures.

This theoretical point must be stressed in view of recent marxist studies in anthropology, not only in France but also in England, the USA, Sweden, and elsewhere. However, to conclude, we now return to the example of socio-economic organization of the Australian Aborigines, since we have not yet exhausted the theoretical analysis of their organization into sections and subsections by simply demonstrating that they function as relations of production and respond to the constraints in the nature of the productive forces themselves. We must also analyse the fact that sections regulate marriage and that their total system of reciprocity is channelled by the system of exchange of women, who are, at one and the same time, irreplaceable producers (since they are responsible for food-gathering and preparation, and for the transport of food, wood, water, and household utensils) and also the means of the biological reproduction of the group, of its physical continuity through the generations. Equally, we must consider in detail the politico-religious functions of the sections and the content and form of their symbolic praxis on social reality, as well as on the imaginary conditions of the reproduction of the world (nature and society). The reciprocal and general cooperation operating between all the sections at the level of relations of production is reproduced in the politico-religious field through this praxis. Just as the basis of the relations of production is the appropriation by the tribal community as a whole of the means of production beyond their appropriation by the local groups and the particular social divisions, so in their symbolic praxis on the imaginary conditions of the reproduction of the world-order, all the sections, groups, and individuals, act as differentiated but complementary parts of the same collective social reality, that is, the tribe. Here we should analyse the phantasmatic nature of these social relations and this symbolic praxis, which is revealed in the fact that the land is not conceived of as belonging to men, but rather that men 'belong' to their section and their section 'belongs' to a supernatural reality, which is represented by, among other things, totems and a multitude of objects and 'sacred' sites. I have attempted elsewhere, with regard to another society of hunters and gatherers, to analyse this inversion and fetishization in the representation of social relations.[14] These problems have yet to be elucidated, but I shall conclude by posing two fundamental questions. (1) What factors control the interval between births and what is their influence on the laws of population of hunting and gathering societies? (2) What is the significance of the existence among other groups of hunters and gatherers of forms of kinship relations different from those characterized by sections but with equivalent functions? Here we touch upon the problem of *the possible*, and the problem of genuine alternatives in history.

For the first point I shall draw on the works of Richard Lee (1968, 1969, 1972) on the Bushmen of the Kalahari Desert, who are also hunters and gatherers living in an arid environment. Bushmen women gather wild plants which provide two-thirds of the food consumed annually in their camp. A camp normally consists of from ten to fifty individuals living less than a mile from a waterhole. Lee has calculated that a female adult covers an average of 2,400 kilometres per year in undertaking her economic activities, and in visits to other bands; for half of this distance she carries heavy loads of water, food, firewood, and of course children. The latter are weaned at around four years of age. During the first two years a child is constantly carried by its mother (2,400 km × 2), it is carried for about 1,800 km in the third year and 1,200 km in the fourth. This means that in the four-year period a woman walks a total distance of about 7,800 km, in the course of which the weight of the child is added to the weight of other loads carried. Given that mobility is one of the necessary constraints on her economic activity as a gatherer and carrier of loads, the effort expended by a woman in carrying a young child must be maintained within limits compatible with the regular and efficient accomplishment of her economic activities. Her work thus depends on the interval between births. It has been calculated that, with a five-year interval between births, in ten years a woman would have had two children and the loads she would carry on average would be reduced to 7·8 kilograms. In the case of an interval of two years (without taking into account the very high rate of infant mortality which occurs between six and eighteen months) the weight to be carried would be 17 kilos and for four of these ten years an average of 21·2 kilos. Theoretically, an interval between births of at least three years appears to be a demographic constraint imposed by the Bushmen's mode of production, and this is verified by statistics. The Bushmen are aware of these demographic constraints and say: 'A woman who gives birth to one child after another—like an animal—has permanent backache.' Furthermore, they kill one of a pair of twins at birth, practise infanticide on those children who are born defective, and

19

abstain from sexual intercourse for at least one year after each birth. Nonetheless, this conscious 'demographic policy' is not sufficient to explain why the interval between births should be statistically of at least three years, since after a year of abstinence women resume full sexual life. Unintended biological factors must therefore intervene, of which the most important is the fact that prolonged breast-feeding of children suppresses ovulation in women. Nancy Howell (n.d.) has suggested that the prolonged period of breast-feeding is necessary for hunters and gatherers because they lack foods that are easily digestible by children. Such foods are not found among the wild food products which the Bushmen eat, but are produced only by agriculturalists and pastoralists (milk, porridge, etc.). The mother's milk is therefore not only indispensable but is the only available nourishment, given the level of development of the forces of production. A similar conclusion has been reached by Meggitt for the Australian Aborigines and is supported by Yengoyan, who shows that the interval between births for them was also three or more years. He identifies the 'economic cause' for this interval as follows: 'the prolonged period of nourishment at the breast not only forces the populations to limit their numbers but also diminishes the complete utility of a woman as an economic partner'.

Richard Lee suggests that the sole fact of a change-over to a sedentary way of life could, by restricting the mobility of women, eliminate the negative biological effects of the nomadic way of life upon the female fertility rate and lead to a population increase even before an increase in food supply. This has been verified experimentally for the Australian Aborigines by E. Lancaster Jones, on whose excellent work Yengoyan relies. The settlement of Aborigines in reservations and the consequent dietary change brought about by the distribution of food by Europeans has been accompanied by an explosion in the birth rate. This, combined with the use of medicines, has produced a population growth rate far higher than that which has been reconstructed for the pre-colonial period. Another interesting aspect of this work is the suggestion that exceptional demographic growth could have taken place in groups of Near Eastern neolithic collectors who relied on dense areas of wild cereals (the ancestors of our cereals), or in populations established on riverbanks or beside the shores of seas in America or Southeast Asia. This demographic expansion could have, little by little, constrained the collectors to grow what they had previously collected, that is to say to domesticate wild plants (Sauer 1952). Wherever these speculations may lead, it must be noted once again, first, that the growth of population is linked to sedenterization and thus to a new mode of subsistence and existence, and, second, that this demographic expansion, even though it could have started without the transformation or expansion of economic resources, could not have continued further without such a transformation, that is to say without a change in the material and social conditions of production.

In this way the study of the hierarchy of levels and of the causes that intervene to 'produce' the demographic structures of Australian societies of hunters and gatherers is being pieced together. More work still needs to be done, but we can summarize some of these relationships in the diagram overleaf. This is the type of research which should in the end lead to the discovery of various types of social and historical rationalities corresponding to the various modes of production and of social organization that have followed one another in the course of history. In this way various forms of 'structural causality' of social relations will also be better understood. In other words, the effects of internal constraints on the functioning of these relations within their internal organization, and on the reproduction of other social relations at other 'levels', will become clear. By using the example of the Australian Aborigines, I hope to have shown that, despite the enormous difference in the form and location of production relations in their modes of production, at the very core of their society, as at the core of bourgeois society, the same law of a functional hierarchy of social structures operates. In this hierarchy of social structures, the most important is, in the last analysis, and in these two cases, that which functions as the infrastructure. This was Marx's fundamental hypothesis, and it has not been invalidated by data from any of the more 'primitive' societies. These may now have disappeared for ever or be rapidly undergoing radical transformations, removing from mankind the evidence it needs to repossess the many facets and forms of its history.

There is an urgent need for many more such studies, but the immense theoretical difficulties standing in the way must be clearly understood. For example, there is the problem of the range of the possible, whether it is a real problem and whether it is amenable to scientific analysis. To refer again to the Australian case, Yengoyan has compared their section system with the kinship system of the African Bushmen and has shown that the two systems, although structurally different, are functionally similar. Both have social relations that ensure, in the economic and political sphere, the same flexibility and the same general reciprocal cooperation, and that guarantee the simple reproduction of societies subject to adverse natural conditions. The Bushmen apply the kinship terms for siblings and relatives of other generations to any individuals with the same name as themselves or that of their kinsmen or affines, even though these people do not belong to these kinship categories. They behave to these 'kinsmen by name' in the same way that they would towards their own kinsmen and affines, and expect the same reciprocity from them.[15] This is what an Australian Aborigine expects from those who belong to the same section, as we know from the works of Radcliffe-Brown, Fry (1934), Elkin, and Strehlow (1965).

So long as we are unable to determine the number and range of compatible possibilities within a system of conditions and constraints,

Diagram of Possible Relationships between Levels

Type and level of development of productive forces	Material life based on specific forms of nomadic hunting & gathering

Necessary division of the group into local bands; units of production and consumption, numbers limited by the relationship between capacity of production/residence/population ↑

Division of labour by sex and age within each local band → position of women in production (gathering, transport) → necessary mobility → practice of regulating intervals between births, infanticide, etc. ↑

Diet of wild foodstuffs → necessity for pro-longed breastfeeding → retarded ovulation → intervals between births ↑

High rate of infant mortality ↑

Necessary reciprocal cooperation within the community as a whole → relations between sections function as relations of production → minimum demographic conditions for the reproduction of sections ↑

Demographic structures and laws of population

etc.

and are also unable to reconstruct in our minds the limited number of transformations that such structures, or combinations of structures, can perform, history, whether of the past or of the future, will appear as nothing but an immense, meaningless mass of facts. If, on the other hand, we succeed in this task, then a science of history will be possible that will also be a science of human populations, from which the fetishized compartmentalization and arbitrary divisions of the social sciences will have been abolished. A science that will serve not only to interpret history but also to make it.

Notes

1 This text is an amended and abbreviated version of a report presented at the symposium on Population and the Family organized by the United Nations and held in Honolulu, 6–15 August 1973.

2 See also Steward (1955), Chapter 3, and especially Chapter 6, which is devoted to a group of hunters and gatherers from the great semi-arid basin of North America, 'The Great Basin Shoshonan Indians, an example of a family level of sociocultural integration'. At the end of his life Julian Steward began to question the existence of such 'familial' levels of integration (cf. Steward 1968: 81).

3 This theoretical position is that of Marx in his famous Introduction to *A Contribution to the Critique of Political Economy*:

> It would seem to be the proper thing to start with the real and concrete elements, with the actual pre-conditions, e.g., to start in the sphere of economy with population, which forms the basis and the subject of the whole social process of production. Closer consideration shows, however, that this is wrong. Population is an abstraction if, for instance, one disregards the classes of which it is composed. These classes in turn remain empty terms if one does not know the factors on which they depend, e.g., wage-labour, capital, and so on. These presuppose exchange, division of labour, prices, etc. For example, capital is nothing without wage-labour, without value, money, price, etc. If one were to take population as the point of departure, it would be a very vague notion of a complex whole and through closer definition one would arrive analytically at increasingly simple concepts; from imaginary concrete terms one would move to more and more tenuous abstractions until one reached the most simple definitions. From there it would be necessary to make the journey again in the opposite direction until one arrived once more at the concept of population, which is this time not a vague notion of a whole, but a totality comprising many determinations and relations (Marx 1971: Ch. 2 section 3).

4 We should note that it was on the basis of data on the Kamilaroi provided by Fison and Howitt, who were also correspondents of Morgan, that Engels set forth in *The Origin of the Family, Private Property and the State* a reworking of Morgan's evolutionary schema of the development of kinship relations and the family, which had been published in *Ancient Society* in 1877 (cf. Fison and Howitt 1880).

5 For lack of space we do not show the statistical methods used in the analysis.

6 Morgan (1877: Part II, Ch. 3, 'The Turanian or Ganowanian System of Consanguinity'). In his notes, Marx noted his approval of Morgan's thesis and generalized it for all 'systems': '*Systems of consanguinity* sind dagegen passiv; *recording the progress made by the family at long intervals apart, and only changing radically when the family has radically changed.*' And he adds: 'Ebenso verhält es sich mit *politischen, religiösen, juristischen, philosophischen* Systemen überhaupt' (Krader 1972: 112).

7 Radcliffe-Brown wrote in 1913 about the Kariera, whom he had studied a few years previously:

> At the present day the natives of the Kariera tribe are nearly all living on the sheep stations that have been established on their tribal territory. They are fed and clothed by the Station owners or at the expense of the Government, and the able-bodied men and women work on the Stations. Their country has been occupied by the Whites for about 50 years and during that time their numbers have steadily decreased. At the present time there are not more than 100 all told, men, women, and children. . . . All of them, except the oldest, can speak fairly good English (Radcliffe-Brown 1913: 144).

8 For a fuller discussion of the concept of 'symbolic work' on the 'imaginary conditions of reproduction', see my analysis of the ritual practices of the Mbuti pygmies (Godelier 1973: 75–9).

9 Firth (1939). But Firth, who has always criticized marxism, or at least what he understands by that term, writes in the preface to the second edition of his book (1965) something that appears greatly similar to the concept of the determination in the last instance of the infrastructure:

> After publishing an account of the social structure, in particular the kinship structure (*We, the Tikopia*, London, 1936), I analysed the economic structure of the society, because so many social relationships were made more manifest in their economic content. Indeed, the social structure, in particular the political structure, was clearly dependent on the specific economic relationships arising out of the system of control of resources. With these relationships in turn were linked the religious activities and institutions of the society (p. xi).

10 We wrote:

> We may thus assume a correspondence between the general structure of the productive forces and the dominant role and complex structure of kinship relations . . . inasmuch as in this type of society, kinship functions in fact as production relations, the determinant role of the economy does not contradict the dominant role of kinship but rather is expressed by means of it . . . (Godelier 1966).

In explaining the dominance of kinship relations in their function as production relations, we adopt a theoretical position which is neither that of the functionalists nor that of Lévi-Strauss; but we are rather surprised by the 'theoretically rigorous manner' in which Terray characterizes our position: 'To stop at this is simply to apply new terms to that functional polyvalence of 'primitive' institutions which has long been known to classical anthropology, and in fact to adopt the structuralist position' (Terray 1972: 143). Not only is this a falsification of the ideas of others but it demonstrates an abysmal ignorance of the structuralist position. Further on, the author notes that 'a lineage often appears to be a productive unit, a political body, and a sort of religious "congregation" . . . amongst them the dominant determinant . . . is the result of a specific structure of the mode of production' (p. 151). This is precisely our point of view. See Godelier (1972: 92–6).

11 Many of the disciples of Althusser have a theoretical interpretation of instances as a hierarchy of 'institutions' and fall back into the positivist error which they claim to have gone beyond 'theoretically'.

12 See the criticism of the limitations of structural analysis of kinship in Godelier (1973: 58–63).

13 To justify his position, Terray has recourse to a letter from Althusser in which the latter asserted: 'Like any social formation, the structure of a primitive social formation is the result of the combination of at least two distinct modes of production, one of which is dominant and the other subordinate' (Terray 1972: 179). We must confess surprise at the dogmatic tone of this assertion. Every 'primitive' society has to combine several modes of production, and, since Althusser says so, these modes of production must necessarily exist. So hunting activities would be christened 'the hunting mode of production' and gathering activities would receive some other title. From there to the invention of a masculine mode of production (hunting), which is dominant over a feminine mode of production (gathering), is just a short step which certain enthusiastic disciples have already taken.

14 Cf. Marx (1970, Vol. I: 71–2), also Godelier (1973, Ch. V, Du caractère fantasmatique des rapports sociaux, pp. 319–92). On the idea of 'belonging', in the strong sense, to the 'higher community' or to the 'highest unity', see Marx: *Pre-Capitalist Economic Formations* in Hobsbawm (1964: 69–70).

15 On the !Kung Bushmen, see the authoritative works of Lorna Marshall (1957, 1959, 1960).

References

BIRDSELL, J. B. 1953. Some Environmental and Cultural Factors Influencing the Structuring of Australian Aboriginal Populations. *American Naturalist* **87**: 171–207.
— 1958. On Population Structure in Generalized Hunting and Gathering Populations. *Evolution* **87**: 189–207.
— 1970. Local Group Composition among the Australian Aborigines. *Current Anthropology*, April: 115–142.
DAVIDSON, D. S. 1928. *The Chronological Aspects of Australian Social Organization.* University of Pennsylvania Press.
ELKIN, A. P. 1964. *The Australian Aborigines: How to Understand Them.* 4th edn, Sydney: Angus & Robertson.
ENGELS, F. 1941. *The Origin of the Family, Private Property and the State.* London: Lawrence & Wishart. Translation of *Der Ursprung der Familie . . .* Zürich: Hottingen, 1884.
FIRTH, R. 1939. *Primitive Polynesian Economy.* 2nd edn, London: Routledge & Kegan Paul, 1965.
FISON, L. and HOWITT, A. W. 1880. *Kamilaroi and Kurnai: Group Marriage among the Australian Aborigines.* Melbourne: Geo. Robertson.
FORTES, M. 1958. Introduction in J. R. Goody (ed.), *The Developmental Cycle in Domestic Groups.* Cambridge: Cambridge University Press.
FRY, H. K. 1934. Kinship and Descent among the Australian Aborigines. *Transactions of the Royal Society of South Australia* **58**: 14–21.

Maurice Godelier

GODELIER, M. 1966. Système, structure et contradiction dans 'Le Capital'. *Les Temps Modernes* (246): 828. English translation in R. Miliband and J. Saville (eds.), *The Socialist Register*. London: Merlin, 1967.
— 1971a. Mythes et histoire: réflexions sur les fondements de la pensée sauvage. *Annales*, special number on 'Structure and History', May–Aug.
— 1971b. Le concept de formation économique et sociale: l'exemple des Incas. *La Pensée* (159), Oct.
— 1972. *Rationality and Irrationality in Economics*. London: New Left Books.
— 1973. *Horizon, trajets marxistes en anthropologie*. Paris: Maspero.
GOODY, J. R. 1972. *Domestic Groups*. Reading, Mass.: Addison-Wesley.
HIATT, L. R. 1966. The Lost Horde. *Oceania* 37: 81–92.
— 1968. Ownership and Use of Land among the Australian Aborigines. In Lee and DeVore, q.v.
HOWELL, N. n.d. !Kung Bushman Demographic Studies: A Preliminary Report. Princeton: Office of Population Research.
HOBSBAWM, E. J. (ed). 1964. *Karl Marx: Pre-Capitalist Economic Formations*. Trans. Jack Cohen. London: Lawrence and Wishart.
JONES, F. L. 1965. The Demography of the Australian Aborigines. *International Social Science Journal* 17: 232–45.
— 1970. *The Structures and Growth of Australia's Aboriginal Population*. Canberra: Australian National University Press.
KRADER, L. (ed.) 1972. *The Ethnological Notebooks of Karl Marx*. Assen: Van Gorcum.
KULA, W. 1972. La Seigneurie et la famille paysanne dans la Pologne du 18ème siècle. *Annales*, special number on 'Family and Society', July–Oct.
LEE, R. 1968. What Hunters do for a Living, or how to make out on Scarce Resources. In Lee and DeVore, q.v.
— 1969. !Kung Bushman Subsistence: an Input-output Analysis. In D. Damas (ed.), *Ecological Essays*. Ottawa: National Museum of Canada.
— 1972. Population Growth and the Beginnings of Sedentary Life among the !Kung Bushmen. In B. Spooner (ed.), *Population Growth*. Cambridge, Mass.: MIT Press.
LEE, R. and DEVORE, I. (eds.) 1968. *Man the Hunter*. Chicago: Aldine.
LÉVI-STRAUSS, C. 1960. The Family. In H. Shapiro (ed.), *Man, Culture, and Society*. London: Oxford University Press.
MARSHALL, L. 1957. The Kin terminology of the !Kung Bushmen. *Africa* 27: 1–25.
— 1959. Marriage among !Kung Bushmen. *Africa* 29: 335–65.
— 1960. !Kung Bushmen Bands. *Africa* 30: 325–55.
MARX, K. 1970. *Capital*. Translated from the 3rd German edition of 1883. London: Lawrence & Wishart.
— 1971. Introduction (1857) to *A Contribution to the Critique of Political Economy*. London: Lawrence & Wishart.
MEGGITT, M. J. 1962. *The Desert People*. Sydney: Angus & Robertson.
— 1965. Marriage among the Walbiri of Central Australia: a Statistical Examination. In R. Berndt (ed.), *Aboriginal Man in Australia*. Sydney: Angus & Robertson.
— 1968. Marriage Classes and Demography in Central Australia. In Lee and DeVore, q.v.
MORGAN, L. H. 1877. *Ancient Society*. London: Macmillan.
RADCLIFFE-BROWN, A. R. 1913. *Three Tribes of Western Australia. Journal of the Royal Anthropological Institute* 43: 143–94.
— 1930–1. The Social Organization of Australian Tribes. *Oceania* 1.
REAY, M. 1962. Subsections at Borroloorla. *Oceania* 33: 90–115.

ROSE, F. G. G. 1965. *The Winds of Change in Central Australia: the Aborigines at Angas Downs.* Berlin: Akademie-Verlag.
— 1968. Australian Marriage, land-owning Groups and Initiations. In Lee and DeVore, q.v.
SAUER, C. 1952. *Agricultural Origins and Dispersals.* New York: American Geographical Society.
STEWARD, J. 1951. Levels of Socio-cultural Integration: an Operational Concept. *Southwestern Journal of Anthropology* 7: 374–80.
— 1955. *Theory of Culture Change.* Urbana: University of Illinois Press.
— 1968. Letter to Yehudi Cohen. In Y. Cohen (ed.), *Man in Adaptation: the Cultural Present.* Chicago: Aldine.
STREHLOW, T. G. H. 1965. Culture, Social Structure and Environment in Aboriginal Central Australia. In R. Berndt (ed.), *Aboriginal Man in Australia.* Sydney: Angus & Robertson.
TERRAY, E. 1972. *Marxism and 'Primitive' Societies.* New York: Monthly Review Press.
TINDALE, N. B. 1940. Distribution of Australian Aboriginal Tribes: A Field Survey. *Transactions of the Royal Society of South Australia* 64: 140–231.
— 1953. Tribal and Intertribal Marriage among the Australian Aborigines. *Human Biology* 25: 169–90.
VON BRANDENSTEIN, C. G. 1970. The Meaning of Section and Section Names. *Oceania* 41 (1): 39–49.
YENGOYAN, A. P. 1968a. Demographic and Ecological Influences on Aboriginal Australian Marriage Sections. In Lee and DeVore, q.v.
—1968b. Australian Section Systems—Demographic Components and Interactional Similarities with the !Kung Bushmen. *Proceedings of the VIII International Congress of Anthropological and Ethnological Science*, Tokyo 3: 256–60.
— 1970 Demographic Factors in Pitjandjara Social Organization. In R. Berndt (ed.), *Australian Aboriginal Anthropology.* Nedlands: University of Western Australia Press.
— 1972a. Biological and Demographic Components in Aboriginal Australian Socio-economic Organization. *Oceania* 43 (2): 85–95.
— 1972b. Aborigines in the Third World. *American Scientist* 60 (3): 367.

Raymond Firth

The Sceptical Anthropologist?
Social Anthropology and Marxist Views
on Society

The title of this paper [1] embodies a reference to Radcliffe-Brown's cita-
tion, at the end of his plea for what he called a Natural Science of
Society, of the Honourable Robert Boyle's work *The Sceptical Chymist*.
Radcliffe-Brown noted that Boyle argued for bypassing 'practical'
problems, what he called 'frugiferous' research, in favour of enlightenment of a theoretical order—'luminiferous' research—and so was able
to found a real science of chemistry out of alchemy and metallurgy.
Radcliffe-Brown would have liked to have been able to emulate Boyle,
and create a 'purely theoretical science of human society' (1957: 147–8),
though he thought that demands for practical results are so insistent
that such an aim will be unlikely of proper attention in our times. Now
this picks out a significant view, and I recall it later. But Boyle saw
theory as basic to practice, not as supplanting it. Granted his concern
for theoretical research, when he published his book in 1661 Boyle had
joined what was called 'a new philosophical college that values no
knowledge but as it has a tendency to use'. This very down-to-earth
body of people afterwards became the Royal Society of London, with
Boyle as a founder Fellow and member of its first Council. What strikes
me also in Boyle's book is his emphasis on experiment, and his refusal
to accept assertion not backed by evidence. A lusty controversialist, he
rejected what he termed the 'intolerable ambiguity' his opponents
allowed themselves in their expressions. If, following Radcliffe-Brown,
we take Boyle as a guide we find he makes two further points. He
believed in flexibility of interpretation. 'It is not necessary that all the
things a Sceptick Proposes, should be consonant. . . . It is allowable
for him to propose two or more several *Hypotheses* about the same
thing. . . .' And in a pre-marxist, even pre-Hegelian, world he dis-
trusted the then version of the dialectic: 'those Dialectical subtleties . . .
are wont much more to declare the wit of him that uses them, than
increase the knowledge or remove the doubts of sober lovers of truth'
(Boyle 1661: A2–4, 14–15; 1964: viii).

Two of the greatest thinkers of the last century, Karl Marx and

29

Sigmund Freud, specialized in the theoretics of confrontation—one might say affrontation. With brutal realism both have forced us to examine components in man's nature and society ordinarily left obscure: Freud to recognize elements of conflict in the self formerly admitted only in secret or veiled behind philosophic discussions of the unconscious; Marx to recognize elements of conflict in society rooted in our material interests. The shock effect of these ideas has diminished with time, and aspects of them have been incorporated—though often distorted—into our common thinking. But now where does Karl Marx stand in the thought of the sceptical anthropologist, trained in the discipline which Radcliffe-Brown did so much to found? Marx, like Radcliffe-Brown later, was committed to a search for general scientific principles underlying concrete phenomena—what Radcliffe-Brown and some marxists have called nomothetic, i.e. law-giving propositions. But Marx, unlike Radcliffe-Brown, was an iconoclast rather than a sceptic, proclaimed dialectical materialism as his method, saw his nomothetic propositions as constant and inevitable, and believed passionately in their practical relevance.[2] How do these propositions, especially those concerned with pre-capitalist society, measure up to anthropological standards of evidence, including (the nearest thing to experiment) the results of field research?

For sociologists and economic historians, consideration of Marx's ideas has long been a commonplace. R. H. Tawney once said that no historian could write as if Marx had never existed. Yet some anthropologists have evaded a parallel conclusion; a recent work on social anthropology and political history has much concern with conflict but little with marxist interpretations of it. Marx's arguments claim to go to the roots of man's economic life, yet economic anthropology has largely ignored his views. Marx propounded a revolutionary theory of social change, yet general works by anthropologists have cheerfully dispensed with all but minimal use of Marx's ideas on the dynamics of society.[3]

In this paper I consider first why Marx's ideas, particularly those concerning primitive society, have been avoided by social anthropologists; then what use has been made of his theories in social anthropology; and finally what I think Marx's work can mean to a sceptical anthropologist. It is a personal view, it is highly compressed, and it deals primarily with Marx and not with his many commentators [4] and apologists.

A simple answer to the question of why such anthropological caution towards Marx's theories might be vested interest—that social anthropologists as bourgeois intellectuals have found themselves unable to face so disturbing a view of man and society as Marx has presented; that they have preferred an idealist, not a materialist, interpretation of history, an integrative, not a conflict, model of society. Some, again, may have been antagonized by Marx's negative attitude to religion. There may be something in this argument, but while simple it is certainly not complete. Another factor could be personal temperament. A disincentive to concur with marxist formulations, even when they might be acceptable, could be the intensity of their polemic. Marx has been called an economist, a historian, a sociologist, a philosopher, a prophet; but Engels in his funeral oration said that Marx was before all else a revolutionist, his real mission was to contribute to the overthrow of capitalist society, and in this fighting was his element.[5] Marx's way of fighting was not only with analytical tenacity but also with a passionate invective inappropriate, so many people have felt, to a scientific presentation. So even where they may have agreed with Marx, social anthropologists seem often to have left this to be read between the lines.

For the early part of this century, social anthropologists might have said they ignored Marx because he was not relevant. Until recently our field has been primarily the technologically backward, economically undeveloped, politically not very complex societies, lacking wage-labour and a clearly identifiable class structure. Influence of an alien government was often remote, of a commercial market peripheral. In structure the Andamanese, the Australian Aborigines, the Trobrianders, the Tikopia, the Tswana, the Tallensi, and many others could be classed only in the area of Marx's amorphous 'primitive communalism'. For classical social anthropology there was not much ethnographically or theoretically of direct concern in Marx's generally known works; and Engels on the family and Lafargue on property represented an outdated arid revolutionary position. As Birnbaum (1960: 104) has mildly said, the traditions of anthropology appear rather remote from the concerns of marxism.

In recent years there has been more convergence. More light has been thrown on Marx's ideas from early draft works, in particular that on 'pre-capitalist formations' to which I refer soon. New issues have been raised as social anthropologists have been confronted with societies in conditions of radical change. Apart from war dislocation, migration of labour and cropping for a commercial market, with the stimulation of new consumer wants, have revealed the shattering effects of an economic system geared to development. The growth of centralized political control, alien or indigenous according to circumstance, has made the bases and structure of power much clearer. The emergence of new religious cults and other indigenous movements of self-expression has reinforced attention to the significance of ideology. Marxist theories about base and superstructure, relations of production, economic determinism, class conflict, exploitation, have therefore tended to draw much closer to anthropological interests.

But anthropological coolness towards Marx's views has been partly due to the influence of another tradition in the interpretation of social phenomena—that of Emile Durkheim. There is a curious parallelism in Marx's and Durkheim's thought which still waits to be fully explained.

31

It concerns the relation of the individual to society, and it emerges for instance in the theory of the sociology of knowledge. Durkheim and Mauss argued that categories of thought are fundamentally social categories, arising from the social relations of men in groups. 'The first logical categories have been social categories. . . . The centre of the first systems of nature is not the individual, it is society. . . .'[6] But chronologically, the theory that what a person conceives he knows is a reflection of his position in society was formulated in essence by Karl Marx. His notion that the material world around us is a materialization of man's *praxis*, man's productive activity in history, is not just an assertion that nature is manmade; it also implies that man's understanding of the material world is a reflection of his own social world. In opposition to Hegel's idea of the concrete as consisting in philosophical thought, Marx's idea of the concrete lay in the relations of men. The relations of men which Marx saw as cardinally relevant for concept formation were those of class, based upon their structural position in an economic framework of production. Hence for Marx ideology was the abstract conceptual form in which members of a class disguised their concrete economic, social, and political interests and position. In Marx's view this ideology took essentially a general form—what were in reality assertions of special class interest were believed to be formulations that applied to the whole of society.[7] The specific political implications of this thesis have tended to obscure its general relevance for many people. But modern studies in what has come to be called cognitive anthropology could find some ancestry in Marx.

This comes out clearly in his early work. In the *German Ideology* (1846) he and Engels held that consciousness, like language, is a social product. In the *Economic and Philosophical Manuscripts* (1844) Marx argued that even what appear to be very private individual actions have a social quality. 'Even when I carry out *scientific* work—an activity which I seldom conduct in association with other men—I perform a *social*, because *human* act. It is not only the material of my activity—like the language itself which the thinker uses—which is given to me as a social product. *My own existence* is a social activity.' And in clarification he specified a further important point, with which the approach of modern social anthropologists is in conformity: 'It is above all necessary to avoid postulating "Society" as an abstraction confronting the individual. The individual is a *social being*. His life, even if it may not appear in the direct form of a communal life carried out together with others—is therefore an expression and confirmation of social life' (Marx and Engels 1933, Abt I, Bd 5: 19–21; Bottomore 1963: 157–8, cf. Milligan 1959: 104). I think that here we get a clue to Marx's whole approach to the evolution of society, coming up again in his ideas about primitive communalism—the idea that basically even ethically, *being* should not be separated from *doing*; activity and existence are one, and it is the demerit of capitalist society that it has promoted such a separation. But note that in some contrast to Durkheim, Marx's merging of society and the individual is countered by his sharp division between different categories of individuals in the production process. Marx's stress on social factors emerges even in his treatment of religion, fore-shadowing in the theses on Feuerbach the main theme of *The Elementary Forms of the Religious Life*. In 1845 (though the *Theses* were not published till 1888) he wrote that Feuerbach resolved the religious essence into the human essence. 'But the human essence is no abstraction inherent in each single individual. In its reality it is the ensemble of the social relations. . . . Feuerbach, consequently, does not see that the "religious sentiment" is itself a *social product*, and that the abstract individual whom he analyses belongs in reality to a particular form of society' (Marx and Engels 1968: 29).

The convergence of the ideas of Durkheim and of Marx has been noted by Sorel, Kagan, Cuvillier, and Gouldner, but it is not easy to decide how far Durkheim was actually influenced by Marx's views. Durkheim knew Marx's work, and according to Mauss he intended to devote a year of his course on socialism to Marx, but instead returned to 'pure science' on undertaking *L'Année sociologique*. But one cannot help forming an impression that Durkheim, with his own brand of social programme and a set of theoretical ideas which, as he saw it, he had arrived at independently, especially through their common ancestor Saint-Simon, was reluctant to discuss those of Marx.[8] He may have tried to reconcile Comte and Marx. But certainly, the few pages he devoted to the class struggle in the *Division of Labour* (1932: 367–9), in which he attributed such conflict as he saw to maldistribution of natural talent and increasing aptitudes in the face of the activities assigned to them, make no mention of Marx's views.

All this has had reflection in social anthropology. Insulated from Marx by the Durkheimian tradition, coming from Cambridge through Jane Harrison and Radcliffe-Brown, and (if only in reaction) from London through Malinowski, British social anthropology stressed solidarity rather than conflict as primary field of study. Symptomatic of one side of this position was Radcliffe-Brown's own omission, from his *Natural Science of Society*, presented in seminars in Chicago as late as 1937, of any reference to Karl Marx or to any principles of radical contradiction within the social system. But the dialectic has been taking its course. Durkheim is pallid by comparison with Marx; if Marx can be crude, Durkheim can seem naïve. In the social and political upheavals of the post-war period, it is perhaps especially to French social anthro-pologists that Marx's propositions have often seemed more relevant than those of Durkheim.

But in some cases attention to Marx's theories, though not absent, has been muted for another reason. Many anthropologists who have not been dazzled by the Durkheimian vision of social solidarity, even some who have not been alarmed by a prospect of a radical re-structuring of

33

Western society, have felt able to give only very qualified intellectual agreement to marxist views, because of the unsatisfactory generalizations offered about the nature of human society.

Take Marx's conception of man (see, e.g., Venable 1946; Fromm 1966; Meszaros 1970; cf. Gramsci 1957: 76–81). In what has been called 'marxian anthropology' Marx's propositions about the nature of man lack that empirical comparative dimension which characterizes anthropology in general. Despite his insistence on the need for a historical dimension in the interpretation of social conditions, Marx's basic assumptions about human behaviour and its meaning seem to be essentially inferential, from postulates concerned with his views on capitalist exploitation. In Marx's view the essential defining character of man is his labour power. Labour is a process going on between man and nature whereby man not only acts on the external world and changes it but also at the same time changes his own nature. Essential to this process are instruments of labour, which are not only tools but also indicators of the social relations amid which labour was performed. As the social relations vary, especially in regard to control of labour power and of instruments of production, so does the character of men vary— it is not general human needs but economic conditions at a particular stage which determine their behaviour (Marx, *Capital*, Vol. 1, 1930: 169–78). Now anthropologists have shared with Marx the realization that in an economy the relations between material things are really an expression of social relations between people. And they may not wish to deny the primacy of labour—though Marvin Harris (op. cit.: 233) has questioned the clarity of Marx's concept of 'work'. But they may wish to set beside it other forces of primary social significance, e.g. exchange, and symbolization. Robert Redfield once asked me to open a seminar on the theme: 'What can one say of a man—any man?' I could have chosen man's propensity to symbolize—in fact I chose his propensity to exchange. All comparative anthropology shows men engaging in forms of exchange, of immaterial as well as material things, of services as well as goods. One has as much right to assert that human culture was born with symbolization and with exchange—often intricately linked in actual transactions—as with labour.

But Marx belittled the primary character of exchange in human society. His explanation in different contexts is not entirely consistent, but basically he seems to have thought that it was through exchange that the possibility of exploitation arose. Marx seemed to think that primitive man shared but did not exchange, or at least engaged only in 'immediate exchange' of use-values without notion of profit. Man, who originally appears as a generic being (*Gattungswesen*), tribal being (*Stammwesen*), herd animal (*Herdentier*), is individualized only through the process of history, and exchange itself is a major agent of this individualization (Marx, *Grundrisse*, 1939: 395–6, cf. 414). Marx held that the value of commodities is nothing but crystallized labour, that a commodity has use-value in its bodily form, and exchange-value in its phenomenal form. But this phenomenal form never occurs when a commodity is in isolation, but only when it enters into an exchange relation with another commodity of different kind. As labour is the cause of value, so labour-time is the measure of value; the idea that value and its magnitude originate in their expression as exchange-value he labelled a delusion (*Capital*, 1930: 32). By associating exchange with interest in commodities as such, including the treatment of labour as a commodity, independent of their producers, Marx believed he had the key to the appropriation of surplus value from the labourer.

Marx's attitude to money was analogous to this. Money as a medium for facilitating exchange; as a means for getting goods and services; as a basis of contract; as a symbol of status—all these were recognized by Marx. But he focused on two functions of money in a capitalist economy which seemed to him to have political and indeed moral implications. One was the treatment of money as a commodity, a demand for money in itself, as treasure, as a general equivalent with special qualities which cause it to be sought and accumulated for its own sake. This hoarding or 'treasurization' (*thésaurisation*) as Suzanne de Brunhoff has discussed it,[9] not only gives a source of power; it is linked with another feature, the quality money has of concealing basic social relationships by developing the productive forces of social labour beyond the limits of ordinary wants. Marx refers to this theme in the *Critique of Political Economy*, then opens it up near the beginning of *Capital* and returns to it again near the end: 'This money form is the very thing which veils instead of disclosing the social character of private or individual labour, and therewith hides the social relations between the individual producers.' What are these social relations? That in a wage-labour system 'the money relation hides the fact that the wage worker works part of his time for nothing' because of the appropriation of surplus value by the employer. Money in various contexts is the absolute commodity; the individual incarnation of social labour; a radical leveller, effacing all distinctions; a social power become a private power; mirroring the antagonism lying between economic conditions of existence at a deeper level.[10] In such a vivid challenging way, with at times an almost lyrical account of the disruption of human feelings by money which transforms and inverts all qualities, Marx saw money as the master not the servant of man in capitalist society.

Marx's conception of early society was linked with all this. Part of a large work written in 1857–8 in preparation for what ultimately emerged as Marx's great study of *Das Kapital* was devoted to forms of pre-capitalist production—*Formen, die der kapitalistischen Produktion vorhergehn*. Known to connoisseurs of Marx familiarly as the *Formen*, this work has become available only recently (first published in Moscow, 1939; [11] in Berlin, 1952; in London, 1964). Till then a conventional listing of Marx's evolutionary stages of society was: 'Asiatic', ancient, feudal, and modern bourgeois modes of production.[12] Each was defined by its economic regime, that of the 'Asiatic' mode being state control; of ancient society being slavery; of feudal society, serfdom; and of bourgeois society, wage-labour. The *Formen* not only gave a broader basis for these developments but also indicated more flexibility in the sequence. The primal material for all these early economic and social forms was purportedly the primitive communal society, which is a subject of special anthropological interest.

Marx seems to have had ambivalent attitudes towards this concept of a primitive society. Early in *Capital* he adopts a lofty tone: 'The social productive organisms of ancient days were far simpler, enormously more easy to understand, than is bourgeois society.' But they were based, he held, either upon the immaturity of the individual human being (who had not yet severed the umbilical cord which, under primitive conditions, unites all the members of the human species one with another) or upon relations of domination and subjugation. They were the outcome of a low grade of the evolution of the productive powers of labour. . . . This restrictedness in the concrete world of fact was reflected in the ideal world, of religion . . . and so on. Later in the same work, in writing on cooperation in the labour process—and lumping together hunting tribes and Indian agricultural communities— he repeated his navel-string analogy, but linked it with communal ownership of the means of production.[13] Modern anthropology has rejected such notions of primitive immaturity, and of individual merged in group. It has also demonstrated that while the structure of production may be simple, the structure of social relationships linked with it can be quite complex and not at all 'easy to understand'. On the other hand, in the *Formen*, loosely expressed and repetitive, Marx presented a view of man in an early social state which allowed him to preserve his human dignity, before the alienation produced by capitalist exploitation—including primarily separation (estrangement) from the means of production. An individual, said Marx, has an objective mode of existence in his ownership of the earth as the original instrument of his labour, mediated by his membership of a community—'his primitive existence as part of a tribe etc.'. Marx stressed the dialectical principle— that activity of production upon the soil changed not only the material environment but also the relations of the producers, who transform and develop themselves with new powers, new conceptions, new modes of intercourse, new needs, and new speech (see Hobsbawm 1964: 81, 93). It is clear that Marx admired such an image of primitive communalism. 'The ancient conception, in which man always appears . . . as the aim of production, seems very much more exalted than the modern world, in which production is the aim of man and wealth the aim of production. . . . Hence in one way the childlike world of the ancients appears to be superior; and this is so, in so far as we seek for closed shape, form and established limitation . . .' (op. cit.: 50, 84–5). Here surely is an echo of the Romantic movement,[14] tempered by a wistful recognition that a world of closed shape cannot last but bears its own forces of change within it. Marx did not stay wistful long. To this mood succeeded an analysis to show how, through the process of history, working through the media of private property in land and exchange, man becomes individualized and parted from the fruits of his labour.

Now Marx's antithesis between communal and private is too sharp, even making allowance for his valid conception of communal ownership and private possession. He clearly failed to realize the complexity of rights over property, including property in land, characteristic of a primitive agricultural community. If Marx had consulted not the Lewis Morgan of *Ancient Society* (1877) as he did later, but the Morgan of the *League of the Iroquois* (1851) published half a dozen years before the *Formen* were composed, he would have found some general statements about the spirit of freedom never having felt 'the power of gain', and about 'absence of property in a comparative sense'; but he would have had nevertheless a complex system of property rights to face. Among the Iroquois, according to Morgan, material property was limited—to planting lots, orchards, houses, weapons, grain, skins, ornaments, etc. But the rights to property of both husband and wife continued distinct through the existence of their marriage, the wife, having inherited matrilineally, controlling and holding her own and in case of separation taking it with her. No individual could get absolute title to land, which was vested in the whole community, but his use of any portion was acknowledged and protected. (Morgan stated that an Iroquois could sell his improvements, which seems like a bourgeois gloss, but perhaps some form of transfer for equivalent was possible; alternatively he could bequeath them to his wife.) The wife's orchards were inherited by her children, while the husband's were not unless he specifically allocated them in the presence of a witness—when presumably his own near matrilineal kin's interests could be raised (Morgan 1851: 139, 141, 326–327).

Attention to this and other available ethnographic information would have enabled what Hobsbawm calls Marx's 'tantalizingly sketchy observations' to have been much more realistic.

But did Marx want them to be realistic? It must be understood that his 'primitive communalism' was a fiction, based, apart from India, on whose social conditions he had read widely, upon very slender ethnographic materials.

The issue comes up squarely with Marx's concept of capital. Many anthropologists have adopted a classification of capital which includes instruments of production in the possession of the producers and helping to yield income when utilized by labour. This is part of a classical economist's category. Marx of course would have none of this, since for him capital can arise only when the means of production are separated from the control of the worker. He rejected the notion of capital as formed from accumulation—saying *inter alia* that little or no accumulation is possible anyway in the simpler production conditions. His view was that the original formation of capital occurs because the historic process of dissolution of an old mode of production allowed value in the form of monetary wealth to buy the objective conditions of labour and exchange the worker's labour for money. (This is part of his elaborate argument on surplus value.) Since this was central to Marx's whole argument he was prepared to treat as capital only the alienated, the disjunctive elements in the production situation. But on any reading, in the *Formen* Marx clearly failed to realize that even in 'primitive communalism' of the structure he described there could be capital in a form analogous to his own sense—production instruments not owned or controlled by the worker who used them. For instance, a man in a 'primitive' Polynesian society could borrow a canoe (which he may not have helped to build) and use it as a necessary fishing aid, by tacit agreement to provide later repayments in fish or labour.[15] If capital be looked at simply as a factor in production, there is no logical reason to class under it only those items of productive equipment which are separated from the worker's possession.[16] Marx's basic thesis, the significance in economic, social, and political structure of capitalism as a system, needs no underlining. But there is a case for considering *conjoined* as well as *disjoined capital* in terms of relation of control over instrument of production by the user of it.

How now is one to judge the *Formen* from an anthropological view? Opinions differ about the value of the work. Marx obviously saw it as historical, though he did say much later (in a letter to Zasulich in 1881) that primitive communities were not all cut to a single pattern but on the contrary they form a series of social groupings differing in type and age, and marking successive phases of development (op. cit.: 144). But even Hobsbawm, who regards this work as 'Marx at his most brilliant and profound' holds that it is not 'history' in the strict sense. There is generally a convention that 'history' can be related to a body of independently verifiable evidence. By this standard, while much of *Das Kapital* is historical writing, those parts of the *Pre-Capitalist Economic Formations* which most concern anthropologists are not. What they do represent is not easy to discover. Linking with the idea of history in non-strict sense we may remember Lévi-Strauss's withdrawal of the line between history and myth, or rather between what is claimed as history and what is rejected as myth. Invoking Marx himself, in combination with Freud, Lévi-Strauss (1962: 336 *et seq.*) reminds us that it is vain to go to the historical consciousness for the truest meaning; both history and myth are selective, serving special interests. Are the *Pre-Capitalist Economic Formations* then myth? Though he does not specifically discuss this work Robert Tucker, a political scientist, would evidently think so. He regards Marx as apprehending and portraying not an empirical set of processes but an inner reality; as projecting an inner drama as a social drama, representing a self-system in conflict in terms of a social system in conflict. On this view, Marx constructed a myth of the warfare between labour and capital, and his account of pre-capitalist society would clearly form part of the background to the myth (Tucker 1961: esp. 218–32). But I think that in the definitional field the question of commitment, of belief, is relevant here, and it is uncertain how far Marx was involved by faith or by logic in this scheme.

Some scholars, including some marxist anthropologists, have held that despite occasional insights, Marx's treatment of pre-feudal society in the *Formen* is highly schematic, superficial, with a loose, sketchy typology which has led Marxists astray—presumably because they felt committed to it (Harris 1968: 227; Meillassoux 1972: 97-8). I see the interest of these pre-capitalist economic formations from another angle —not as history, not as an empirical contribution to a typology of social forms, certainly not as Hobsbawm does, as a work of 'unbroken internal logic' of elegant form, but not just as myth. I think that in the modern idiom it may be called a model, and not without interest, though rather old-fashioned and adopted without proper ethnographic testing. It is a model which is interesting because it is articulated at every point with the much more complex and powerful construction in the study of *Capital*; moreover, as Tucker has indicated more generally, it reveals almost as much about Marx as about the subject he discusses. In essence, as I see it, what Marx drafted in the *Formen* was a mirror-image of what he wrote in *Capital*—to put it crudely, he wrote the dialectic backwards.[17] I think this is exemplified by Marx's treatment of cooperation in a passage in *Capital* dealing with pre-capitalist conditions. He writes of cooperation in the labour process in the dawn of civilization, but attributes it to a type of collectivity analogous to that of a hive of bees; primitive cooperation is sharply distinguished from capitalist cooperation. In Marx's view, clearly, primitive cooperation is an almost instinctive reflex of community membership, while capitalist cooperation presupposes free wage workers who sell their labour power to capital. Then contrasting capitalist cooperation with the arrangements of peasant agriculture and independent craftsmanship he makes the paradoxical statement that cooperation manifests itself as a historical form peculiar to the capitalist process of production, and specifically differentiating that process. The change to cooperation is the first change undergone by the actual labour process when subjected to the dominion of capital (Marx, *Capital*; 1930: 351). To anthropologists who have observed cooperation in primitive economies this appropriation of the term to capitalism seems very odd (cf. e.g. Firth 1939: 115–16, 134–9, 275–6, 298). It could be argued that capitalist cooperation, though falling under the same category as primitive cooperation, is so complex as to constitute a different order, but Marx does not argue so. For him the essential criterion of cooperation is the simultaneous occupation of numerous wage workers in the same labour process. What he really had in mind, it would seem, was cooperation in the sense of side-by-side reduplication of activity, not the fitting together of labour and skills. Because the former gave the conceptual base for his analysis of capitalism—'the starting point of capitalist production'—he minimized the latter in the primitive field, and ignored the significance of decision-making in the primitive community.[18]

This is further illustrated in some argument about exchange in economic anthropology. From a marxist viewpoint exchange in primitive society is of essentially different quality than in an industrial society where the economy has separated the means of production from the worker. Here, it is argued, things exchanged have become simple commodities stripped of their human relevance; transactions are profit-seeking and so can operate as a means of extracting surplus value from the worker over and above the return he gets from his labour on them. In a primitive society, as Karl Polanyi and others have often held, exchange, like other economic relations, is 'embedded' in social relations. Put another way, as Maurice Godelier has stated it, kinship is dominant and serves as both infrastructure and superstructure. Correspondingly, universals in economic process are denied—capital, cooperation, exchange, scarcity can be only the product of historical conditions. So the principles of economics themselves must be different for pre-capitalist and capitalist economies—for primitive economies the formulations of what is called 'utility economics' have no meaning.[19]

Now I myself, with other anthropologists, have emphasized the social character of exchange in primitive societies, and examined the limitations of contemporary formal economic analysis in such conditions. But for orthodox marxists much of their argument, if taken literally, is self-defeating. For instance, if exchange is completely socialized in a primitive economy, then this destroys the contention that value is simply crystallized labour—symbolic elements must be included in the scheme. It is sometimes held that to speak of exchange or capital—perhaps even cooperation—as applying to a primitive economy is to import anachronistic categories more proper to capitalism. But the reverse is also true—to insist that primitive exchange is essentially different from our own, that a primitive society knows no capital relations, that true co-operation is peculiar to capitalism, is a kind of dialectical negation which denigrates the economic perceptions and judgement of non-capitalistic man.

The pre-capitalist economic formations are not an empirical outline of early types of economy and society, but an imaginative sketch, selecting out the main themes which Marx regarded as foils in his war against capitalism. The work is not literal Marx, it is Marx in figurative dress. It does call attention to critical elements in the economic fabric and raise significant questions. The idea of value as crystallized labour is a metaphysical assertion.[20] Taken literally, the question: where is value really bred, in the muscles or in the head?—is futile. But figuratively, it calls up difficult problems of relation between effort and estimation that students of economic anthropology continue to ponder over.[21]

Then take the so-called 'Asiatic' mode of production. This has presented problems to marxists who hold to the conventional evolutionary scheme since its relation to the Western series, e.g. feudalism, is not clear. Marx's views on the 'Asiatic' mode of production seem to have been based mainly on his reading of the situation in India. In 1853 he agreed with Engels that the absence of private landed property was effectively the key to all the Orient, and added as indices that all public works were controlled by the central government, and the villages were 'little worlds' of their own. Now many social anthropologists know from their own field experience that this is a caricature—the range of variation is great. But Marx's assertions about the main themes—control of public works versus private enterprise; role of central government versus local community—like his examination of communism in the *Economic and Philosophical Manuscripts*—have provoked illuminating discussion about the relations between political and economic forms. The cryptic possibilities of the 'Asiatic' mode, however, have made some modern interpreters inquire whether it may not have had universal validity at an early stage of history, or, forebodingly, when all capitalist modes of production have been socialized the result may be not the end of exploitation but the spread of the 'Asiatic' mode to all mankind.[22]

Relevant to a model or figurative interpretation of Marx's observations on pre-capitalist formations is the marxist argument, rather loftily advanced, that Marx's theory is not an empiricism, is not concerned with patterns of events, but with theoretical conceptions of an inner structure of relations lying behind the events and explaining them. While ignoring Marx's own concern, in his truly historical studies, for correlation of theory with observed fact, this is in line with his stress on the characteristics of the system as responsible for the apparently free acts of the individuals within it.

Marx's own attitude to this whole set of problems is also relevant to the interpretation. It seems quite clear that Marx regarded his basic postulates about humanity as having a definite moral component, of absolute, not simply historical value. He was not simply analytical, he was indignant about man's treatment of man in capitalist society—though it was the system, not the individuals, who bore the responsibility. It is Hobsbawm's view that Marx found himself increasingly appalled by the inhumanity of Western capitalism, after earlier welcoming it as an inhuman but progressive force compared with the stagnant pre-capitalist economies. But as Hobsbawm pointed out, Marx's thought cannot be interpreted as merely an ethical demand for the liberation of man (Hobsbawm 1964: 12, 50; cf. Tucker 1961: 14–21). Yet his belief in 'the triumph of the free development of all men' has no trace of relativity about it; the inevitable was also the desirable. Likewise, the appeal of doctrines about labour and value and alienation rests largely upon their moral implications, their passionate sentiments, as Alfred Espinas said nearly a century ago; or as a recent writer (Lewis 1965: 187) has put it concerning *Capital*, it is to be seen not as a treatise upon economics but as a dramatic history designed to involve its readers in the events described. There is no suggestion either that Marx regarded his values as determined by his own class position.[23]

The upshot of all this is that where they particularly concern social anthropology, I contend, Marx's own theories have no special claim to be 'scientific' or 'historical'. And, parenthetically, a successful revolution does not prove the correctness of Marx's theories any more than—as Marx himself would have argued—the success of the Christian Church proves claims to the divinity of Christ. On the other hand, as a model, a series of systematically articulated propositions subject to variation and testing, Marx's theories deserve continued scrutiny. If only as an irritant, they stimulate the collection and reinterpretation of data which may modify their conclusions. It is the literal interpretation of Marx, the 'vulgar marxism' of intellectual as well as political commitment which does not belong to our discipline. For social anthropology, literal marxism is intellectual atrophy.

This is evident from some of the work of Marx's followers. Neither Engels's *Origin of the Family, Private Property and the State* (1884) nor Lafargue's *Evolution of Property from Savagery to Civilization* (1890) is of much theoretical interest to modern social anthropologists.[24] In professional marxist anthropology, the work of Soviet ethnographers suffered for long from a literal interpretation of marxism. An interest in substantiating the methodology of historical materialism led to an immense accumulation of data but a cramping of theoretical exploration, in what Emmanuel Terray has described as developing in a 'closed vessel' (*vase clos*). But some modern Soviet anthropological work has been intellectually stimulating as well as ethnographically up to date, treating Marx and Engels more flexibly.[25]

The development of contemporary Western anthropological interest in the work of Karl Marx I put down to three main considerations. One is a broadening of theoretical interest as the ideas of other major sociological figures have been worked through. More important is the confrontation of anthropologists with radical changes in the character of their material, which the existing body of theory has not yet been able to handle adequately. Then a questioning of established institutions and values, and a deep sense of their contradictions, has led to a search for a theory to correspond. Marxist doctrine offers a coherent diagnosis and systematic explanation of the world's disorders, founded upon what claims to be a philosophical approach understanding the principles of the inner reality of social existence.

The question whether or how far any individual anthropologist is a marxist is not of much relevance. But among Western professed marxists one may differentiate what may be colloquially called 'gut-marxists' from 'cerebral marxists'. 'Gut-marxists' are those who feel deeply about the world situation, hold that it conforms broadly to Marx's theories of class conflict, base and superstructure, etc., and espouse his interpretation of historical development with moral fervour. Such an overt orientation, with elements of literal marxism, has recently come to expression in Western social anthropology. In 1971, in an attempt to infuse anthropological discussion with a greater sense of relevance for problems of radical change, several open sessions of the American Anthropological Association annual meeting in New York were devoted to symposia on marxism. Critical appraisal was made of contemporary anthropology in the light of historical materialism as an explanatory method, and of the social relations of imperialism as a body of relevant but neglected fact. Discussions of problems created by Western economic and political dominance of less developed societies, of the significance of migratory labour for a colonial regime, of the genesis of proletarian consciousness, of class identity and struggle, of the political role of a peasantry were pointers to the desire for a re-orientation of anthropological theory towards a more explicit ideological position. Out of this somewhat confused set of empirical data and general formal propositions one sensed the concern of many anthropologists, including students, that our discipline was being used to support an exploitative system.

Linked with such intellectual positions has arisen a body of opinion calling for a much more direct involvement of anthropologists in the socio-political situations they study, primarily in terms of marxist interpretation. Reiterating the fallacy of a claim to a disinterested social science, such views call for an awakening of anthropology to its social responsibilities and for active participation in change. As some of my colleagues will remember, such positions are not altogether new in British social anthropology.

In the present climate of the discussion I think some of the polemical issues should not be entirely avoided. It is becoming a popular cliché now to write of anthropology, particularly social anthropology, as the child—or the grandchild, or the stepchild—of colonialism. British social anthropology here is an easy mark because unlike the Americans or the Russians we have acknowledged our colonies as such; and unlike the French and the Dutch we produced between the wars a new and fruitful body of anthropological theory which has since been used as a vigorous analytical instrument. Criticism has been levelled at the whole discipline of social anthropology, and at leading figures personally, for having adapted their studies in the interests of colonial rule. Ironically in the light of what I quoted earlier from Radcliffe-Brown, he among others has been described as always desiring that anthropology be a relevant, practical science, in order to win funds and recognition by government,

43

and for the purposes of British imperialism. In the light of the strategy of British colonialism to maintain control over their subject peoples, far-sighted anthropologists, it is said, regarded with alarm the symptoms of social change, and considered it their mission to provide colonial authorities with the knowledge needed to allow them to retain their political control. While such charges have been made sincerely, much of this is a travesty, argued from a point of view as partisan as that which is stigmatized.[26] While it may be true, as Schumpeter has stated, that political criticism cannot be met effectively by rational argument, a brief comment is in place.

To begin with, anthropology is not the bastard of colonialism but the legitimate offspring of the Enlightenment. Interest in the practical relevance of social anthropology over the last forty years has been very uneven, but has been definitely very secondary to comparative general theoretical interest. The study of social change has long ceased to be confused with applied anthropology. In the applied context, while it has seemed to make sense to advocate that knowledge of the structure and functioning of African and other alien institutions was preferable to ignorance, this knowledge has been regarded by anthropologists primarily as means to securing more respect for peoples' own values, not as a means of controlling them more effectively. Some anthropologists have explicitly rejected the idea that they should be expected to serve administration policy or proselytizing campaign, or refused to accept a claim of the absolute validity of Western moral standards invoked to enlist anthropological assistance.[27] Many have recorded the disruptive effects of a colonial situation upon the societies they studied, and some have specifically examined the significance of colonialism as a social type.[28] Indeed I would argue that one role of social anthropology has been to supply ammunition for the forces of contradiction within the system. Governments have supported anthropology, but anthropology is dedicated to exposure of the structures and values of the societies studied. This includes making clear the aims and interests of the people as stated by themselves and revealed in their own behaviour, in terms of their own conflicts as well as integrative ties. In the history of the subject this has been recognized by some members of the societies concerned who have come to anthropology for analytical tools to aid them in their search and struggle, or who have appreciated the record anthropologists have made of their institutions at a given point of time. In this whole historical context, it is well to remember what Karl Marx wrote of the factory inspectors, the medical reporters on public health, and other officers in Britain on whose observations he drew so heavily for his generalizations on their capitalist society. He did not accuse them of subjectivism or of supporting the system; he praised their competence, their freedom from bias and from respect of persons, and their power to search out the truth. I suggest that despite their failings, social anthropologists have on the whole been at least as competent and perceptive as factory inspectors—and perhaps have worked harder and suffered more.[29]

There is also a comparative issue. Kathleen Gough has pointed out that social anthropologists from the beginning have inhabited a triple environment, involving obligations first to the people we studied, second to our colleagues and our science, and third to the powers who employed us in universities or who funded our research. She says, justly, that in many cases we now seem to be in danger of being torn apart by the conflicts between the first and the third set—the peoples and the governments; while the loyalties to our science, as an objective and humane endeavour, are being severely tested and jeopardized. Now much crude marxist argument speaks as if these issues were quite clear and their identification simple. But as Ioan Lewis (1968: 405, 418) has pointed out in comment, the anthropologist's duty to side with the 'oppressed' rather than with the 'oppressor' may have great poignancy for those who work in the contemporary 'Third World'. The interests and aspirations of local societies may be at complete odds with wider needs for economic development and viability, or unification on some broad political or religious platform. Lenin held that in conditions of colonial oppression nationalist movements should be encouraged for their revolutionary importance (though Marx, who looked on colonialism as historically inevitable, did not express very definite opinion on this point); (see introd. Avineri 1969: 13–14). But in modern states the issue of encouragement may be highly complex. Among peoples well known in anthropological literature the Micronesians want self-determination from the United States, who holds them in the firm grasp of a strategic Trusteeship Territory. The issue here is fairly clear. But what about the Nagas of Assam, who are fighting for independence from India, who, they say, is their oppressor; is there neo-colonialism in this situation?

It is from such point of view that to a so-called 'liberal' anthropologist of socialist interests, the successful revolutionary societies such as the USSR, the Peoples' Republic of China, or Cuba, are still part of the problem, not part of the solution. They still present the basic dilemma—of maintaining relative freedom and creativity for individuals in the course of securing centralized decision or common action on matters of public import. Problems of power and hence potentials of conflict occur in all large-scale organizations. One solution—a guiding party of the elite with a rigorous discipline, may mean the crystallization of a privileged bureaucracy, intent on keeping power but using the name of the people. Another solution—of trying to maintain a continuing revolution by the masses—can generate enthusiastic participation but can involve undiscriminating criticism and impulsive waste of skills and resources. Marxists have their vocabulary and interpretations for all this. But for social anthropologists the underlying issue remains: anywhere where control of information has become an overt instrument of public policy, freedom of scientific opinion is at risk. This may apply especially to 'grass-roots' sciences such as ours, which explore and expose dissidence and conflict at an empirical, often local, level.

In the West, 'gut-marxists'—or 'organic intellectuals', if the term be preferred—have the function of stimulating anthropological awareness of relevant political variables in the social situations we study. But it is significant that nowhere as yet in the writings of Soviet anthropologists, nor of post-revolution Chinese anthropologists in the Peoples' Republic, by any evidence that has reached the West, does one find the depth of critical scrutiny of the effects of revolutionary process on the structure of their local communities, in terms comparable to those in which Western anthropologists have written of the transformation of the less-developed societies in Africa, Oceania, and elsewhere.

The work of 'cerebral' marxists—some of it clearly revisionist—can be best exemplified from French anthropology, which has opened up problems of a highly theoretical order. Predictably, the issue has been raised of how the thought of Lévi-Strauss, claiming some ancestry in Marx, can be fitted to Marx's conception of history; can the structures of Lévi-Strauss conform to a theory of change? Alternatively, how far are Marx's theories of the origin and development of social forms consistent with modern structuralist concepts? Some marxists have been uncompromising and rejected Lévi-Strauss's structuralism as a variant of bourgeois ideology. Others have sought a reconciliation. Godelier, for instance, has argued that while the traditional analysis of Marx's work on the dialectic is hopelessly wrong, the essence of the treatment of *Capital* is its perception of structure in terms not of visible relationships but of their hidden logic; hence Marx is clearly a forerunner of the modern structuralist movement. Moreover, Godelier buttresses this view by holding that a correct interpretation of Marx's work would show that the study of the internal functioning of a structure must precede consideration of its origins and development.[30] Basic to much of such argument is a clash over the meaning of history—whether it is to be understood as a demonstrably empirical continuous working out of human activities by dialectical process in specified time contexts, as in Sartre's version of the Marxist view; or whether it is to be seen in a more abstract way as a series of discontinuous choices of incidents and processes fitted by men into a logical order in terms of general modes of thought. Hence the contrasting contentions: that the structuralism of Lévi-Strauss is a-historic, or universally historic; or that what Sartre calls history is to Lévi-Strauss another form of myth (see Rosen 1971; cf. Diamond 1964). It could be an interesting exercise for anthropologists to translate into such alternative terms of event and conceptualization the Marx–Engels statement that the history of all past society has consisted in the development of class antagonisms.

A related set of issues concerns Marx's well-worn proposition that the aggregate of production relations constitutes the economic structure of society, the real basis on which a juridical and political superstructure is erected, to which correspond definite forms of social consciousness (Marx 1859: v). Sophisticated marxist interpretations reject a crude determinism in the relation of the social to the economic, and offer other formulations for the connection. Godelier argues for example that in a 'primitive' society kinship does not grow out from relations of production but actually functions as such; that there is an internal correspondence between economy and kinship until in social evolution they separate in functional differentiation. But some of the modern marxist argument about what is popularly known as the problem of infrastructure and superstructures (Marx himself wrote *Basis* and *Ueberbau*) tends to be only a reformulation in more abstract terms of what other social anthropologists have given in analyses of relationships between such interdependent variables.[31]

Lévi-Strauss has taken another line. Starting from the idea that myths are an expression, disguised in language, of fundamental principles of social conflict, his impressive analysis aims to interpose between base and superstructures a mediator, a synthesizing operator, in the form of a conceptual scheme of defined structures of thought, which incorporate such principles. So the development from basic activity into behaviour patterns (*praxis* into *pratiques* in his play upon words) becomes more intelligible. So he has enlarged the theory of superstructures, which as he notes, has been scarcely sketched out by Marx (Lévi-Strauss 1962: 173: trans. 1966: 130).

More concrete concern has been given to modes of production in 'pre-capitalist' societies, and their interaction with social factors. Claude Meillassoux, for instance, has examined production, distribution and alliances in a segmentary lineage society, the Guro of the Ivory Coast. Tracing the change from subsistence economy to commercial agriculture, he identifies the most significant determining forces in the social relations in each phase of the economic transformation, placing particular emphasis on the controlling role of the eldest male sibling in a household.[32] In a more general context Meillassoux has also pointed out the inadequacy of Marx's own generalizations about pre-capitalist societies. He advocates more systematic exploration of their economic formations, using theoretical insights from Marx's own more developed analysis in *Capital*. So, starting from Marx's notion of land as an instrument of labour in self-sustaining agricultural communities, Meillassoux develops an argument that it is not control of the means of production that is of prime significance for exercise of power, but control of the means of *r*eproduction by wealth—over subsistence and over women. He looks to continuity and change over time, e.g. the generation succession, as essential to the socio-economic organization. He also places such economic formations in a historical frame by considering the radical transformations that take place in conditions of modern capitalist development. His treatment is sometimes doctrinaire, mis-

47

conceptions about 'universalism' and other theoretical issues in the views of 'liberal' economic anthropologists seem apparent. But the approach is critical, of Marx as well as of others; concepts are re-formulated in a lively systematic way. As with Godelier and the Baruya of New Guinea or Terray and the Dida of West Africa, so with Meillas-soux and the Guro—there is association of theory with intensive field research that refreshingly puts Marx's thought in its proper light as material for scientific use.

Yet Marx's militancy is not forgotten. In his confrontation of marxism with studies of primitive society, Emmanuel Terray spiritedly sets out as a final objective the capture of social anthropology. It is the present task of marxist researchers, he notes, to annex the reserved domain of social anthropology to the field of application of historical materialism, i.e. to prove the universal validity of concepts and methods elaborated by it. The aim is to replace social anthropology by a par-ticular section of historical materialism consecrated to socio-economic formations where the capitalist mode of production is absent (op. cit.: 173). Though it is envisaged that ethnologists will collaborate with historians on this work, nothing is said about possible demarcation problems and power structures that might be involved.

If the older marxist combination of outworn evolutionary schemes, economic determinism, apocalyptic vision and demand for total intellectual commitment has alienated many social anthropologists, some theoretical propositions of marxism have had effect. Ideas about the political significance of relations of production, about class structure and class formation, about alienation, about ideology, with some aspects of the dialectical method, have seeped through the traditional walls. Some years ago I myself drew attention to the significance of Marx for 'dynamic' theory in social anthropology: the importance of seeking an economic dimension in social action; of scrutinizing power relations for contradiction and conflict as well as for adjustment; of examining moral formulations in terms of interests underlying them (Firth 1964: 19–26). Others have pursued such themes more systematic-ally or more forcefully.

In the last half-century, but especially since the war, while there has undoubtedly been much diffusion of marxist thought in Western social anthropology, its effects are often impossible to identify in particular cases. In general terms, however, from a concept of predatory lineage, or a reinterpretation of landlord–tenant relations, to the more direct relation of religious beliefs and ritual acts to power structures, there has been a sharpening of anthropological perceptions which has inclined towards rather than away from marxist ideas.

For example, it would be hard to trace the influence of Marx's concept of ideology in social anthropology. Though certainly some stimulus came through Karl Mannheim, early students learned from Malinowski to take peoples' statements about values, ethical expressions, judgement on conduct as part of the instrumentality of their society, to be held up to the light like lantern slides so that they could be related to the social structure in definable ways. But while Marx's own theory of interests remained unspecified (Birnbaum op cit.: 94, 117), and while few anthropologists would accept a rigorous determinism, it seems probable that knowledge of the marxist position on ideology has reinforced the anthropological view of ideas representing and disguising interests, and so giving a partial view of society. That ritual may conceal basic conflict, and that ritualization of relations may help to maintain a power structure at the same time as it may help to protect an individual by specifying his role as he acts it out—ideas which Max Gluckman has long advocated—is clearly related to the concepts of Marx as well as of Simmel.[33] In the study of millenarian movements, by adopting a marxist position, Peter Worsley gave a fresh turn to the interpretation, stressing their significance as a form of political protest. Despite an overemphasis in this direction—many of these cults or movements seem to have been as much forms of symbolic economic activity—this analysis stimulated scrutiny of them in terms of historical circumstances of alien political control.[34]

Some overt effect of Marx's ideas has emerged in recent years in analyses of the structure and role of a peasantry as a social type in changing economic and social conditions. Much anthropological work on peasant society has not been politically oriented. But recently a problem has emerged in the context of international events, since contrary to Marx's ideas, though not to those of modern marxists such as Gramsci, a peasantry rather than an urban proletariat has provided much modern revolutionary material. So anthropologists concerned with peasant institutions, especially in the Mediterranean area, the Caribbean, and Latin America, have focused not only on peasant traditionalism and ideology, peasant household, peasant marketing, but also on the political awareness and role of peasants, the quality of their leadership in a situation of radical change, and their relation to urban class structures. Even Marx's famous 'sack of potatoes' analogy, which stressed the relative autonomy of peasant households, has been invoked, with an eye to their revolutionary potential.[35] Contrasting in a general way with such peasant studies has been a series of analyses of social relationships in a plantation system (as by Mintz, Wolf, Jayawardena), where alignment of power and class according to production role are displayed in structural terms which invite reference to marxist theory.[36] More generally, in political anthropology, there has been a shift of emphasis from traditional functional and structural studies through more dynamic interactional and organizational studies to analysis of the implications of principles of contradiction in the body politic based upon implicit opposition of interest between social categories rather than explicit conflict between individuals (e.g. Asad 1972: 74–94).

Some anthropological reactions to marxism have been concerned not so much with substantive issues as with Marx's method of approach—primarily his dialectical materialism. We know that neither Marx nor Hegel invented the dialectic, which in some form of argument by examination and resolution of contradictions goes back to the Greeks. We know too that the form of the dialectic chosen can vary according to the discipline of the scholar, the use he wants to make of it, and the kind of intellectual baggage he is prepared to tolerate with it. In its basic expression, much broader than the crude thesis–antithesis–synthesis concept commonly associated with it, it embodies two main modes or emphases of primary interest for anthropologists. One is the assumption of a principle of intrinsic contradiction in the nature of phenomena, leading to inevitable change; the other is an assumption of the possibility of contradiction in the set of ideas by which the phenomena are envisaged. The first standpoint, basic to the materialism of Marx and Engels, has been epitomized in Joseph Stalin's version (1947)—the dialectic was a method of regarding nature holistically, in a state of continuous movement and change, continuous renewal and development, with internal contradiction inherent in all things, as a process of development in which changes can occur abruptly and radically. Running to some extent athwart this is another marxist view, as expressed for example by Gramsci (1957: 61; cf. Zitta 1964: 72; Rosen 1971: 270–4), of conflict between thought and act, with co-existence of two conceptions of the world, one affirmed in words and the other explaining itself in effective actions. For the second, Hegelian standpoint, turn to a philosopher, J. N. Findlay. In his framework the essence of the dialectic is higher-order comment on a thought-position previously achieved. One sees the possibility of contradiction in the position, what can be said about it that cannot be said in it. So it is the mode of conception that is criticized rather than the actual matter of fact that has been conceived. In this form of the dialectic, then, a series of deepening analyses is obtained going beyond ordinary commonsense terms (Findlay 1963: 219–20).

It is a fair presumption that anthropologists who have made use of the dialectic have often been stimulated by marxist ideas, upon which they have commented, or from which they have implicitly dissented. Marvin Harris (1968: 230–6), one of the most explicit on such issues, has accepted Marx's materialism in a cultural frame, but rejected Marx's use of Hegelianism. He has granted some value to the dialectical mode of thought as hypothesis about human cognitive process, but has denied its significance for world evolutionary process. For Harris, the metaphysical influence of Hegel, as he sees it, was the 'Hegelian monkey' on the backs of Marx and Engels. Another view has been to reject Marx for his materialism but to accept the dialectic, albeit in a Hegelian mode in which ideas, not material forces, are the generative elements. This Burridge (1969: 136–40) has done in his examination of millenarian movements, envisaging conflict in the world of ideas with a transcendent power (*Geist*) admitted to the operations. More broadly, Robert Murphy (1971) has also embraced a non-marxist dialectic as a fundamental postulate for the understanding of human thought and social life. For Murphy, drawing to some extent upon Findlay, the principal character of a dialectic is that it is critical and sceptical of received truth and established fact, an iconoclasm that follows from its premises. It is not Burridge's version of Hegel, for there is no *Geist*, but neither is it the dialectic of Marx, for Murphy accepts elements of phenomenology and an explicit recognition of subjective states. Murphy sees his use of the dialectic as enabling him to identify infrastructures that are logical products of the investigator's mind, beyond the ordinary empirical structures derived from observation. (In some of these analyses it is hard to distinguish the specific use of the dialectic from scientific method in general.) In Lévi-Strauss again the analysis has taken another turn. Though explicitly not calling himself a marxist in the ordinary sense, he has emphasized that what he found in Marx when a young man was a model for the study of social phenomena, by which, to understand consists in reducing one type of social reality to another, that which is true being never the most manifest.[37] This guiding principle, enunciated in *Tristes Tropiques* (1955: 44), reappeared in another form in *La Pensée sauvage* (1962: 336), where the combined lesson of Marx and Freud is given, somewhat dismally, as being that the meaning people attach to their acts is never the right one; superstructures are faulty acts which have been 'successful'. In his subtle treatment of these difficult issues Lévi-Strauss points out that a basic problem is to ascertain the relation between the surface presentation, the sense-experiences, and the underlying reason. In a kind of scientific model of the sacrifice syndrome he argues that we must first repudiate experience (*le vécu*) in order to attain reality—though they must be re-integrated later in an objective synthesis.[38]

Behind much of such reaction to Marx, whether positive or negative, lies a wish to go beyond what is thought to be the traditional empiricism of functional and structural social anthropology. There is dissatisfaction with so-called 'common-sense' definitions and interpretations of social phenomena, and a view that greater adequacy is to be found in principles of deductive reasoning—whether dialectical or more generally analytical in form—to reveal the 'inner reality' of social life. Criticism is directed against the empiricist lack of systematic framework of ideas— and so on. Some of this may be an intellectual's response to the frustrating inconsistencies of our ordinary social relationships. But whereas Marx always tried to marry the abstract to the concrete, some anthropologists seem bent on divorcing them. But there is sometimes confusion among the more ardent exponents of such views, between empiricism as a stress upon the importance of experience in establishing the validity of theory, and empiricism as opposed to theory. In the empiricism of British social anthropology it has long been recognised that structures are not seen but inferred; that observation alone is useless without a theoretical framework; and that the relation between them is the cardinal problem.

I take it that all anthropologists would agree with Robert Boyle that it is one thing to be able to help Nature to produce things, and another to understand well the nature of the things produced (1661: 167–8). I much doubt if Radcliffe-Brown, often termed an empiricist, 'always saw the principle as directly distilled from the data' (Murphy op. cit.: 172) when he constructed that model of the social organization of Australian tribes on which so much later work has drawn. To rephrase what I pointed out years ago: there is structure at all levels—in the phenomena, as in the perceptions which order them and in the concepts which interpret their logical relationships; and it is presumptuous to assign to one level more 'reality' than to another. To return to Boyle and the problem of evidence—an anthropologist is not a Jonathan Swift, picking out some mode of human thinking as an abstract principle and constructing a society around it; he observes and describes, in generalized form by the use of abstraction, the verbal and non-verbal behaviour of actual people in particular societies. As amateur philosopher or analyst of language he may speak grandly of modes of thought but as anthropologist he does not escape the problem of authenticity.

This is where the relevance of marxist theory of society lies for social anthropology. Many marxists now recognize that much of Marx's theory in its literal form is outmoded, an essentially nineteenth-century historical product of a bourgeois intellectual able to transcend his class limitations. In many ways industrial society has not developed as Marx predicted: the working class is not in increasing misery; wages are not being forced down to a minimum; a managerial bureaucracy has often succeeded the capitalist entrepreneur; the Western working class does not unite with the masses of the less-developed countries but connives in the widening gap between them; the revolutionary societies have their own power struggles, if anything more bitter in accusation, more brutal in treatment of the defeated than in the capitalist world. Marx was a critic and a prophet, not a planner; he gave a vision not a blueprint of the Promised Land. But some of his major issues and his conclusions are still with us—the almost inevitable logic of technical improvement, with its concomitant drive for economic development, omnivorous consumption of resources, and irreversible destruction of forms of human society, is linked in the West with commercial incentives of profit-seeking which threaten so many of our aesthetic and moral values. In the relations between the more and the less developed societies the same expansive tendencies, not limited to capitalism, seem paramount (Birnbaum 1969).

What Marx's theories offer to social anthropology is a set of hypotheses about social relations and especially about social change. Marx's insights—about the basic significance of economic factors, especially

production relations; their relation to structures of power; the formation of classes and the opposition of their interests; the socially relative
character of ideologies; the conditioning force of a system upon
individual members of it—embody propositions which must be taken
for critical scrutiny into the body of our science. The theories of Marx
should be put on a par with, say, those of Durkheim or Max Weber.
Because they imply radical change they are more threatening. But they
need not be treated as dogma, as a received scientific system (e.g.
Gramsci op. cit.: 117); nor should they be embraced as a set of symbolic forms for an inner social reality. Some of their basic postulates are
assumptions of a metaphysical order and as such untestable, but they
provide initial theoretical standpoints, while others can be subjected to
the usual testing methods of our science. I am advocating then, not so
much a dialogue between non-marxist and marxist anthropologists—
whoever they may be—as a metaphorical translation of Marx's
memorial from Highgate Cemetery to where it really belongs, the scene
of his *praxis*—in the Reading Room of the British Museum. And on it
I suggest we might put the motto with which Karl Marx himself ended
the preface to the first edition of his volume on *Capital* just over a
century ago:

SEGUI IL TUO CORSO; E LASCIA DIR LE GENTI
Follow your own bent, and let people say what they will.

Notes

1 This paper presents the complete text, unchanged save for the omission of two
   introductory paragraphs and three minor verbal alterations, of the inaugural
   Radcliffe-Brown Lecture in Social Anthropology read before the British
   Academy, 3 May 1972. The lecture explored and brought up to date my thinking
   on the significance of Karl Marx's writings for social anthropology, a topic to
   which I had made brief reference earlier (see my 'Comment on "Dynamic
   Theory" in Social Anthropology', in Firth 1964).
      But the paper was delivered before the publication of several writings relevant
   to my theme (e.g. Meillassoux 1972; Godelier 1973; Asad 1973), and I have not
   been able to take account of them in the present paper. More generally, the major
   biography of Karl Marx by David McLellan, and that of Emile Durkheim by
   Stephen Lukes, would have added to my understanding of the background of
   my lecture, had they been available at the time.

2 Marx's flexibility in the matter of theory has often been stressed, with justice.
   But leaving aside inconsistencies of statement which occur in his work, his flexibility seems to have applied primarily to his caution in coming to conclusions;
   once arrived at, his conclusions were put forwardly very firmly, without alternative.

3 Some American works refer to Marx and Engels, but primarily to criticize their

theory of social evolution. Paul Bohannan (1963: 172–6) credits Marx with original thinking on the subject of rank, but views his theory of class structure critically. Marvin Harris (1968) is the only major American anthropologist to deal fairly fully, if somewhat idiosyncratically, with the relevant range of Marx's views, though Leslie White, Stanley Diamond, Morris Opler, and Marshall Sahlins are familiar with Marx's ideas. Morton Fried (1964: 49–61) has examined 'core' and 'superstructure' in marxist thought.

References to Marx in British social anthropology have usually been brief. See e.g. Firth 1939: 361 (1965: 20); 1951: 168–9; 1964: 19–26; Gluckman 1963: 10–11; Frankenberg 1967: 47–89; Lloyd 1967: 164, 272, etc.; 1968: 29–33.

4 But I wish to acknowledge the stimulus of Raymond Aron's study of Marx, and also of T. B. Bottomore's writings.

5 Frederick Engels, Speech at the Graveside of Karl Marx (Marx and Engels 1968: 430).

6 Durkheim and Mauss (1901–2: 67, 70–1; trans. 1963: 82, 86). They cite De la Grasserie only as having developed, obscurely, analogous ideas (in 1899).

7 Karl Marx, 'The Eighteenth Brumaire of Louis Bonaparte', 3rd edn 1885, in Marx and Engels (1968: 117, 120); cf. Karl Korsch (1938: 74–6). Norman Birnbaum (1960: 91–117 etc.) is illuminating on this theme.

8 Robert Merton (1949: 226, 392) has pointed out that in the sociology of knowledge there have been parallel French and German traditions. Durkheim may not have seen some of Marx's early writings—though the *Economic and Philosophical Manuscripts* were published in Paris in 1844, in the socialist journal *Vorwärts*.

Bottomore and Rubel write that though Durkheim expressed reservations about 'economic materialism' he followed closely the publications of the Marxist sociological school. 'It was under Durkheim's direction that the early volumes of the *Année sociologique* devoted a considerable amount of space to the discussion and critical examination of the sociology of Marx, and of his disciples and interpreters' (1963: 47, 54). This seems to apply, however, mainly to volume i of *L'Année sociologique* (1896–7), which contained reviews by R. Lapie (270–7) of A. Labriola's essays on the materialist conception of history; by E. Durkheim of E. Grosse's study of forms of the family and economy (319–32); and by F. Simiand of R. Stammler's work on economy and law (488–97). Simiand's review was appreciative, those of Lapie and Durkheim much less so; Marx was mentioned only incidentally, and by Durkheim not at all. Later volumes of the journal had very little reference to Marx's work or that of his followers—e.g. D. Parodi on A. Loria's sociology (*AS*, v, 1900–1: 129–33); C. Bouglé in a general review of theories of division of labour (*AS*, vi, 1901–2: 93, 113). A translation, *Critique de l'économie politique*, was warmly greeted (*AS*, iii, 1898–9: 544), but *La Lutte des classes en France*, and *Le XVIII brumaire de Louis Bonaparte* were noted without comment, while volumes II and III of *Le Capital* were coolly received merely as 'so necessary to the true comprehension of the doctrine, the essential work of Marx' (*AS*, iv, 1899–1900: 564; v, 1900–1: 558–9). And whereas *La Lutte des classes* and *Le XVIII brumaire* were entered under the head of 'Socialism', the two volumes of *Le Capital* appeared merely under 'Divers' in the economic sociology section. Presumably all this was a reflection of the view (*AS*, iii: 542–4) that *L'Année sociologique* restricted itself to discussing works which studied socialism scientifically.

In a new section on the sociology of knowledge in Volume xi of *L'Année sociologique* (1906–9: 41) Durkheim and Bouglé claimed to have been occupied with such questions for a long time though most of the works reviewed so far had come under the head of the sociology of religion. But bearing in mind Merton's phrase (op. cit.: 223) about marxism in various respects being the storm centre of *Wissenssoziologie*, it is interesting that the introduction to this new section made no reference to earlier thinkers in this field.

For general discussion of Durkheim's views I am indebted to Talcott Parsons (1937: 301–450; Raymond Aron (1968) and Alvin W. Gouldner (1959). See also G. Kagan (1938); Armand Cuvillier (1948).

9 Suzanne de Brunhoff (1967); Marx's term was *Schatzbildung* (Marx 1859: 104–116).

10 *Capital* (1930: 49, 113, 117, 120, 589); see also Marx's views in *Economic and Philosophical Manuscripts* (trans. Bottomore 1963: 189–94).

11 *Grundrisse* (Heft v: 375–413). The valuable introduction to the English edition (Hobsbawm 1964) gives the history of the work.

12 Preface to *Kritik der politischen Oekonomie* (1859: vi).

13 *Capital* (1930: 53, 350–1). Cf. J. Suret-Canale (1964), who insists that 'primitive' refers only to hunters and collectors, not agriculturalists.

14 Cf. Ernest Seillière (1911: 207 *et seq.*)—a work mentioned to me by Julian Pitt-Rivers.

15 Raymond Firth (1939: 62, 319). Marx held that 'primitive' instruments of labour were only property in the sense of being part of land ownership (*Formations*: 99) —but empirically this was not so; they were often separate.

16 e.g. Robert Szereszewski (1965: 22–3) discusses manmade assets of the traditional economy: the stock of dwelling units, simple tools, canoes, etc.—some of them on the borderline of capital goods owing to high depreciation rates. The main analytically interesting feature, in his view, is that these were simple transformations of tool-aided labour into capital assets. 'This is the simplest case of capitalisation, without the structural problems of capital-formation; the problems of conveying and integrating several flows of inputs and factor services into a final structure.'

17 Perhaps this is what Hobsbawm meant by a passage which is still obscure to me —that the draft work attempts to discover in the analysis of social evolution the characteristics of *any* dialectical, or indeed of any satisfying, theory on any subject whatsoever! (op. cit.: 11).

18 J. Suret-Canale (1964) argues that ethnologists have misunderstood Marx on primitive communalism because the only definition one can give to such societies is that they do not and cannot allow of exploitation of man by man, and so of antagonistic classes, from the low level of productive forces. 'Nothing is more false than to imagine such people as deprived of individuality.' But this not only sidesteps the basic issue of mode of property-holding, in empirical terms; it also ignores Marx's own 'worker bee as part of the hive' analogy, for members of a primitive community.

19 Ronald Frankenberg (1967: 51–70); Maurice Godelier (1970: 355; 1971: 96); Claude Meillassoux (1972; and introd., 1971: 68–9).

20 See the opinion of Joan Robinson (1962: 34–41). R. H. Tawney traced this assertion back to the Middle Ages—'The true descendant of the doctrines of Aquinas is the labour theory of value. The last of the Schoolmen was Karl Marx' (1938: 49, 52). Ernest Seillière (1911: 281–90) writes of Marx's 'divinization' of simple labour-power.

21 e.g. for anthropological discussion of labour-time as an arbitrary measure of value in non-monetary economic conditions, see C. S. Belshaw (1954: 149–50); R. F. Salisbury (1962: 106–11, 186); Ronald Frankenberg (1967: 70–4).

55

22 See <u>Ferenc Tökei, Maurice Godelier</u>, *et al.* in *La Pensée* (114, 1964: 3–73). An attempt to provide the 'Asiatic' mode of production with universal value at an early stage in the marxist scheme was given by Jean Suret-Canale (op. cit.), but criticized by Catherine Coquery-Vidrovitch (1969: 61–78), who argues for a specific African mode of production.

23 Eugene Kamenka (1962: 28) holds that Marx's concept of freedom was largely moulded by Hegelian philosophy, reinforced by an outstanding character trait— an almost Nietzschean concern with dignity, seen as independence and mastery over things. For the problem of transcendence of class position, see e.g. Norman Birnbaum (op. cit.: 93), Raymond Aron (op. cit. I: 218). Cf. also Marx *Capital* (1930: 864).

   I have used transcendence in the ordinary secular sense of surmounting a particular in favour of a more general aim. Raya Dunayevskaya (1958: 319) discusses transcendence more technically, in relation to alienation. Cf. Robert Tucker (op. cit.: 57) on the Hegelian concept of self-realization through successive transcending of limits.

24 Paul Lafargue (a son-in-law of Marx) credits Vico with having been the first to apprehend 'the great law of historical development' of the universal stages in human society. Engels, who seems to have been mildly paranoid about his work, said in his preface to the 4th edition (1891) that 'the chauvinistically inclined English anthropologists are still striving their utmost to kill by silence the revolution which Morgan's discoveries have effected in our conception of primitive history, while they appropriate his results without the slightest compunction'.

25 e.g. on an Asian theme J. V. Maretin (1961: 168–95) has shown the Minangkabau system of Sumatra to have been changing from its matrilineal form, not due, as had been alleged, to a more consistent application of Islamic law, but rather to economic developments, including a move to production of commercial crops. More generally (I know only the translations) interesting work has appeared in *Sovietskaya Etnografia* and in international congress and other essay papers, under the names of, for instance, O. Akhmanova, V. P. Alexeiev, I. L. Andreiev, M. S. Butinova, L. V. Danilova, V. Kroupianskaia, D. A. Olderogge, A. I. Pershits, L. P. Potapov.

26 For a vivid controversy on these issues, see Bernard Magubane *et al.* (1971: 419–43).

   For a reasoned argument, see Jack Stauder (1971; my copy by courtesy of Mr Stauder).

27 For some of my own views, see Firth (1936: 599; 1946: 230–2).

28 See, e.g., G. Balandier (1963: 3 *et seq.*). Balandier gives a reasoned consideration of Marx's views in his *Anthropologie politique* (1967).

29 Marx, *Capital* (1930: 863–4; preface to 1st edition). I find that Lévi-Strauss has also appreciated this passage (1958: 417n.)

30 Maurice Godelier (1970: 340–58; 1971). For a general theoretical treatment, see Lucien Sebag (1964).

31 Cf. E. R. Leach, to the effect that kinship systems have no 'reality' at all except in relation to land and property (1961: 305 *et passim*).

32 Claude Meillassoux (1964). Cf. review by Emmanuel Terray (1972, Pt II) arguing *inter alia* against a concept of any unitary 'mode of production' at this pre-capitalist phase; and critical review from a more orthodox standpoint by Jean Suret-Canale (1967).

33 I omit complications, such as the notion of integrative conflict put forward by Gluckman, related to a distinction between conflict within a system of which the premises are generally accepted, and conflict about the premises themselves (Gluckman 1955: esp. Ch. VI; 1965: 109 *et seq*.). This again may differ from contradiction, not overtly perceived, between the premises or their implications. Cf. F. G. Bailey (1960: 7, 239). As Chandra Jayawardena has pointed out, the concept of conflict can have theoretical significance only when the system to which it refers has been clearly specified (1963: 132–3).

34 Peter Worsley, *The Trumpet Shall Sound* (1957; in the introduction to the second edition of this work Worsley has modified his commitment to a determinist marxist orientation). Worsley's analysis was closely followed by that of Vittorio Lanternari (1960); he adopted a dialectical interpretation of relations between prophet and cultural conditions in political terms, but without a specific marxist theme. Much in these positions was anticipated by Jean Guiart (1951).

  For an examination of 'marxist' explanations of millenarian activities, see Kenelm Burridge (1969: 130–6).

35 e.g. especially Eric R. Wolf (1966; 1969; and review by Jayawardena 1971). See also Mintz (1971); cf. Worsley (op. cit.: 229). See also Gramsci (op. cit.: 30–1).

36 e.g. Mintz and Wolf (1959); Jayawardena (op. cit.). Cf. Larson (1971).

37 Cf. Georg Lukács (1954: 1914): 'Vom lebendigen Anschauen zum abstrakten Denken *und von diesem zur Praxis*—das ist der dialektische Weg der Erkenntnis der *Wahrheit*, der Erkenntnis der objektiven Realität' (Lenin).

38 Lévi-Strauss has stated that in addition to a Marxist hypothesis on the origin of writing, his studies of Caduveo and Bororo were 'efforts to interpret native superstructures based upon dialectical materialism' (1958: 365).

References

ARON, E. 1968. Karl Marx. In *Main Currents in Sociological Thought*. New York: **1**: 145–236.
ASAD, T. 1972. Market Model, Class Structure, and Consent: A Reconsideration of Swat Political Organization. *Man* **7**: 74–94.
— (ed.) 1973. *Anthropology and the Colonial Encounter*. London.
AVINERI, S. 1969. *Karl Marx on Colonialism and Modernization*. New York.
BAILEY, F. G. 1960. *Tribe, Caste and Nation*. Manchester.
BALANDIER, G. 1963. *Sociologie actuelle de l'Afrique noire*. 2nd edn, Paris.
— 1967. *Anthropologie politique*. Paris.
BELSHAW, C. S. 1954. *Changing Melanesia: Social Economics of Culture Contact*. Melbourne.
BIRNBAUM, N. 1960. The Sociological Study of Ideology (1940–60): A Trend Report and Bibliography. *Current Sociology* **9**: 91–117.
— 1969. *The Crisis of Industrial Society*. London.
BOHANNAN, P. 1963. *Social Anthropology*. New York.
BOTTOMORE, T. B. 1963. *Karl Marx—Early Writings*. London.
BOTTOMORE, T. B. and RUBEL, M. 1963. *Karl Marx: Selected Writings in Sociology and Social Philosophy*. Harmondsworth.

Raymond Firth

BOYLE, R. 1661. *The Sceptical Chymist*. Everyman edn introd. E. A. Moelwyn-Hughes, London 1964.

BRUNHOFF, S. DE 1967. *La Monnaie chez Marx*. Paris.

BURRIDGE, K. 1969. *New Heaven, New Earth: A Study of Millenarian Activities*. Oxford.

COQUERY-VIDROVITCH, C. 1969. In *La Pensée* (144) 61–78.

CUVILLIER, A. 1948. Durkheim et Marx. *Cahiers internationaux de sociologie*. **4**: 75–97.

DIAMOND, S. 1964. What History Is. In R.A. Manners (ed.), *Process and Pattern in Culture*. Chicago: 29–46.

DUNAYEVSKAYA, R. 1958. *Marxism and Freedom . . . from 1776 until Today*. New York.

DURKHEIM, E. 1932. *De la division du travail social*. 6th edn, Paris.

DURKHEIM, E. and MAUSS, M. 1901–2. De quelques formes primitives de classification. *L'Année sociologique* **6**: 67, 70–1. Trans. introd. R. Needham as *Primitive Classification*, London, 1963, pp. 82, 86.

FINDLAY, J. N. 1963. *Language, Mind and Value*. London.

FIRTH, RAYMOND. 1936. *We, The Tikopia*. London.

— 1939. *Primitive Polynesian Economy*. London, 2nd edn, 1965.

— 1946. Colonial Societies and their Economic Background. *Colonial Review*, Dec.: 230–2.

— 1951. *Elements of Social Organization*. London.

— 1964. *Essays on Social Organization and Values*. London.

FRANKENBERG, R. 1967. Economic Anthropology: One Anthropologist's View. In R. Firth (ed.), *Themes in Economic Anthropology*, ASA Monographs 6, London.

FRIED, M. 1964. Ideology, Social Organization and Economic Development in China: a Living Test of Theories. In R.A. Manners (ed.), *Process and Pattern in Culture*, Chicago: 49–61.

FROMM, E. 1966, *Marx's Concept of Man*. New York.

GLUCKMAN, M. 1955. *Custom and Conflict in Africa*. Oxford.

— 1963. *Order and Rebellion in Tribal Africa*. London.

— 1965. *Politics, Law and Ritual in Tribal Society*. Oxford.

GODELIER, M. 1970. System, Structure and Contradiction in *Das Kapital*. In M. Lane (ed.), *Introduction to Structuralism*. New York: 340–58.

— 1971. Myth and History. *New Left Review* (69): 93–112.

— 1973. *Horizon, trajets marxistes en anthropologie*. Paris.

GOULDNER, A. W. 1959. Introduction to Emile Durkheim, *Socialism and Saint-Simon*, trans. C. Sattler. London.

GRAMSCI, A. 1957. What is Man? *The Modern Prince*, trans. L. Marks. London.

GUIART, J. 1951. Forerunners of Melanesian Nationalism. *Oceania* **22**: 81–90.

HARRIS, M. 1968. *The Rise of Anthropological Theory*. New York.

HOBSBAWM, E. J. 1964. Introduction to Karl Marx, *Pre-Capitalist Economic Formations*, trans. J. Cohen, London.

JAYAWARDENA, C. 1963. *Conflict and Solidarity in a Guianese Plantation*, LSE Monographs on Social Anthropology **25**. London.

— 1971. Review of Wolf (1969). *American Anthropologist* 73: 869–71.

KAGAN, G. 1938. Durkheim et Marx. *Revue d'histoire économique et sociale*: 233–4.

KAMENKA, E. 1962. *The Ethical Foundations of Marxism*. London.

KORSCH, K. 1938. *Karl Marx*. London.

LANTERNARI, V. 1960. *Movimenti religiosi di libertà e di salvezza*. Milan. Trans. as *The Religions of the Oppressed*. New York, 1963.

LARSON, E. H. 1971. Neo-Colonialism in Oceania: Tikopia Plantation Labor and Company Management Relations. In J. D. Colfax and J. L. Roach (eds), *Radical Sociology*, New York: 322–40.

LEACH, E. R. 1961. *Pul Eliya*. Cambridge.

LEVI-STRAUSS, C. 1955. *Tristes Tropiques*. Paris.

— 1958. *Anthropologie structurale*. Paris.

— 1962. *La Pensée sauvage*. Paris. Trans. as *The Savage Mind*. Chicago, 1966.

LEWIS, I. M. 1968. In Social Responsibilities Symposium. *Current Anthropology* **9**: 405, 418.

LEWIS, J. 1965. *The Life and Teaching of Karl Marx*. London.

LLOYD, P. C. 1967. *Africa in Social Change*. Harmondsworth.

— 1968. Conflict Theory and Yoruba Kingdoms. In I. M. Lewis (ed.), *History and Social Anthropology*, ASA Monographs 7. London.

LUKÁCS, G. 1954. Kunst und objektive Wahrheit. *Deutsche Zeitschrift für Philosophie*, 2 Jahrg. 1954.

MAGUBANE, B., *et al.* 1971. A Critical Look at Indices used in the Study of Social Change in Colonial Africa. *Current Anthropology* **12**: 419–43.

MARETIN, J. V. 1961. In *Bijdragen tot de Taal-, Land- en Volkenkunde*: 168–95.

MARX, K. 1939 (1857–8). *Grundrisse der Kritik der politischen Ökonomie (Rohentwurf)*. Moscow.

— 1859. *Zur Kritik der politischen Oekonomie*. Berlin.

— 1930 (1867). *Capital (A Critique of Political Economy)* Vol. I. Trans. from the 4th German edition of 1890 by Eden and Cedar Paul. London.

MARX, K., and ENGELS, F. 1933. *Die deutsche Ideologie* (1846). In *Marx-Engels Gesamtausgabe*. Moscow.

— 1968. *Selected Works*. Moscow (London, 1970).

MEILLASSOUX, C. 1964. *Anthropologie économique des Gouro de Côte d'Ivoire*. Le Monde d'outre-mer, I ser. xxvii. Paris.

— 1971. Introduction, *The Development of Indigenous Trade and Markets in West Africa*. London.

— 1972. From Reproduction to Production: a Marxist Approach to Economic Anthropology. *Economy and Society* **1**: 93–105.

MERTON, R. K. 1949. *Social Theory and Social Structure*. Glencoe, Ill.

MESZAROS, I. 1970. *Marx's Theory of Alienation*. London.

MILLIGAN, M. 1959. *Karl Marx—Economic and Philosophical Manuscripts of 1844*. Moscow.

MINTZ, S. W. 1971. Marx's Potato Sack and the Social Origins of the Cuban Revolution. Paper presented to American Anthropological Association meeting, New York, Nov.

MINTZ, S. W. and WOLF, E. R. 1959. In *Plantation Systems of the New World*. Washington, DC.

MORGAN, L. H. 1851. *League of the Ho-De'- No-Sau-Nee, Iroquois*. Rochester.

MURPHY, R. 1971. *The Dialectics of Social Life*. New York.

PARSONS, T. 1937. *The Structure of Social Action*. Glencoe, Ill.

RADCLIFFE-BROWN, A. R. 1957 (1948). *A Natural Science of Society*, Glencoe, Ill.

ROBINSON, J. 1962. *Economic Philosophy*. London.

ROSEN, L. 1971. Language, History, and the Logic of Inquiry in Lévi-Strauss and Sartre. *History and Theory* **10**: 269–94.

SALISBURY, R. F. 1962. *From Stone to Steel*. Melbourne.

SEBAG, L. 1964. *Marxisme et structuralisme*. Paris.

SEILLIÈRE, E. 1911. *Les Mystiques du néo-romantisme*, 2nd edn, Paris.

STALIN, J. 1947. Dialectical and Historical Materialism. *Problems of Leninism*. Moscow: 569–95.

STAUDER, J. 1971. The Function of Functionalism: The Adaptation of British Social Anthropology to British Colonialism in Africa. Paper presented to American Anthropological Association meeting, New York, Nov.

SURET-CANALE, J. 1964. Les sociétés traditionelles en Afrique tropicale et le concept de mode de production asiatique. *La Pensée* (117): 21–42.
— 1967. In *La Pensée* (135): 94–106.
SZERESZEWSKI, R. 1965. *Structural Changes in the Economy of Ghana, 1891–1911.* London.
TAWNEY, R. H. 1938. *Religion and the Rise of Capitalism.* Harmondsworth.
TERRAY, E. 1969. *Le Marxisme devant les sociétés 'primitives'.* Paris.
TUCKER, R. 1961. *Philosophy and Myth in Karl Marx.* Cambridge.
VENABLE, V. 1946. *Human Nature: the Marxian View.* London.
WOLF, E. R. 1966. *Peasants.* New Jersey.
— 1969. *Peasant Wars of the Twentieth Century.* New York.
WORSLEY, P. 1957. *The Trumpet Shall Sound: a Study of 'Cargo' Cults in Melanesia.* London.
ZITTA, V. 1964. *Georg Lukács' Marxism: Alienation, Dialectics, Revolution.* The Hague.

Stephan Feuchtwang

Investigating Religion

This is an essay. It is an attempt to set out a marxist means of investigating ideology and in particular religion as ideology. It starts with a criticism of certain sociological theories of religion, claiming that, because they take individual subjectivity as axiomatic, these are theories of what one might call a philosophy of subjective idealism. This is followed by a formulation of a way of studying the social formation of subjectivity, using marxist theories of ideology. The second part of the essay is such a study, the investigation of religious ideology in late imperial China.

What do we need in order to explain religion? First of all, we need a general theory, which can be made more precise by criticism and from which a concept of religion can be deduced. This essay will suggest where such a theory may be found. Marxism is a historical and social science which matured with the writing of *Capital*, but was preceded by Feuerbach's and the Young Hegelians' critiques of religious thought and by Marx's and Engel's critique of Feuerbach and the Young Hegelians themselves in *The German Ideology*. In that book and the later *Capital* a theory of religion was in use—for instance in the section of *Capital* on the fetishism of commodities—but it was never formulated. Since then few marxists have done more than repeat Marx's figurative approximations to a theory of religion—an up-turned reflection of reality, an opiate. Non-marxist social science, on the other hand, including some marxologizing sociologists, has given special attention to religion. For decades, exponents of the sociology of religion have sought their starting-point in a definition of religion as a universal fact. But theories from which a concept called religion can be derived, and statements of what empirically it does and does not do, when it is and is not necessary, have been noticeably absent. Definitions abound. In the end most can be traced in a theoretical derivation either from Durkheim's 'sacred', with its dependence on his general theory of society as a moral fact, or from Weber's 'ethic' and 'orientation', with their dependence on his definition of sociology as a study of meaning and action.

In the last fifteen years social anthropologists have made attempts to rethink the explanation of religion. This has been part of a general reappraisal taking place in social anthropology as a result of a swing away from ideas of structure towards ideas of action. This itself is a result of renewed interest in 'social change' brought about by politically effective anti-colonial movements. The fact that new nationalisms and internationalisms have been preceded, accompanied, or followed by religious movements has no doubt stimulated deeper thought about religion, as has the part religion seems to have played in the conservation of forms of hierarchy and order now as well as in the colonial past. Has social anthropological reappraisal been an adjustment to a new state of social affairs or a radical theoretical step after which political, ideological, and religious movements can be explained as the products and phenomena of social processes?

Let us look at some recent writing on religion by social anthropologists to see what theory of religion can be deduced from them. In doing this it is convenient and perhaps necessary for the sake of exposition to adopt the standard practice of starting from a preliminary definition of what we can call religion. I think we can agree, without contradicting any of the anthropologists I shall consider, that religion is a shared reality: it is both a system of ideas about reality and a means of communicating those ideas. This can be put in a more structural and cultural way: a religion is a system of categories, or an articulation of several systems of categories, and their representation as symbols and rituals. By its means definitions or classifications of the world as a whole are reproduced. Whether or not we choose in addition to accept the proposition that totalization characterizes religious ideas more than other kinds of ideas, or that totalization combined with moral prescription is their peculiarity, religion is a kind of ideology. And for a definition of ideology let us take for a starting-point the one given by Dumont in his book on the religious formation of Indian society, a formation apparently resistant to colonial and post-colonial changes:

> The word 'ideology' commonly designates a more or less social set of ideas and values. Thus one can speak of the ideology of a society, and also of the ideologies of more restricted groups such as a social class or a movement, or again of partial ideologies bearing on a single aspect of the social system such as kinship. It is obvious that there is a basic ideology, a kind of germinal ideology tied to common language and hence to the linguistic group of the global society (Dumont 1970: 263, n. 1a).

In treating religion as a kind of ideology we would also be adopting a procedure similar to Geertz's treatment of religion as a cultural system. According to this treatment, religion is a system of symbolic action. To study it is to find out how it works as the interpretation of experience and a commitment to a certain orientation for action (Geertz 1966; 1968: 97, 99).

One religious idea presents a peculiar problem to social science. That is the idea of the supernatural, and the supersocial. Does the sociological study of religion have to accept in some way this non-material reality? For instance, Spiro's definition of religion is as 'an institution consisting of culturally patterned interaction with culturally postulated superhuman beings' (Spiro 1966: 96). The insertion of the qualification 'postulated' before 'superhuman beings' apparently avoids acceptance of a non-material reality. But it only postpones the business of producing a concept of religion in which 'superhuman beings' are not necessary and by which, on the contrary, their postulation can be explained. Spiro only comes half way to such a concept in seeking to explain what he himself conceives to be a cultural, and therefore social, postulation as a psychological need. The belief or postulation is a reality to be explained. But the believed-in reality of superhuman beings is included with the belief as soon as we take the subject's view of reality and then include it in a definition of religion as the interaction with it. Unless we find a means of dealing with subjectivity itself as an object instead of leaving it outside the bounds of our competence as so much social science does, superhuman beings in various guises will be postulated in social science.

It is perfectly true that no social scientist, as far as I know, explains social life as the work of gods. But many accept religious beliefs as unproblematic or beyond their competence, so that they are treated as a given factor according to which social life may be explained. Statements of the kind that the X people have this custom because they have that theme or belief in their conception of the world, assert that religion, ritual, and myth are a self-defining reality. An assertion of this kind could be a preliminary step towards producing a theory of religion, ritual, and myth. But when the assertion is coupled implicitly or explicitly with an assumption that the self-defining reality of religion, ritual, and myth is not related to the rest of social reality in any necessary way which can be known, it endows ideas of gods with an explanatory force which is but the pale agnostic substitute for gods themselves. Confronted with ideology, the social scientist does in fact usually limit him- or herself to its elucidation as an independent variable. But there have at least been a few attempts in social anthropology to know what is specific to religion as a kind of social reality.

THEORIZING ABOUT RELIGION

Firth (1964) posed the problem of explaining religion as a distinct category and kind of institution. His lecture was a step away from treating religion along with other presumed-to-be-basic systems in society—the social, economic, and political, as Firth enumerates them—as a functional prerequisite of the Social Whole. Religion, according to Firth, is of course related to the other systems, but in itself it is a system of symbols by which individuals make sense of experience in terms of basic human goals. So religion presented itself to Firth primarily as a problem of meaning, both in its relation to the other systems and also in itself as a system of symbols which refer to each other.

Analysis of religion is therefore the finding of cognitive and affective referents. The system of symbols that is religion refers, on the one hand, to the social system, which is, according to Firth, a reference to human action and the experience of it. On the other hand it refers to the possibility of extra-human action and experience. The extra-human reference is, according to Firth, unlike the other because its assumptions cannot be empirically tested (1964: 231). We may argue that it does not follow that the assumptions are not to be explained. But Firth included the basic assumption of extra-human action in an empirical description of religion as a universal fact, which was the configuration of religion as he conceived it, and so turned the assumption into an unproblematic given. Only what followed from it and its logical implications in each of its instances were to be analysed.

Now, Firth and other social scientists keep the idea of the superhuman because social actors think something exists which sociologists and other scientists cannot experience and test. First, we have a decision to treat thought and ideas as an independent variable. Second, this particular idea is generalized as a universal fact of humankind. As a result, the idea of non-empirical and non-material reality is retained as an independent fact of social life, and defined negatively according to whatever sociology and other sciences can test and know.

This is doubly unsatisfactory. First, we should be able to explain the idea, as well as its effects and functions. Second, we should be sure what ideas are actually held by social actors without imputing to them a distinction that assumes the methodological categories of our science. Some years after Firth, Worsley faced this problem in considering 'Religion as a category', the heading of a section on theoretical issues which he added to the 1968 edition of *The Trumpet Shall Sound*. He took up the problem in a Weberian way, which is a sociology founded explicitly upon the individual human subject. In it ideology is an orientation to action, and religion is action according to an otherworldly orientation. To pinpoint religion as a category, Worsley, like Firth, sought to save it from functional analysis in which it was engulfed as part of a seamless social whole. He asked what is peculiar to specifically religious values, and so to specifically religious behaviour. These questions were put as an empirical test according to which the category of religion was assumed to be a universal fact and its nature was to be found by reference to human subjects themselves, acting religiously. So the scientific distinction between technical or empirical and mystical acts was referred to the actors and the question put whether in all cases reported the actors made this distinction. They did not. One of the reports Worsley took up was Nadel's study of Nupe religion, in the light of which he found that most of the religious actors were not concerned with high gods, with ethics, or with after-life. So, if religion was to be an empirical as well as a universal category, such concerns could not constitute its core either.

Worsley rejected Nadel's own conclusion that religion is a kind of experience, William James's 'thrill' and the assurance it gives. Most religious people have not had the experience. He looked instead for a special kind of meaning, not for an experience. The special kind of meaning turned out to be, after much intellectual soul-searching, a belief in superhuman powers or in a superhuman realm! These he could define only by making a distinction between empirical–technical and non-empirical–technical domains. So, despite attempting to reach a theory of religion which did not distort or reduce the actors' own categories of thought, Worsley had to resort to 'an analytical distinction *not* necessarily present in the minds of the believers themselves', a distinction peculiar to '*our* scientific culture' (Worsley's stresses, 1970: 310, 311).

Why was it necessary to introduce this distinction into an empirical definition centred on the actors and their own categories? It was because the actors' categories included beings the existence of which, defined as they were, could not be known by any science which seeks demonstrable and not just declared truths. Sociology aims to be such a science. So why in the case of religion does the subject-matter have to include a category which is by definition the scientifically unknowable? Why could the sociological category of religion not define the actors' postulations and categories in terms of material and experienced subject-matter and testable theories? It is because of the reliance of this sociology on a *primary* reference to the *ideas* of social actors, that is to their subjectivity. The motivations and the modifying experiences of social actors are of the essence, the primary essence, in the analysis of social life according to this sociology. Yet the sociologist can only know his own experience, and can only interpret the motivations of social actors by imaginative empathy and proximate rational patterning of his insights and understandings or of records and traces of their behaviour. The subject, and subjectivity, are the starting-points of this sociology, which respects the privacy, the unknowable nature of the essence of social action, the subject, his worship, his imaginative orientation.

There are various kinds of subjectivity, such as the acting subject, the contemplating subject, the consumer of experience, assumed as given in this sociology, but which can in fact be investigated sociologically and historically. We can ask what social formations provide the conditions in which these subjectivities are possible as categories and assumptions, in the same way that Marx was able to ask what were the historical preconditions for the category of labour (Marx 1973: 103 ff.). A reconsideration of the social anthropology of roles and units of social identity would also be enough to indicate that the social and historical definition of subjectivity is on the cards for social science. To begin with, it is by no means a fact that the biological individual is the most signifi- cant unit of action and subjectivity in all social systems. A great deal of social anthropology is a study of different kinds of culturally produced identities—ethnic, kin, and individual, to mention the most common. Were they not also posited as universal facts, the facts of ethnicity, of kinship, and of the individual, it would be possible to know them as various historically produced systems of defining social subjects. In other words, the definition of units of common experience, the sharing and non-sharing of material conditions, and the instituted units of social action and mobility are specific to each social system. They are not unknowable, and we do not have to preserve the superhuman in their name.

THE STUDY OF IDEOLOGY

The study of religion is part of the study of ideology, indeed it is the part of that study which represents it *par excellence*. As Worsley wrote, and emphasized himself, religion 'is *ideal* as well as social' (1970: 305). Ideology is the subject-matter of *Homo Hierarchicus*. In this book Dumont was not concerned to find an empirically universal category of fact. His concern with ideology was explicitly methodological. But the implications of his approach are similar to Worsley's and Firth's, and it illustrates the methodological principles that hamper the study of religion in the type of sociology they share. For Dumont, the task of social study is to find the complementary and variable relation between the ideological aspects and the non-ideological aspects of social reality.

'The distinction between the ideological (or conscious) aspects and the others is required methodologically', and 'methodologically, the initial postulate is that ideology is *central* with respect to the social reality as a whole (man acts consciously and we have *direct* access to the conscious aspect of his action)' (Dumont's own stresses and parentheses, 1970: 263–4). He wrote much the same on another page (p. 282). In both places he was careful to note that ideology is the *methodological* starting-point. It is not necessarily primary in existence. Nevertheless, a reading of his methodological postulates will, I think, reveal that he has loaded them inevitably towards finding that ideology is actually primary, however much he has professed to leave open 'the question of the place or function of the ideology in society as a whole' (p. 263).

One of the main reasons Dumont gave for starting out with ideology is the methodological requirement of explaining the parts of a society by the whole. Here ideology is decisive because, he asserted, ideology orders and logically encompasses a raw material that is non-ideological. When we turn to inquire what the nature of this raw material is, we find it to be both methodologically and ontologically, according to Dumont, a residue. It is formlessness, the negative of the category 'ideology' defined as form. Ideology is also defined, as the passage from page 263 already cited shows, as consciousness. The raw material is its residue, the unconscious (p. 28 and p. 273, n. 22c). Dumont pointed out that the consciousness of their social reality produced by the ideological subjects of a society is not necessarily the correct one (pp. 36–7). But since social phenomena are what appear to consciousness and have no other charac-ter, they must be the concomitants either of the ideology of the social subjects under study or of the ideology of the student (p. 38). Dumont divides social reality into consciousness and that which appears to be its concomitant. Small wonder that for Dumont 'it is hardly conceivable at present' that the non-ideological aspects of social reality, in which are included politics and economics, 'will be shown to be in reality the fundamental ones, and the ideology secondary' (p. 39). No sooner is the contemplating subject separated out as an independent variable of social life, than social reality becomes an appearance to this subject, not a system of social formation, that is determinate appearances to deter-minate subjects.

The following sections of this essay are attempts to show what a study of socially determinate appearances to socially determinate subjects would be.

MARXISM AND IDEOLOGY

The separation of consciousness or the 'ideal' from non-consciousness or the 'social' as independent factors of human reality either takes ideas and consciousness out of social reality or divides every social unity into two 'aspects' on these same categorical lines. It is often thought that Marx's historical science does this and therefore that the categorical lines are a common battleground upon which his materialist assump-tions can be challenged and tested. But Marx's materialism precisely is not a fundamental categorical separation of thought from material human being.

Every human practice—all production—is social, intentional, and significant. Consciousness is the selective mental reflection on social practices, including the practices of thought and theory. It is determined and formed by what has already been produced and by the relations of production already in existence (as Marx's notes on production and consumption in general make clear; 1973: 90 ff.). Ideas and thought are to be known both in their specific character as thought and ideas, and also in the instance of some social systems in which they are separated as a special preserve or level of practice. But always they are to be known within the complex unity of a social system. If thought were not a *distinct*, as well as a dependent, practice there would be no possibility of initiating a struggle to change a social system. And if it were not a *dependent* as well as a distinct practice, knowledge and consciousness themselves could not be known and corrected.

67

Ideological production, the production and communication of ideas, is no more purely ideal a practice than economic production is purely material. It is nothing if it is not social. Social scientists recognize as much in their concern to elucidate the structure or pattern or internal coherence of ideologies as systems—systems of priorities, or of classification, or of signification. Since they are social, they are qualities of historically specific relations between concrete individuals, and so they are material. Ideological production is determined within the social unity of which it is a distinct part, and, in the last instance, it is determined by the capacity of the individuals in that unity of their relations to produce and reproduce their, and so those relations', material being.

Marxist analysis produces a theory of the system of practices, a theory from which can be derived all the forms which make up the complex unity of the society in question. This must involve marking its difference from other societies. A theory of a specific socio-economic formation shows it to be repeatable. That is to say it shows it to be the constitution of a specific set of conditions, and not any other set. But marxist analysis neither starts from nor seeks to discover some universal object, like Human Nature, or Society, or Power, or Ideology, or Religion, which is a non-historical 'fact'. Rather, it produces theories and concepts by which historical reality can be known and changed.

IDEOLOGY IS THE FORMATION OF SUBJECTS

Althusser (1971) produced a marxist theory of ideology both as a specific social practice and as part of a kind of socio-economic formation. The first thesis of his theory is that 'ideology represents the imaginary relationship of individuals to their real conditions of existence' (p. 153). It is an imaginary relationship because it is that of individuals, material *units*, thinking about the social *relations* which are their very conditions of existence. Only by means of ideology are individuals constituted as subjects, that is to say as sources of action able to relate to the whole of which they are parts.

An ideology is a structure which has a social and a historical existence. In it, individuals not only imagine their relations to each each other to be those of interacting subjects. They also (we also) treat their (our) conditions of existence as subjects with which they (we) interact. That is to say, the individual subject recognizes as another subject with which he or she can interact what would, in a subject-less discourse, be known as a set of relations of which the individual is a constituent physical, biological, psychological, and sociological form. Put in yet another way, this means that, in an ideology and its institutions, the individual enacts a relation of inclusion and social representation as if it were an interaction between subjects, one of which is him- or herself and the other the inclusive social unit itself.

Let me illustrate the point with Taiwanese religion. In Taiwan, one of the most common forms of association in which individuals agree to act jointly is a feast. The feast is a formalization of social unity. An association of individuals not previously united in a group seal their association in one of many bonds in their ideological vocabulary by means of a ritual of toasting each other at a feast. They may only drink wine when they have found a partner. And they find partners by discovering a common identity—of name, of place of ancestral origin, of work, of school, of military service. One of these standard forms of identity is itself the principle for the organization of an association, a common identity sealed and regularly re-sealed in freely drinking together on fixed occasions. It was common, and is still a frequent procedure in Taiwan now, to constitute the association itself in a symbolic form as an incense burner, through which to establish communication with a patron deity before whom solidarity is sworn. Merchant guilds in imperial times would, for instance, hear cases of members' misconduct before the guild's patron deity and the sanction was often to give a feast, as an offering both to the association's god and to its members.

The relationship, it should be noted, is not so simple as a one-to-one projection of the association into a god. The god is not just the god of that particular association. He or she is the god of a kind of relation—whether of a craft, of commerce, of sea-travel, or of location in a place. The particular association has specific to it only the incense burner and whatever other ritual property may have been added to it—perhaps a figure of the god, a temple to house it, and land, the rent from which is used for its upkeep.

The Taiwanese illustration indicates three terms in the imaginary relationship of subjects to their social conditions of existence. The associated individuals treated their social unity as a subject with which each could interact as a sanctioned petitioner or celebrant. This is not to say that the god was the social unit itself. The incense burner, which specifically was the property of that social unit, was a medium by which the unit's constituent individuals interacted and communicated with the relation of association itself as a supersocial subject.

The achievement of Althusser's article on which I have so far concentrated is the singling-out of the subject as the constitutive category, not of society in general, but of ideology in particular. Now I want to turn to the historical nature of ideology itself. Althusser argues that not only is ideology made up of basic categories which are imagined as subjects of eternal truth, but that ideology has no history. Even if it was only in bourgeois society that the subject first appeared as a category in philosophy, 'the category of the subject (which may function under other names, e.g. as the soul of Plato, as God, etc.) is the constitutive category of all ideology, whatever its determination (regional or class) and whatever its historical date—since ideology has no history' (Althusser 1971: 160). This seems to agree with sociological statements that the subject and ideology are universal, ahistorical facts. But in fact we are to understand by 'history' itself a limited concept (p. 152); ideology is limited to those societies with history, which is characterized by class struggle and a state apparatus. Althusser says no more, but the implication here is that the concept of ideology and its theory are parts of the theory of hierarchical social systems. They are true, that is, of those social systems in which the organization of labour and exchange is no longer on one plane in its relation to the natural environment. They are true only where the organization is on two planes, the second being a special 'division of labour', a division made by accumulators, redistributors, directors, exploiters by rights—that is, holders of the ideology.

Such systems are hierarchical in the sense that part of society controls the whole and represents the whole to itself while being supported and replenished by the other parts. The extent of exclusion from the means of control and representation varies greatly. But in terms of thought and signification all hierarchies are structures of graded generality in which the higher level of generality and inclusion is constituted by means of a mechanism of representation which is metonymic. Let me explain what I mean by 'metonymic', a term borrowed from Lévi-Strauss (1962: 297 ff.) and Mendelson (1967: 135–6). In a hierarchy the inclusive level of organization is itself a part and not the combination of the parts that constitute the included levels. So the part represents the whole by virtue of being a part, of being continuous with and dependent on the rest of the whole which it represents. But *as its representative* it is discontinuous with the other parts, representing to them the whole. In brief, hierarchy is the principle 'by which the elements of a whole are ranked in relation to the whole' (Dumont 1970: 66).

Hierarchy obviously determines the way in which an individual imagines his relationship to the conditions of his existence. But that can surely not be taken to mean that in non-hierarchical societies individuals would not imagine their relationships to their conditions of existence at all. If that were all we meant by ideology then it would surely be as true of all societies as purposive behaviour is true of humanity as an animal species. We may, however, use a more restricted concept of ideology, as the way in which individuals imagine their relationships to the conditions of their existence in a social hierarchy. In that case the social conditions of existence are imagined as other collective conscious and active subjects. And the ideology of the dominant division or class as well as of the social order in which the class is perpetuated is the most characteristically ideological since it defines the present social conditions as eternal or natural.

IDEOLOGY IS BELIEVING WHAT YOU EXPERIENCE TO BE THE TRUTH AND THE ONLY TRUTH

In considering the relation of ideology to the rest of a social formation Dumont can again take us part of the way. It is the relation of appearance to consciousness. But if we are not to go round in ideological circles we have to abandon his thesis that the order of the whole social formation comes from ideology. Order is first of all the order of the social formation itself, its combination of relations.

The social relations we seek to know are not self-evident. They have an appearance; they have phenomenal forms which are their immediately perceived reality. But the record of their perception does not explain their appearance. If social relations were self-evident there would be no need for social science. One can accept the appearance of things and relations as if they were self-evident or one can search for a reality behind the appearance. The difference between doing the one or the other is the difference between justification and investigation, the more and the less ideological. Ideological discourse makes of appearances the categories of reality.

One kind of sociological discourse would question an ideological statement of reality, but only to make it relativistic: reality is the appearance to an ego according to his or her situation and world-view. It would add by way of demonstration the behavioural indices of perception and expression. The regularities and frequencies of these behavioural indices would be known as the phenomenal forms of subjective realities. The subjective realities would be the essential reality and one which can only be typified, modelled, guesstimated, or known intuitively.

A marxist social science would find that the apparently thinglike phenomenon is the form of a complex of relations of production and the exchange of products. Both the form and its reproduction in the complex of relations are real. Relations within that complex also combine with other relations and have other phenomenal forms. None of these forms would be explained as the material residue of subjective realities. Nor would they be explained as the one reality of the human psyche in a variety of cultures and systems of values. On the contrary, they would be explained as a distinct order of relations and their forms. Once the order has appeared it constitutes the preconditions for the appearance of another. This is how history is conceived in a marxist social science. Each order is itself the thinglike form of processes in whose movement and self-transformation are the preconditions of the next apparently stable formation.

To sum up: the most ideological discourse bears the message that there is nothing more to know, that everything is as we experience and perceive it with its characteristic property. To a non-marxist sociology, experience is to be known as an organized pattern, the society and the culture of concrete individuals who are active subjects of experience. To a marxist sociology, a complex of social relations and processes makes a social formation and its ideology. Experience is to be investigated as the way in which a social formation appears to the subjects defined in the ideologies of that social formation.

IMPLICATIONS OF THE THEORY OF IDEOLOGY FOR THE INVESTIGATION OF IDEOLOGIES AND RELIGIONS

A definition of religion which sums up the anthropological texts I have cited and interpreted would be as follows. Religion is a system of symbols orienting action with reference to ultimate ends and to a higher-order reality. Now let me reformulate it in a way that would enable us to investigate rather than to assume the conscious and active subject. Religion is ideology and the system of symbols and institutions in which it is shared and communicated. The peculiar property of ideology is the category of the subject. Concrete individuals think and act in relation to their conditions of existence by means of ideologies. Ideologies constitute them as individual or collective social subjects. Ideologies constitute the social relations of existence as subjects. So active subjects imagine themselves to be in relation both to equivalent and to higher, inclusive orders of reality known also as other thinking and active subjects.

An ideology is a system of symbols. That is to say, it is the means by which an interrelated set of social forms is reflected in thought. Part of its investigation must therefore consist in finding out how those forms are the necessary appearance of the underlying order of social relations which are the social conditions of the existence of the concrete individuals with whom we are concerned. In one social formation there may be many ideologies, and they may be more or less systematically related. An ideology is then the categorization of the sets of forms which the social system reproduces in one particular point of view. The points of view, points of similar and potentially shared experience, are themselves formed in the divergences and contradictions, the groupings and classes, of the social system.

But in addition a system of symbols, as sociologists and anthropologists have pointed out, has its own kind of coherence as a system of categories and their representation. The system has its own internal contradictions and its own pace of internal change. Contradictions and divergences in the formation of society will be recognized and disguised, represented and misrepresented, not only according to the various points of view but also according to the very structure of the ideology. So a second part of the investigation of an ideology must be to lay bare its particular structure. It is here that social anthropology has its greatest strength. Lévi-Strauss, especially, stimulated the development of means of studying signification as such, so that one can take practices and texts and analyse them as constituting a system instead of making sense of them piecemeal, by finding for each practice a functional attribute of one or another social institution.

Every social activity has an ideological content in that it is carried out with certain intentions and a certain consciousness. In that consciousness the relations of production of the social formation are repeated and reproduced. But there are also definite organizations and defined occasions, such as a calendar of festivals, a system of local shrines, or an educational system, which are set apart particularly for the rehearsal and reproduction of the ideologies otherwise embedded in social activity. They are at once the concrete representations of the ideologies and the institutions in which they are formed. The ideologies represent in various ways, from various points of view, the general system of dominance and of defiance towards it. Through their specific institutions they are subject to other kinds of institution which control and provide for them as well as being informed by them. A third part of the investigation of an ideology must therefore be to see how it has effects in the rest of the social formation. Conflict, the containment of conflict between classes, and the emergence of new classes in the social formation will not only have an effect in the system of ideological structures and their institutions. The ideological institutions will also themselves be objects of struggle in any struggle for hegemony, or new systems of dominance and resistance to domination. There will be ideological conflict in which divergent points of view and shared experience, as well as divergent ideological structures, will develop coherence. These conflicts will be reproduced as the consciousness and as the subjects themselves of further conflict. They will thus in turn have their effects on social activity in general.

In sum, I am suggesting that the three elements of an investigation of an ideology are:

1 the presentation of social forms to the ideology, and the formation of points of view and shared experience which are the fields of ideological operation;
2 the internal coherence of the ideology, in which social forms are structured as categories and subjects;
3 the constant formulation of identities and actions by the ideology and the effects of this formulation in the rest of the social practices —that is the practices of domination, or economic production and exchange, or science.

In order to give these rather grimly fashioned instruments some life in use I will outline an investigation of religion in late imperial China.

FORMS AND POINTS OF VIEW OF A SOCIAL FORMATION

Obviously, only a brief sketch of late imperial China can be given here, and I will concern myself mainly with forms of political domination.

Units of production in late imperial China were extremely small. They were households, loosely organized for mutual help in families and neighbourhoods. They were linked by participating in exchange through an elaborate marketing system and a commercial organization for processing and accumulating products. Processing, accumulation, and redistribution were organized by merchants, some working for the state, most working privately.

The imperial bureaucracy organized certain monopolies (salt, silk) and the large-scale transportation of grain obtained through taxation. Landlords and literati organized hydraulic and other public works. In short, the main classes of non-labourers in late imperial China were landlords, literati/bureaucrats, and merchants, while the labourers were peasants and artisans. Ownership of land was a basic relation of production and from it were derived most of the other forms of domination in imperial Chinese society.

Fei Hsiao-t'ung (1946) makes the point that Chinese peasant social organization 'stops at the loosely organized neighbourhood', whereas gentry organization is much more comprehensive. 'Those who stay at the peak of the social pyramid are the leisure class—the gentry—a minority who live on rent collected from the peasants' (p. 1). The difference between these two groups is manifest in kinship organization and in the different size of gentry and peasant families. The peasant producer was concerned with the maintenance of a minimum unit needed for self-reproduction, and this was very small in China. The rentiers were concerned with maintaining enough ownership of land so as to provide rent to live on. In a system of private property and of partible male inheritance, as was the case, this involved kinship organization going beyond the immediate family. In fact, it meant family organization concerned not only with the land itself but with other sources of accumulating surplus to ensure the necessary continuing investment in family property and education to maintain class position. The determinants of organization for the leisure class were not the reproduction of the unit of agricultural production. They were of a political order and concerned reproduction as part of the leisure class. The social unit had to withstand threats to the minimum amount of property it would need for the next generation. These threats were the rules of partible inheritance and of competitive succession to those offices where great accumulation of wealth was possible.

For the leisure class, reproduction implied three strategies of organization. One was the maintenance of wide affinal links. The second was extended family budgeting with a social and economic dispersal of brothers and collateral kin cooperating in various ways to provide social and economic credit. The third was lineage organization: that is the formation of trusts in the name of an immediate ancestor, since trusts were excluded from partition. It is important to note the general effects of these strategies in social organization. One was a combination of landlordism with a movement towards centres of accumulation of surplus by other means than rent. Another was the possibility for peasant farmers of vertical social mobility, but this process required the passage of a number of generations. 'The average farm in China,' as Fei wrote (1946: 6), 'is only a few acres. Small farming makes accumulation of capital impossible. Villagers put it neatly: "land breeds no land".' In one generation a few poor peasants out of thousands could move up to the level of middle and perhaps rich peasant, hiring labour to farm some of the land or letting some of it. Movement at one stage in the domestic cycle up to the level of a stem family was frequent, but partible inheritance broke it down again. It was frequent enough to have enabled a few peasants to begin to apply the aforementioned leisure-class kinship strategies and for the rest to have experienced the possibility of mobility.

Lineage organization meant that inclusion in a lineage could give security of tenure on trust land to a member tenant and the right to send his children to its school for the few months when they might be spared from production. It might even mean the rare chance of leisure-class lineage managers deciding to sponsor a poor child for further education. These factors too were reinforcements to the hope of upward mobility for the peasant and meant his acceptance of descent organization, the norms of marriage, ancestor worship, and the attendant morality of filial piety, all beliefs to which the leisure class adhered as a necessary part of *their* strategy. Peasant producers, however, could only share these beliefs with a large number of modifications in marriage and adoption customs, since they could not afford the excessive dowry system and other encumbrances involved in maintaining alliances and a line of descent. For the peasant producers such modifications resulted in a much narrower range of alliance.

It was still a kinship-based organization and an ideology founded in agricultural production with all its concomitants of storage and continuity of a fixed means of production. However, it supported forms of political organization for a leisure class which were on a much wider scale. The peasant remained in his small bounded social system. The rentier belonged to the same social system, living on the surplus from ancestral lands, but also on surplus accumulated in other ways. This meant that the rentier lived near or in the centres of accumulation from a wide area. To maintain his position he could not rely on land if he was not to suffer the fate of the peasant at partition. As Fei Hsiao-t'ung put it (ibid.: 6), 'after a few generations the big (gentry) house will break down into a number of petty owners again. Therefore it is essential for the rich to keep away from the village. The place where they can keep their power and wealth is the town.'

The town was the seat of tax accumulation and of accumulation of mercantile surplus. The central town of a qualified person's native administrative region, however, was not the best place for him to accumulate surplus through commerce or tax. It was all right as the first place in which to invest rent, profit, and fees in an education for his children, to qualify them for a place in the imperial bureaucracy. But to receive the bureaucratic post and the salaries and other forms of payment based on tax which went with it he could not be in the capital of his native area. According to an integral rule of the system, bureaucrats above a certain rank were not allowed to serve where they had near kin.

Moreover, they, and the merchants too, were able to practise tax and profit management more ruthlessly far away from the place where they were honoured as patrons and filial sons.

Let us now turn to the system itself, reproducing itself according to the rules discussed above. It was a state system in which the ultimate authority was vested in a royal dynasty. It was administered through a bureaucracy recruited from a rentier class whose organization was kin-based but which could not pass on these offices by descent. In fact, the rule against an official serving in his native area and the rule of partible inheritance had been introduced to break the power and prevent the re-emergence of a feudal nobility and thus safeguard central monarchy.

The state in China constituted the largest and virtually the only military organization, the taxing authority, and the keeper of public security. A division between the organization of military protection from the rooted organization of production and property is, I think, an inherent probability of settled agricultural communities, since these are so vulnerable to raids and pilfering of their grain stores. The military organization for protection is likely to have been in the past an organization for plunder. There is likely to be military competition for—and defence of—the right to plunder, and it is therefore likely that the military organization will not be that of the owners of the land. The plunderers may even be classified as 'alien' or 'outcast' by the landowners. However, once they are in a position to *defend* the right to plunder they become part of the political system of the agriculturalists. Logically the first to organize protection is the class that derives its livelihood from production on its property, but should a separate class of owners emerge for whatever reason and live on the surplus production it appropriates from the producers, this class can then be replaced by an external organization seeking plunder. The external organization may be one of agricultural property-owners or of another kind of production and property altogether. In the latter case the organization of protection will be distinct from the organization of production itself. In such a case another form of accumulation of surplus, not derived from ownership of land, will support the military organization separately: as tax is distinct from rent. The two organizations will divide the ruling class into a minority of protectors (plunderers) and a majority of production managers (rentiers).

Conflict between the two may lead to one of two results. Either it may lead to the extension of military rule by the central authority so that it expropriates the land as its property, in which case tax and rent coalesce. Or landlords may develop their own military forces and divert tax into their own hands as warlords. There is a third possibility: the two groups remain separate while supporting each other in a mutual transformation. In China's case this was, on the one hand, the rule of partible inheritance designed to limit and break up the power of the class of owners, and, on the other hand, it was participation by the owners in centralized protection, subject to the rule against serving as protector, as agent of the military authority, in their ancestral home. Loyalty both to the ancestral home and to the native rulers was maintained and encouraged in the plundered by the possibilities offered by mobility. The role of ruler was thus split into two, but there were many ways in which the two sides supported each other. To cite Fei again, 'For a local government official the gentry (i.e. the local, native, gentry) are his opposition'. But as Fei also wrote, 'Although an official he is in his private capacity one of the gentry. He will write letters to his fellow-officials asking favour for his own kin, relatives or local people. The gentry-official is the pivot in the traditional Chinese power structure' (ibid.: 9). The splitting of the ruling class in any one place into several insiders and one outsider made political use of the small-scale character of peasant producers' organization and helped to maintain it as such. By its means the leisure class maintained hegemony over each unit and over China as a whole.

The regions of shared experience which are the points of view in this social formation are most broadly the gentry, as a class, and the peasantry. What could have united the peasantry was the potentially shared experience of rural toil and of the gentry, but the peasantry was broken into small regional and subregional units of communication—standard marketing areas (see Skinner 1964) and the loosely organized neighbourhoods Fei mentioned. What united the leisure class in extent [1] was its literacy and the administrative and jural codes, even though a small minority of them held office at any one time. The smallest sub-units of the gentry, as of the peasantry, were households. For the gentry they were often subunits of extended families. For the peasantry they were usually coextensive with small families. Between the two were the institutions and groups constituted by the forms of domination themselves—administrative units in a nested hierarchy, and beside them individual and corporate landlords, lineages and other local organizations of public works, all usually managed by members of the leisure class.

The forms of political domination by the leisure class are the opposed roles of native landowner and of official protector of law and order against rebels, bandits, and invaders. Their order of appearance at any point of view was through the mechanism of relative interiority—the us/them contrast, which is characteristic of all ideology. In this case it distinguished officials from native patron as relative outsider, but distinguished bandits as ultimate outsiders from both officials and native patrons taken together.

THE FORMS AS CATEGORIES IN IDEOLOGICAL STRUCTURES

Two linked structures run through the ideological institutions of imperial China as well as present-day Hong Kong and Taiwan. These are a structure of filial devotion and protection and a structure of political loyalty and protection. The constitutive categories of the former structure are ancestor and its hierarchical corollary, descendant. Those of the latter structure are god and follower, or client, for he is no mere supplicant. Each structure has distinct though similar deferential ritual and institutions. In the ancestral structure the principles of lineal ascription, segmentation, and family strategy are conceptualized and rehearsed. In the god structure the principle of residential ascription, neighbourhood organization, and the administration of law and order are conceptualized and rehearsed.

A third category has the dual function of being the negative of these two structures. That is the category of *kuei*—translated as ghosts or demons. As the negative of ancestor, *kuei* is 'orphan soul' or 'spirit without descendants'. As the negative of god, *kuei* is malicious influence, demon or soul in purgatory. It is a category of isolated and cut-off subjects without structure, let alone a hierarchy, of its own. Indeed it is the category of being both outside structure and controlled by means of the structure of gods.

Homes, neighbourhood, and larger localities are favoured (or not) by gods, and they are also protected (or not) by gods against *kuei*. The image of gods controlling *kuei* is a religious metaphor of a heavenly court hierarchy, of purgatorial judges and their courts, of physicians, magicians, and of generals and their troops. The whole moral and hierarchical order itself is conceptualized and given deference as a fourth category: heaven, ultimate ruler, emperor, arbiter of lifespan. At this point we may note how each higher and more inclusive order of reality is itself categorized as a subject with which subjects in lower orders interact: heaven, or the god of heaven, through lower-order gods of localities control *kuei* and favour and protect the central places, neighbourhoods, homes, and individuals of the social world.

An example of the combination of all these categories in practice is the twice-monthly domestic ritual which I observed in Taiwan in 1966–8 and have described more fully elsewhere (Feuchtwang, forthcoming b). This is a ritual performed in each household to renew its protection and that of the territory which included it, and was focused on the local god and his temple. Incense was burnt and minor offerings presented in deference facing outwards at the main door to heaven, inwards at the domestic altar, stage left to the local god, and stage right to the ancestors, and then outwards again to provision the military retinue of the local god and to propitiate *kuei*. Of those subjects addressed when facing outwards, heaven was first and the offerings were elevated. The god's retinue was penultimate and the offerings were placed on the ground but within the threshold. *Kuei* were last; the offerings were placed also on the ground but beyond the threshold.

We should note here how the mechanism of relative interiority, by which the forms of domination in late imperial China appeared to their subjects, is translated in ideological practice. Ancestors are unambiguously inside; gods are not ancestors and are partly inside and partly outside, represented within the home, but as the god of the locality which includes the home; heaven is completely outside but positively so, at the highest order of inclusion; and *kuei* are completely outside and negatively so, at the lowest point of isolation and exclusion.

The imagery and practices of the ideological structures have been described so far from the point of view of the peasantry, and their local gentry, the patrons of the local temples and festivals. From the point of view of the gentry as officials, the same categories are ordered in a different way with different practices and imagery. The practices of the state religion, as observed in every administrative city at all levels of the hierarchy, excluded the common people. The temples and gods of the common people, outside the walls of the administrative city, were treated as crudely conceived and lesser in status within a minutely ordered hierarchy of gods and spirits, bureaucrats and functions, whose apex was the imperial metropolis, the emperor and his ritual preroga- tives (Feuchtwang: forthcoming a). Chief among the emperor's ritual prerogatives was the worship of heaven. The open altar to heaven, out- side the walls of the imperial metropolis, had its equivalent in lower- order administrative cities in the open altar, also outside the city walls, for worship addressed to the local mountains and streams, thunder and rain, soil and crops. Outside the walls of every administrative city was another open altar, to the local orphan souls. From the official point of view, the other senses of *kuei* did not exist. Within the walls were the temples to Confucius and the patrons of literacy, to other gods incor- porated into the state religion, and to the city god himself. The city god was treated as equivalent to the official at the head of the local adminis- trative bureaucracy in his dealings with the subjects under his adminis- tration. The imagery of the city god was that of a judge ruling souls in purgatory. Here, then, the mechanisms of relative interiority excluded ancestors completely, for they were in another region altogether; the gods were inside, heaven and *kuei* remained outside, in their respective positions in the hierarchy. From this point of view, then, the same ideo- logical categories as were worshipped by peasants and local gentry were differently ordered, even though the ordering mechanism was the same.

The differences were determined by the positional differences in the relations of domination themselves. The forms of domination were the same but appeared differently from different sides.

IDENTITIES REPRODUCED IN THE IDEOLOGICAL STRUCTURES

Family name and the social units of family and lineage were reproduced as identities and social subjects in the ancestral structure. In the god structure, place of residence and the social units of household and locality were reproduced as identities and social subjects. Out of their combination were reproduced place of origin and groupings of compatriots, such as migrants who formed settlements or street neighbour-hoods as communities centred on a shrine to the god of the place-of-origin they had in common. I have already given the example of the use of name and place-of-origin in forming feast associations. They were vehicles for whatever non-ideological practice their subjects wanted to organize—trade, political mobilization, public works. But in them all, the ideological structures served to reproduce the relations of patronage and protection which ensured the forms of domination by a leisure class. The larger the organization and the greater its corporate property and activity, the more scope there was for both investment in it and manage-ment of it. And a disparity of investments by its members would take the form of patronage, its management the form of protection of the less wealthy.

The negative category *kuei* was a site containing struggle ideologically within the dominance structures described. Peasant grievances, occa-sions of extraordinary suffering, were identified in a great elaboration of different kinds of *kuei* and of ambivalent figures on the categorical border between gods and *kuei*. These could become the subjects of secret cults and of secret societies, organizations of rebellion. In them they could be further elaborated into an alternative hierarchy of super-social subjects. But at the same time, name and place-of-origin formed peasant action against rulers and exploiters into local action against particular gentry and officials. Gentry identified themselves not only as local patrons and protectors but also as officials incorporated in a centralized hierarchy united under the emperor, identified as the son of heaven, while *kuei* continued to be reproduced as a category in which rebels were identified with bandits, foreigners, and barbarians, beyond the social pale. The pale was the imperial system of domination.

As the social formation was transformed by a new invasion and domination, that is the armed commerce of capitalist nations, new points of view, new groups and classes, emerged—a bourgeoisie with a national concentration of banking capital; an industrial proletariat and its unions; a party of the bourgeoisie, landlords, and new military rulers, and a party of the proletariat and peasantry. So new ideologies from these points of view impinged on the old religious ideological system and had their effects in it. I cannot now describe this process of trans-formation and the new ideological struggles and systems it produced. I offer just this description of late imperial China as an extended illustra-tion of ideologies which are specific to a certain social formation, and cannot be abstracted from it into a discipline of comparative religion. An ideology is a system of categories and their representations in which social forms are imagined as subjects and the relations between subjects. The imperial relations of tax and rent had the political forms of pro-tector, patrons, and plunderers. These were imagined as a structural coupling of outsider/insiders/outsiders, and as a hierarchy of singular over plural subjects. The subjects were categorized in a basic set of four:

heaven–gods–ancestors–*kuei*. Through them all kinds of associations, and the family, neighbourhood, and marketing organizations of peasant households, were identified as territorial, ancestral, and compatriotic subjects. In other words, individuals acted in units as households and on the larger scales as families, lineages, surname associations, localities, and native-place groups. These were the units of subjectivity in which individuals imagined their relationships to their conditions of existence as the patronage and protection of ancestors and gods, on the one hand, and as the threatening opposition to the whole order of units by structureless, individual subjects: *kuei*.

I began this essay by arguing that the peculiar property of ideological practice is the formation of subjectivity. Its use as an assumption was illustrated in the second part. I have not shown what is peculiar to religion as a kind of ideology. But I have argued and sought to show that subjectivity can be exposed to investigation by methods which deny subjective idealism or any idealist philosophy and do not hold the individual subject to be a given social truth.

Note

1 That is, over the whole extent of the social system, but not including every family that lived on rent. Many landlords were not literate though they aspired to literatus status in the next generation.

References

ALTHUSSER, L. 1971. Ideology and Ideological State Apparatuses: Notes towards an Investigation. *Lenin and Philosophy and Other Essays*. London: New Left Books.

DUMONT, L. 1970. *Homo Hierarchicus: the Caste System and its Implications*. London: Weidenfeld & Nicolson.

FEI HSIAO-T'UNG. 1946. Peasantry and Gentry. *American Journal of Sociology*.

FEUCHTWANG, S. forthcoming a. City God and School Temple. In G. W. Skinner (ed.), *The City in Late Imperial China*. Stanford: Stanford University Press.

— forthcoming b. Domestic and Communal Worship in Taiwan. In A. Wolf (ed.), *Religion and Ritual in Chinese Society*. Stanford: Stanford University Press.

FIRTH, R. 1964. Problem and Assumption in an Anthropological Study of Religion. In *Essays on Social Organization and Values*. LSE Monographs on Social Anthropology, No. 28. London: Athlone Press.

Stephan Feuchtwang

GEERTZ, C. 1966. Religion as a Cultural System. In M. Banton (ed.), *Anthropological Approaches to the Study of Religion*. ASA Monographs, 3. London: Tavistock Publications.

— 1968. *Islam Observed*. New Haven: Yale University Press.

LÉVI-STRAUSS, C. 1962. *La Pensée sauvage*. Paris: Plon.

MARX, K. 1973 (1857–8). *Grundrisse*. Translated by M. Nicolaus. Harmondsworth: Penguin.

MENDELSON, E. M. 1967. The 'Uninvited Guest': Ancilla to Lévi-Strauss on Totemism and Primitive Thought. In E. R. Leach (ed.), *The Structural Study of Myth and Totemism*. ASA Monographs, 5. London: Tavistock Publications.

SKINNER, G. W. 1964. Marketing and Social Structure in Rural China, Part I. *Journal of Asian Studies* **24**: 1.

SPIRO, M. 1966. Religion: Problems of Definition and Explanation. In M. Banton (ed.), *Anthropological Approaches to the Study of Religion*. ASA Monographs, 3. London: Tavistock Publications.

WORSLEY, P. 1970. *The Trumpet Shall Sound*. 2nd edn, London: Paladin.

CLASS AND
CLASS CONSCIOUSNESS

Emmanuel Terray

Classes and Class Consciousness in the Abron Kingdom of Gyaman

Translated by Anne Bailey

Five years ago, I somewhat aggressively concluded a critical study of Claude Meillassoux's *Anthropologie économique des Gouro* (1964) with the following statement:

> Marxist researchers now face the task . . . of bringing the field so far reserved for social anthropology within the ambit of historical materialism, and thus demonstrating the universal validity of the concepts and methods developed by the latter. By doing this they should ensure that social anthropology becomes a particular section of historical materialism devoted to socioeconomic formations in which the capitalist mode of production is absent and in which ethnologists and historians collaborate (1972: 184).

It seems to me that this programme was consonant with Marx's avowed intentions and with the idea he had of the scope of his discoveries. As early as the writing of *Capital* Vol I, Marx actually protested against interpretations of historical materialism which would restrict its application solely to societies dominated by capitalist production (1967: 81–2n.). If he greeted the 1877 publication of Morgan's *Ancient Society* so enthusiastically, it was surely because, for him, this book demonstrated in practice the universal vocation of the new science and its capacity for explaining the whole of humanity's social and historical evolution (see Engels's letter to Kautsky of 16 February 1884; Marx and Engels 1965: 368).

But in the eyes of disbelievers, mere reference to the will of the Founding Fathers has never constituted proof. Here as elsewhere, movement cannot be proved except by moving forward. In other words, we have only one *de facto* if not *de jure* means of convincing our interlocutors that the ambitions of historical materialism are legitimate: effectively to put it to the test in concrete cases which until now have been confined to the scrutiny of social anthropology and ethno-history. Since the appearance of the study cited above, some important steps have been taken along this line, notably in the recent works of Claude Meillassoux and Pierre-Philippe Rey. For my part I would like to make a small contribution to this endeavour, using the research I have undertaken on the history of the Abron Kingdom of Gyaman to this end. To be more explicit, in the following article I shall offer a broad outline of what a marxist analysis of this social formation could be: it is for the reader to judge the results of this attempt and the efficacy of the tools it employs.

A rapid inventory of these tools should be drawn up. At this initial stage of the journey, I do not intend to embark on a general presentation of the fundamental categories of historical materialism. It will be sufficient to indicate the meaning I am giving to certain terms—'class', 'mode of production', 'reproduction', 'social formation', 'domination of a mode of production within a social formation'—which will continually appear in this article, and I only ask for the provisional acceptance of these definitions until the account is completed.

Subject to this proviso, I should like to answer an initial question. My project is to outline a marxist explanation of the Abron social formation. Why have I chosen the theory of social classes for this project? Because the concept of class is what one could call a 'totalizing' concept: one must refer to all aspects of social reality in order to define it. When Marx wrote on the first page of the *Communist Manifesto*, 'The history of all hitherto existing society is the history of class struggles' (Marx and Engels 1969, Vol, I: 108), he *also* gave us an indication of an epistemological nature. If all history may be regarded as the history of class confrontation, it is because class is, as it were, the place where the various dimensions of social life—economic, political, ideological—intersect. In other words, within the field of social relations, class is the product of the conjoined action of different structures—economic, political, ideological—the combination of which constitutes a determinate mode of production and social formation (Poulantzas 1972: 70–1, 73). In this respect class plays within marxist theory a role similar to that which Mauss attributed to the 'total social fact' in an entirely different context. All the determinations that characterize a given social formation at a given period are concentrated in it. This is why the viewpoint of class is a privileged perspective for the marxist researcher. It is why the study of classes represents the royal road to a marxist analysis of society and history.

What, in fact, is a social class? Lenin tells us:

Classes are large groups of people differing from each other by the place they occupy in a historically determined system of social production, by their relation (in most cases fixed and formulated in law) to the means of production, by their role in the social organization of labour, and consequently by the dimensions of the share of social wealth of which they dispose and the mode of acquiring it. Classes are groups of people one of which can appropriate the labour of another owing to the different places they occupy in a definite system of social economy (1971: 231).

Three aspects of this passage should be noted:

(*a*) First of all, a class never exists on its own. What one always encounters is, by definition, a plurality of classes. I shall not emphasize this point, since it is obvious and can be deduced from the general meaning of the term class. In botany as in logic, a class is always a sub-division within a larger set. A set in which only one class existed would in fact be a classless set. Similarly, in this context, a social class is an internal part of a whole, an element internal to a system. It is defined by the role that it plays within this whole, by the function that it takes on within this system. One must therefore start from the whole or the system in order to understand the part or element.

(*b*) What is this whole or system? It is, Lenin replies, 'a historically defined system of social production', i.e. a determinate mode of production. In other words, the different places which classes occupy within a given mode of production define them and distinguish them from one another. An extremely important, but too often ignored, consequence follows from this. Beyond the very general, abstract indication given by Lenin, it is not possible to give class a universal definition, valid for all modes of production. If a class is characterized in a differential manner by its position within a determinate mode of production, it conversely follows that a specific definition of class corresponds to each particular mode of production. In other words, the question whether the concept of class is useful in studies other than those bearing on the capitalist mode of production is divested of meaning. If by 'class' is understood classes such as they exist in the capitalist mode of production, then the answer is obviously no. But this does not mean that there are classes in this mode of production alone. Classes may be found in other modes of production: only then their reciprocal relations and indeed their very nature will be defined by the structure of the mode of production. For each mode of production the concept of class that is appropriate to it must be constructed.

(*c*) Lenin states that the position of a class within a mode of production should be understood as the relationship it has to the means of production. This relationship is manifested on two levels: at the level of the productive forces, a class formed by producers or non-producers can or cannot set to work the means of production. At the level of the relations of production, a class can either control and dispose of the means of production or else be separated from them. Depending on the circumstances, this relation may be translated as a relation of property or non-property at the level of the legal superstructure.

The combination of these two distinctions produces four types of possible classes:

1 Producers disposing of the means of production (self-subsistent community production, petty commodity production).
2 Producers separated from the means of production (slave, serf, worker).
3 Non-producers disposing of the means of production (slave-owner, feudal lord, capitalist).
4 Non-producers separated from the means of production (social classes and categories that are said to be unproductive).

This last type provides a precise definition of what might be called secondary classes. Even if secondary classes of a specific nature are found in each mode of production, their specificity is but a derivative effect of the specificity of the fundamental classes, i.e. the classes that have an actual relation to the means of production at one or the other level.

As for the three other types, they actually refer to two distinct situations:

In the first, one and the same social group uses and controls the means of production. In this case, the mode of production comprises only one fundamental class, which is of the first type.

In the second, the control and use of the means of production are the function of two different social groups. Here the mode of production comprises two fundamental classes, one of which belongs to the second type, the other to the third type.

In both situations the setting apart of a proportion of the surplus provided by the producers ensures the livelihood of the non-producers. But in the first case, the producers are the ones who decide what proportion of the surplus should be set aside. The non-producers have no means of compelling them to divide the surplus into definite proportions. Consequently the non-producers are entirely dependent upon the producers. On the other hand, in the second case the control of the means of production gives to those non-producers who exercise it the means of determining the amount of surplus allotted to themselves. This control renders the producers subordinate to the non-producers.

This last situation represents exactly what one would call a relationship of exploitation. For one class to exploit another, not only must its subsistence be secured from the surplus labour of the other, which is true for all non-producers, but, furthermore, the exploiting class has to be in a position to dictate its conditions to the exploited class and to determine the amount of surplus which it appropriates.

In the first case—where there is only one fundamental class—we would normally speak of a classless society. In the second—where there are two fundamental classes, direct producers and owners of the means of production—we would on the other hand speak of a class society. The term class obviously acquires a new meaning in such expressions: henceforth it denotes the two opposing poles in a relationship of exploitation.

In the light of the preceding remarks, we are now in a position to return to the concept of 'mode of production', which as we have seen is extremely important for an exact understanding of what classes are. The way in which I previously expressed this concept (1972: 97–8), while not incorrect, today appears to me inadequate, at least on one point: It was indecisive as to the respective roles of the two aspects of 'productive forces' and 'relations of production' in the definition of the mode of production. Where in the last analysis should we look for the specific distinguishing mark of a given mode of production, for that which distinguishes it from other modes of production and lies at the foundation of its particular economic, political, and ideological character? For reasons that were otherwise valid, but that were linked to the particularities of the case under analysis, I had been led to see the evidence for the identification of the mode or modes of production realized in the socio-economic formation in the forms of cooperation between the producers (op. cit.: 107). In so far as this was true, I might have given the impression, despite my denials, that for me the origin of the differentiation of modes of production lay within the domain of the productive forces. Moreover, as I also refused to admit the existence of relations of exploitation in the society in question,[1] this impression could only have been confirmed by the remainder of the study.

Now, it would obviously be wrong to attribute a role to the productive forces which Marx expressly indicated belonged to the relations of production. Marx wrote a passage which today seems to me decisive for a correct definition of the concept of mode of production:

> The specific economic form, in which unpaid surplus labour is pumped out of direct producers, determines the relationship of rulers and ruled, as it grows directly out of production itself and, in turn, reacts upon its as a determining element. Upon this, however, is founded the entire formation of the economic community which grows up out of the production relations themselves, thereby simultaneously its specific political form. It is always the direct relationship of the owners of the conditions of production to the direct producers —a relation always naturally corresponding to a definite stage in the development of the methods of labour and thereby its social productivity—which reveals the innermost secret, the hidden basis of the entire social structure, and with it the political form of the relation of sovereignty and dependence. . . . (Marx 1967, Vol. III: 791).

The specific form in which unpaid surplus labour is extorted from the direct producers is exactly what I have called a 'relation of exploitation' in my preceding remarks. For Marx, this relation constitutes the heart or nucleus of the mode of production. It is at the very foundation of the set of determinations that characterize the mode of production at its various levels: economic, political, and ideological. Consequently, the siting of the various modes of production in a social formation will necessarily proceed by a preliminary inventory of the different forms taken by the relation of exploitation in this social formation, since a particular mode of production would correspond to each of these forms.

In thus defining the mode of production from the perspective of the relation of exploitation, do we not run the risk of excluding the possibility of modes of production that would not in fact rest on exploitation, i.e. on the total or partial transfer of surplus to benefit a minority of non-producers? To my mind we may eliminate this risk if we retain as the basis of defining modes of production and discriminating between them, *not* the relation of exploitation in the strict meaning of the term, *but*, more generally speaking, the *specific mode* of the drawing-off, allocation, and utilization of surplus. Among the various possible modes, those which give rise to exploitation would then form a particular family.

How does the way in which surplus appears and is allocated determine the political and ideological superstructures that are linked to it? Once and for all, we must rid ourselves of metaphors of reflection—according to which the superstructure would be a reflection of the economic base—as well as metaphors of 'begetting'—according to which the economic base gives birth to the superstructure by some mysterious process. In every mode of production the motive and goal of social activity is not only the creation of use-values necessary to the life of the society, but also the maintenance and consolidation of the social relations through which this creation is carried out. Referring to the capitalist mode of production, Marx wrote:

> . . . if the capitalist mode of production presupposes this definite social form of the conditions of production, so does it reproduce it continually. It produces not merely the material products, but reproduces continually the production relations in which the former are produced . . . (Marx 1967, Vol. III: 879).

The superstructures appear then as the political and ideological conditions of the orderly reproduction of the relations of production. In fact, this reproduction is liable to interruption for various reasons, some of which at least are of a political or ideological nature. Institutions operating at these two levels may therefore be regarded as so many means open to the society—or in the case of a society divided into classes, to the dominant class—for coping with these threats. Thus, each specific mode of extraction of the surplus presupposes a determinate superstructure as a condition of its own reproduction. And, as Louis Althusser writes: '. . . this superstructure is necessarily *specific* (since it is a function of the specific relations of production that call for it)' (Althusser and Balibar 1972: 177).

But a mode of production does not itself exist in isolation. The development of the productive forces—which includes not only what we would normally think of as technical progress, but also the improvement of all manner of means available for the concentration of producers and bringing them into large-scale cooperation—leads to the wearing away of certain modes of production and the simultaneous advent of other more productive modes, or rather modes that are more capable of producing a surplus. Thus, at each specific moment of history, we can see the coexistence of the old and the new. In other words, what we find in empirical research are not modes of production, but social formations, the structure of which is 'the result of the combination of at least two distinct modes of production, one of which is dominant and the other subordinate' (Althusser, cited by Terray, op. cit.: 79). Here again, the indications given in my 1969 text (English translation 1972), while not wrong, were inadequate. By not having taken the perspective of reproduction, I did not satisfactorily manage to uncover the meaning of the domination of one mode of production over another. Once again, Pierre-Philippe Rey's work today allows us to go further and to offer the following definition: a mode of production is dominant within a social formation when it subjects the functioning of other modes of production represented in this social formation to the requirements of its own reproduction.

Some important consequences follow from this definition. First of all, as the example of colonialism clearly shows, the functioning of dominated modes of production is modified and deformed by the action of the dominant mode of production. But conversely, the subordination of dominated modes of production to the requirements of the reproduction of the dominant mode in turn transforms the functioning of the latter. Thus the persistence of small independent production and commerce enables large firms and stores in the sectors concerned to set higher prices than would be possible if capitalist production had totally taken over the economy. Therefore, when a mode of production, whether dominant or subordinate, combines with other modes of production within a social formation, its functioning necessarily differs from what it would be if this mode of production existed 'in a pure state'. We have consequently to abandon considering this mode of production in isolation. Since the mode of production is to the social formation as the element is to the system, it is also determined by the properties of the set in which it is enclosed.

To define a class one must therefore begin not only from the mode of production, but also from the social formation of which it is a part. Not only the economic infrastructure, but also the political and ideological superstructures, must be taken into account. Indeed, we have seen that a class is the product of the combined action of all these structures. We must emphasize this point. By confining oneself to the economic base alone, one will only grasp what Marx calls classes 'in themselves', characterized by their function within the mode of production, their position at one end or other of a relation of exploitation. But even when it is a case of an exploited class, a class 'in itself' is not necessarily simultaneously a class 'for itself', conscious of itself and capable of collective decision and action. To be sure, where there is exploitation there is always some form of revolt and struggle, but such struggles may remain fragmented, temporary, and defensive. In such situations the class does not constitute a genuine historical force liable actively to determine the course of events. Illustrative of this distinction is the famous passage in the *Eighteenth Brumaire of Louis Bonaparte* (1852) where Marx portrays the peasants cultivating small land-holdings:

> The small-holding peasants form a vast mass, the members of which live in similar conditions but without entering into manifold relations with one another. Their mode of production isolates them from one another instead of bringing them into mutual intercourse . . . In this way the great mass of the French nation is formed by simple addition of homologous magnitudes, much as potatoes in a sack form a sack of potatoes. In so far as millions of families live under conditions of existence that separate their mode of life, their interests and their culture from those of the other classes, and put them in hostile opposition to the latter, they form a class. In so far as there is merely a local interconnection among these small-holding peasants, and the identity of their interests beget no community, no national bond and no political organization among them, they do not form a class. They are consequently incapable of enforcing their class interests in their own name . . . They cannot represent themselves, they must be represented (Marx and Engels 1969, Vol. I: 478–9).

What we want to know next are the conditions and circumstances in which a class 'in itself' becomes and remains a class 'for itself'. We can give a preliminary answer of a general nature: classes 'in themselves' are transformed into historical subjects, and as such capable of reflection and initiative, by struggling and fighting against each other. But this transformation, which may be more or less deep-seated, more or less lasting, will vary with the mode of production. These variations are not arbitrary; they are a function of the nature of the relations of production basic to the mode of production in question. In other words, the specific way in which surplus is created, drawn off, and allocated—the specific form the relation of exploitation assumes—determines not only the nature of the classes present, but also their ability to organize themselves and act as classes, the forms and intensity of confrontation between them, and the possible outcome of such confrontation.

It would seem to me that two elements play a particularly important role in this area: the specific methods according to which the class is recruited and the stability or growth in the intensity of exploitation.

As far as the first element is concerned, we have seen that Lenin defined classes as 'large groups of people' occupying a determinate position in a mode of production. We may then ask ourselves how these large groups of people are recruited. In other words, the existence of classes implies a series of different positions within a mode of production, on the one hand, and the division of a population into various categories, each of which is assigned to one of the positions in the series, on the other. Now this division may present itself in different ways: it may use pre-existing divisions like the 'given' differences of sex, age, position in the kinship network, or socio-historical differences based on ethnic differences—or it may constitute a new division, entirely independent of previous ones. Thus two situations may occur:

Either the division of the society into classes reproduces or repeats 'given' or socio-historical differences present in that society, in which case classes coincide with the sexes, the generations, kinship categories (sons, nephews, etc.), or ethnic groups. The composition and recruitment of classes depends upon the composition and recruitment of these groups. In such a situation, one might speak of classes with closed or predetermined recruitment.

Or the division of the society into classes is distinct from 'given' or socio-historical forms of differentiation, and cross-cuts them. Each class reproduces these differences within itself. The composition and recruitment of a class are independent of the categories which they generate. Here, one might speak of openly recruited classes.

Of course, the open character of class recruitment may be hidden in certain cases by the fact that the class division uses socio-historical distinctions that appear as if they were independent of the class division, but that are really directly produced by it. For example, Bukharin demonstrates clearly how the hierarchy of the orders, conditions, and estate of the Middle Ages is but a legal representation of the class division in certain modes of production of a determinate structure:

> In precapitalist forms of society, all relations are far more conservative; the tempo of life is slower; alterations are less significant than under capitalism . . . This striking *immobility* in conditions makes possible a consolidation of class privileges—as well as class duties—by means of a series of legal standards; this immobility enabled classes to be enveloped in the garment of the 'estate' (Bukharin 1969: 280).

Here again, the 'choice' between the possibilities of closed and open recruitment is not an arbitrary one, but one that is determined in the final analysis by the relations of production. In 1969, I tried to show why classes in 'the pure state', i.e. which are openly recruited, appear only in the capitalist mode of production (Terray 1972: 148 ff.). A class is defined by the function its members fulfil in social production, but that function can only become the direct principle in the formation of concrete social groups if the economic instance is the dominant instance in the mode of production. Such is the case in capitalism. There, even if a class is politically organized and ideologically united, it is first of all and originally an economic group. On the other hand, when the relations of production are not exclusively of an economic nature, the economic function cannot by itself account for the identity of concrete social groups, nor can it directly serve as the basis of the distinctions between them. Referring to the feudal mode of production, Marx wrote:

> The direct producer, according to our assumption, is to be found here in possession of his own means of production, the necessary material labour conditions required for the realization of his labour and the production of his means of subsistence. He conducts his agricultural activity and the rural home industries connected with it . . . Under such conditions the surplus-labour for the nominal owner of the land can only be extorted from them by other than economic pressure, whatever the form assumed may be (Marx 1967, Vol. III: 790–1).

In my opinion this remark may be extended to cover all pre-capitalist modes of production. In the latter, the extra-economic bonds, i.e. political and ideological, of which Marx wrote are not just the realization of the superstructural conditions of the reproduction of the relations of production, they are present in the very constitution of these relations, since in their absence no surplus, regardless of the way it is used, could be drawn off. The political and ideological bonds are thus the preliminary condition for the production process itself. In other words, the superstructure is introduced at the very centre of the economic base as a presupposition.

In these modes of production economics, politics, and ideology are inextricably linked. This interconnectedness represents what one might call the functional multivalence of institutions and groups. In contrast to the capitalist mode of production, where a whole series of functions is divided among different units, here they are concentrated in the same groups and institutions at their respective levels. Thus in the lineage mode of production, the lineage and the segment in their respective concerns are simultaneously units of production, consumption, political organization, and religion. We could say as much for the feudal manor, *mutatis mutandis*. The economic division of society therefore merges with the political and ideological divisions; it is indeed the same division which appears multivalent. In my opinion the number of divisions of this kind operating in a given society depends upon the stage of the division of labour. If this is little advanced, limited to the allotment of different tasks to the different sexes and age groups, a group modelled on the family—band, segment, lineage, etc.—can form an autonomous unit. Consequently, if we are dealing with a subsistence economy, defined not by the lack of exchange or the basic autarchy of communities, but by the homology between units of production and consumption and the absence of a market acting as a screen between them, then a single division occurring in the kinship system could constitute the sole framework of the whole social structure. In each case, the specific concrete forms of this system are determined by a whole series of economic, political, and ideological variables. When the division of labour is more advanced, for example when there are specialized branches of the economy, e.g. agriculture and stock-raising, then a new division is superimposed on the pre-existing one without abolishing it. Two communities, each organized on the principles described, are bound together within the same totality, be it by relations of equal exchange and complementarity, or, on the contrary, by relations of domination and exploitation, such as those prevailing between Tutsi herdsmen and Hutu cultivators in Ruanda. Ethnic cleavages might then be used to distinguish the two communities. But in each case the different positions or functions discerned within the mode of production are assigned to groups the recruitment of which is predetermined by differences in sex, age, kinship category, or ethnic affiliation. In other words, the class division remains, as it were, entangled in these differences.

The importance of this distinction between closed and open recruitment to classes lies in the consequences it entails for the nature and outcome of class conflict. Where closed recruitment obtains, classes in fact have no distinct, autonomous existence, since they merge with the sexes, age groups, kinship categories, or ethnic groups. Simultaneously, class conflict takes the form of conflicts between the sexes, generations, individuals, and groups occupying such and such a position in the kinship network or between tribes. In other words, classes and class contradictions do not succeed in emerging as such: their manner of appearance checks their expression and limits their development. At this point, I would like to refer to a discussion which I had with Pierre-Philippe Rey on the presence of exploitation and classes in what we have called the lineage mode of production (Terray 1972: 166–7).

Today I am ready to admit their presence when the conditions posited by Rey obtain: when the extortion of surplus labour from the direct producers permits the dominant minority, either directly or through exchange, to acquire prestige goods, the control of which constitutes the guarantee of its power. Indeed, how did Marx and Engels define exploitation? In *Anti-Dühring*, Engels wrote:

> Surplus-labour, labour beyond the time required for the labourer's own maintenance, and appropriation by others of the product of this surplus-labour, is therefore common to all forms of society that have existed hitherto, in so far as these have moved in class antagonisms (Engels 1969: 248).

For exploitation to exist, it suffices that there be extortion, i.e. the forced levy and appropriation of surplus labour by others, regardless of the purpose to which the product of this surplus labour is put, whether it be used for expanded reproduction of the mode of production, the immediate or conspicuous consumption of the non-producers, or whether it merely circulates under their control or is hoarded by them. In other

95

words, as we shall see, even if the intensity and social effects of exploitation vary according to the use made of extorted surplus labour, the fact of exploitation is itself independent of such use.

On the other hand, the existence of exploitation by itself only establishes the presence of classes 'in themselves', in the previously defined sense of this term. The problem of how these are transformed into classes 'for themselves' still remains. For example, in the lineage mode of production, women, youths, or whatever the category of persons occupying a definite position in the kinship system, may be regarded as constituting classes. But all actual communities regardless of their scale are cross-cut by age and sex differences and include various categories of kin. These distinctions may serve as the foundation for various kinds of groups—age-sets, women's associations, etc.—but no autonomous community can be based on these groups. As far as the sexes are concerned, the physiological and economic division of labour creates such close bonds between them that neither could conceive of itself without the other, nor set as its goal the liquidation of the other. As for age differences, the normal functioning of the society enables at least some of the youths to become elders, and every elder was once a youth. In other words, some of the exploited one day in turn become the exploiters, and the hope of such a promotion inevitably reduces the sharpness of conflicts. With respect to kinship categories, if Ego is exploited in his position as son, sister's son, or matrilateral cross-cousin, he is necessarily at the same time an exploiter in his position of father, maternal uncle, or patrilateral cross-cousin. This is not to say that there are no contradictions within the lineage mode of production or that the classes which it implies are not antagonistic. As we shall see, the quarrels accompanying the transmission of inheritance and social privileges or witchcraft accusations may quite legitimately be interpreted as class conflicts. But the characteristics described above prevent these classes—women, youths, sons, or nephews—from becoming conscious of themselves as classes, from organizing and acting as classes, from collectively proposing the reorganization of society on the basis of their class interests. For the most part the conflicts that set them against the dominant class remain confined to each actual community. Class conflicts therefore remain fragmented and dispersed and cannot be forged to produce a general confrontation at the level of the total society.

We can therefore understand why the presence of classes within the lineage mode of production is not accompanied by that of the state, i.e. a specialized institution constructed by the dominant class in order to guarantee the reproduction of the exploitation of the dominated classes. For the state to exist, i.e. for there to be a relatively centralized apparatus of oppression and repression, class antagonisms must be manifested as such, divorced from other sorts of conflict and extending beyond the limits of local communities to give rise to conflict in the larger society. At the same time, we understand why class contradictions inherent in the lineage mode of production cannot lead to a revolution, or to the overthrowing of one class by another, to the seizure of power by one class to the detriment of another, and hence to a transformation of social relations. Only a development internal to the productive forces can result in overcoming these contradictions, for example, through the introduction of slavery, or the increasing gap between the noble and commoner lineages, or through outside intervention linked to the action of another mode of production.

When classes take the form of ethnic communities, the situation is already visibly different, since the latter actually have a distinct, autonomous social existence. Here we already find an initial type of state, which anthropologists have designated the conquest state. There class conflicts appear as conflicts between peoples or tribes, and we shall see the limitations stemming from this form in our analysis of the case of Gyaman.

But as we have already briefly indicated, there is a second element that determines the transition from a class 'in itself' to a class 'for itself' and therefore the nature and the outcome of class conflicts: it is the use to which extorted surplus labour is put and the effects this utilization has on the intensity of exploitation. In *Capital*, Marx wrote:

> It is, however, clear that, in any given economic formation of society, where not the exchange-value but the use-value of the product predominates, surplus-labour will be limited by a given set of wants which may be greater or less, and that here no boundless thirst for surplus-labour arises from the nature of production itself (Marx 1967, Vol. I: 235).

In an economy dominated by exchange-value, i.e. a market economy, the motive of production is the acquisition of exchange-value. Now, exchange-values can only be distinguished from one another by quantity. The entrepreneur and the merchant can have no other goal than to obtain greater and greater quantities of exchange-value. This is why the intensity of exploitation in such an economy is always raised to the highest degree compatible with the development of the productive forces, and necessarily grows with this development. Marx observed that:

> in antiquity over-work becomes horrible only when the object is to obtain exchange-value in its specific independent money-form; in the production of gold and silver (ibid.).

This is also why the organizers of production must constantly strive to create new needs, so that they can realize increasingly greater quantities of surplus labour extorted from the direct producers. On the other hand, the domination of use-value means that production is determined by consumption, therefore by existing needs. Here, the master of production seeks to obtain, either directly or by means of exchange, a determinate quantity of objects with determinate utility, which are destined either for his immediate consumption or for conspicuous consumption. Surplus production is only a means for him to acquire these objects. Since production is here subordinated to consumption, it does not prompt the appearance of new needs. Without external intervention, needs remain unchanged, and consequently the intensity of exploitation also remains uniform.

For example, this stability of exploitation enables us to understand why ground-rent in the feudal mode of production could remain relatively constant for very long periods, and why the rate of ground-rent could be set either by customs that were considered immemorial or by long-term contracts. Likewise, this stability enables us to understand why we may witness an autonomous economic development of the dominated class when rent is appropriated in labour or in kind (Marx 1967, Vol. III: 792 (labour rent), 794 (rent in kind)). This occurs when the productive forces and the productivity of labour progress, while the intensity of exploitation remains stationary.

On the whole, a kind of equilibrium in exploitation is realized in societies dominated by use-value which is unfavourable to the aggravation and explosion of class conflicts. Indeed, the absence of change in the conditions and intensity of exploitation over time makes it appear as an inescapable, natural phenomenon, free from the vicissitudes of history and the action of man. Pushed by the desire and necessity of accumulating more and more profit, the capitalist bourgeoisie, as Marx wrote in the *Communist Manifesto*:

> . . . cannot exist without constantly revolutionizing the instruments of production and with them the whole relations of society . . . Constant revolutionizing of production, uninterrupted disturbance of social conditions, everlasting uncertainty and agitation distinguish the bourgeois epoch from all earlier ones (Marx and Engels 1969, Vol. I: 111).

But in so doing the bourgeoisie labours towards its own undoing, for it exposes the historical and transitory nature of the social relations that form the basis of its power:

> All that is solid melts into air, all that is holy is profaned, and man is at last compelled to face with sober senses, his real conditions of life, and his relations with his kind (ibid).

On the other hand, all pre-capitalist modes of production are to varying degrees characterized by the continuity and immutability of the social relations that constitute them, and Marx's statement on the feudal mode of production can be applied to them:

> . . . it is evident that tradition must play a dominant role in the primi-

tive and undeveloped circumstances on which these social production relations and the corresponding mode of production are based. It is furthermore clear that here as always it is in the interest of the ruling section of society to sanction the existing order as law and to legally establish its limits given through usage and tradition. Apart from all else, this, by the way, comes about of itself as soon as the constant reproduction of the basis of the existing order and its fundamental relations assumes a regulated and orderly form in the course of time. And such regulations and order are themselves indispensable elements of any mode of production, if it is to assume social stability and independence from mere chance and arbitrariness . . . Under backward conditions of the production process as well as the corresponding social relations, it achieves this form by mere repetition of their very reproduction. If this has continued on for some time, it entrenches itself as custom and tradition and is finally sanctioned as an explicit law (Marx 1967, Vol. III: 793).

This strength of tradition, which is proportional to the permanence of social relations, does not necessarily prevent the dominated class from becoming conscious of itself, but it at least leads it to doubt its capacity to transform a situation that appears to it to be the effect of the 'nature of things'.

Nevertheless, two points should be clarified. First of all, the stability of the intensity of exploitation does not mean that pre-capitalist modes of production are necessarily doomed to what Marx called simple reproduction, the perpetual reconstitution of the same conditions and relations of production. In fact, they may undergo and may actually have experienced periods of growth and rapid transformation preceded and accompanied by an intensification of exploitation. But these periods are the result of determinate historical conjunctures: in contrast to the capitalist mode of production, the worsening of exploitation does not constitute a tendential law inherent in the actual structures of these modes of production. On the other hand, one may also witness a general deterioration of the relations forming the mode of production and of the situation of the classes it entails. For example, usury in the feudal mode of production produces this kind of deterioration. It corrodes the condition of the landlord as well as that of the peasant, and undermines the whole social structure. Here again, there is certainly an intensification of exploitation, but the landowners do not profit from it since the surplus siphoned off by usury benefits the classes around which the capitalist mode of production is beginning to organize itself.

These various considerations at least partly explain why the domination of the 'Asiatic', slave, and feudal modes of production, in which classes are clearly constituted as such, was not overthrown by a revolution conducted by the exploited classes in these various modes of production. Indeed, if we examine the way in which the supremacy of one mode of production gives way to that of another, we may ascertain that the elements—relations of production, classes—of the subsequent mode of production are formed at the boundaries, 'in the margin', of the previous mode of production and the global and uniform wearing-away of the latter has permitted the former to be imposed at a particular time.

By developing the considerations offered above, we would arrive at a kind of typology of modes of production based both upon the nature of the classes they entail and upon the character of the conflicts opposing these classes. According to the first meaning of the term class—a group of men occupying a determinate position in social production—we would find classes in all modes of production. According to the second sense of the word—class as one of the two terms in a relationship of exploitation—we would distinguish modes of production without exploitation and classes from those with exploitation and classes, according to the way in which surplus is created, drawn off, and allocated. Among the latter, one may furthermore distinguish modes of production where classes are recruited in a closed manner, where the division into classes is buried under 'given' or socio-historical differences, and consequently where classes remain classes 'in themselves', unable to transform themselves into forces open to historical initiatives, from those where classes achieve consciousness of themselves and are able to organize themselves and act as such. Finally, among these last types, we may distinguish modes of production where exploitation generally remains uniform from those in which it is, as it were, accelerated. We note in passing that, had we been dealing with one of those *combinatoires* so dear to the structuralists, we would have had to envisage the possibility of modes of production in which only classes 'in themselves' would exist and in which exploitation would nevertheless be accelerated. But, clearly, there can be no such possibility, since the accelerated character of exploitation presupposes the domination of exchange-value over production, and consequently an important development in exchange. This in turn is a result both of the private character of production and of the development of the division of labour. Now, classes remain 'classes in themselves' when they are moulded into 'given' or socio-historical differentiations, and this conversely implies a low degree of development of the division of labour.

In terms of this classification, the state, as the centralized instrument of repression, would only appear with classes in the third sense, classes conscious of themselves and capable of collective action. As for revolution, understood as the overthrow of existing social relations through the action of the exploited class, it would be a possible outcome of class contradictions only in modes of production where exploitation was accelerated.

These distinctions will allow us to avoid the debate over whether or not exploitation and classes exist in such and such a mode of production, a debate that today appears to me quite sterile. Sterile, because in the last analysis its outcome depends upon the definition which the debaters in question give to the term class, and since in agreeing to enter this sort of debate, they presuppose that this definition is universal and independent of the specific characteristics of the mode of production that encompasses the various classes. Instead of persevering on this path, in my opinion it would be more worth while to consider the concept of class as a 'derivative' concept, admitting that classes are the product of the structures of the mode of production, and thus to begin from the mode of production in order to understand the classes. Only by employing this strategy may we proceed to comparisons and, if circumstances permit, elaborate a general definition. At any rate, this is the manner in which we will proceed in our examination of the Abron kingdom.

Located on the boundary between the savanna and dense forest, the territory occupied by the Abron Kingdom of Gyaman is situated northeast of what is now the Ivory Coast and northwest of present-day Ghana, in the region of Bondoukou, which lies between the Komoe and the Black Volta.

Established about 1690 by the *Gyamanhene* (king of Gyaman) Tan Date, the Gayman kingdom fell under Ashanti domination in 1740. Ashanti hegemony lasted until 1874 despite numerous uprisings (in 1750, 1764, 1798, 1800, 1818). Gyaman was not to regain its independence until 1874, when Sir Garnet Wolseley's English troops defeated the Ashanti and destroyed Kumasi. From 1875 until 1882, the kingdom went through a period of rapid territorial expansion, followed by a period of internal disorders that ended around 1890. Then it was invaded by Samori in 1895; the French and English occupied the western and eastern areas of the kingdom respectively at the end of 1897.

The first administrators estimated the population at around 80,000 inhabitants (Clozel 1906: 63), a figure which to my mind is only a rough indication of size. As regards ethnic groups, this population was extremely mixed. Indeed, the Abron kingdom was in fact a political unit encompassing linguistic and organizational features from very different cultures and the number of actual Abron was quite small. According to Captain Benquey's 1902 census in the French part of the kingdom, there were only 8,000 Abron out of a total population of 54,000. Let us briefly list the groups [2] represented:

(a) The *Gur*-speaking peoples belonging to the *Grusi* groups: *Loron, Kulango, Degha* or *Senufo*, and the *Nafana*.

(b) The *Mande*-speaking peoples: the *Guro* and *Gan*; the *Ligbi* accompanied by the *Numu* blacksmiths who transmitted their language to the indigenous *Huela*; finally, the *Dyula*, some settling in Bondoukou, others in the western province of Barabo.

(c) The *Akan*-speaking peoples: the *Anyi* occupying the southern borderlands of the *Bini*, *Bona*, and *Asikaso*; and finally, the *Abron*, who were undoubtedly formed by the fusion of two groups: the indigenous Guang-speaking *Brong* peoples from south of the route going from Bondoukou to Wenchi, and a small group from Akwamu, to the north of Accra, which by itself made up the dominant group: it provided the kingdom with the lineages of the king, provincial chiefs and most of their political officials.

These peoples arrived in several waves. Except for the Dyula of Barabo, who were summoned by the first *Gyamanhene*s, the Abron of Akwamu were the last to arrive. Although the Kulango and the Anyi dominate the north and south respectively, the various groups are closely inter-connected. Separation between them operates at the level of villages or even at the level of neighbourhoods in larger towns.

In the economic sphere, the yam is the staple agricultural crop. The Abron kingdom produces only a small crop of kola nuts and does not export this product. On the other hand, the wealth of its gold mines has been known from early times.

A very important trade route passes through Gyaman, joining the Niger with the Gulf of Guinea, passing through Bobo Dioulasso, Kong, Bondoukou, and Kumasi or Anyibilekru. The following products are transported along this route:

From south to north: kola nuts, gold (which, at the beginning of the nineteenth century, would be diverted to the Hausa), sea-salt, and finally, European trade goods: iron and copper rods, cloth, alcohol, guns, and powder.

From north to south: Bobo Dioulasso iron manufactures, Buna cotton, Saharan salt, livestock, ivory, and captives.

At the heart of the kingdom is a large town, Bondoukou, which sprang up at the beginning of the eighteenth century, following the decline of Bighu. From 1879, travellers reaching the town claimed that the population was anything from 4,000 to 8,000 inhabitants. It is simul-taneously a stopover place, an unloading-point (where the means of transport of goods changes from animal to human); a decisive point in the trade network (many Dyula merchants go no further south and many Ashanti merchants go no further north); a monetary frontier (between the gold-dust and cowrie zones); and, finally, an 'industrial' centre with many artisans and in particular Hausa dyers.

As far as the productive forces are concerned, we shall confine ourselves here to two remarks:

The Abron social formation allocates its social labour-time between several types of activity: agriculture, hunting, animal husbandry, handicrafts, and the extraction of gold. But in each of these branches, with the sole exception of handicrafts, labour-power is the principal factor in the labour-process. As far as handicrafts are concerned, we know that this role is played by the union of the labourer and his means of production, the weaver and his loom or the blacksmith and his bellows, etc. As Étienne Balibar, writing on this question, states:

> On the one hand, the means of labour (the tool) must be adapted to the human organism; on the other, a tool is no longer a technical instrument in the hands of someone who does not know how to use it: its effective use demands of the worker a set of physical and intellectual qualities, a sum of cultural habits (an empirical knowledge of the materials, of the tricks of the trade, up to and including the craft secrets, etc.) (Althusser and Balibar 1972: 238).

But handicrafts in the Abron social formation represent a unique case: in all other branches labour-power is in fact the dominant element in the labour-process. First of all, with the exception of fire, which is used when clearing the fields, and of donkeys allocated for the transport of cargo, muscle power is the only available source of energy. The tools of labour (hoe, machete, the miner's small pick) are rudimentary; generally it is a matter of individual tools, mere extensions of the human arm, the productivity of which varies little. Therefore what I wrote about the Guro also applies:

> . . . their very simplicity makes most of these implements polyvalent—their nature does little to predetermine the use to which they will be put. Here, the worker is the effective 'site' of the labour process (Terray 1972: 104).

Thus the efficiency of the labour-process and the scope of its capability to transform nature are a direct function of intensive human labour. Consequently, the control of men and thus the possibility of organizing their cooperation on a large scale is the key to economic power.

But what might the foundation of this control be and what forms can it take? In the *Grundrisse*, Marx distinguished between two kinds of submission of one individual to another or of one class to another, which can be called 'personal dependence' and 'material dependence' respectively:

> Relations of personal dependence (entirely spontaneous at the outset) are the first social forms, in which human productive capacity develops only to a slight extent and at isolated points. Personal independence founded on *objective* (*sachlicher*) dependence is the second great form . . . Patriarchal as well as ancient conditions (feudal, also) thus disintegrate with the development of commerce, of luxury, of *money*, of *exchange value*, while modern society arises and grows in the same measure (Marx 1973: 158).

In the first type, subordination is direct and immediate, as in the relation of a servant to his master. In the second, the control of the producer is mediated by the control over the means of production which the producer needs in order to subsist. Now, land is abundantly available in Gyaman.

103

In 1889 Freeman estimated that the kingdom covered 9,600 square miles,[3] which for a population of 80,000 inhabitants would give us a density of fewer than nine inhabitants per square mile. Of course, this figure only makes sense when related to the technical conditions of land-use, but it seems clearly lower than in neighbouring regions (Ashanti, Indenie) where these conditions are identical. In other respects, even though shifting agriculture requiring a considerable amount of land was practised in Abron territory, Abron immigration at the end of the seventeenth century does not seem to have produced a land problem, if we believe traditional accounts. The Abron were able to settle either in the 'empty' zones in the south of the country or in the north on land left vacant by their Kulango predecessors. Accounts gathered from both the Kulango and the Abron mention neither conflict over land nor expulsions. As for the instruments of labour, they are made of materials (wood, iron) easily obtainable either directly or by exchange, and their simplicity makes them openly available to the great majority of the population. Iron ore is not mined in the Abron territory; blacksmiths living in Bondoukou and other large towns use iron rods from the coast or iron ingots from the Bobo Dioulasso region in forging their wares. Many finished products are also imported from Bobo: knife and hoe blades, containers, etc. (Binger 1892, Vol. II: 194; Joseph 1915: 204–5; Tauxier 1921: 146). As trading is unrestricted, everyone can acquire such goods. Thus the subjugation of the producer cannot rest upon the appropriation of the material factors of production as is the case with land in the feudal mode of production or with machines in the capitalist mode of production. Therefore, the establishment of bonds of direct personal dependence is the preferred means of controlling men and their labour and hence of the extortion of surplus.

Thus it is an inventory of the various forms of *personal* dependence in the Abron kingdom that will provide guidelines for 'siting' the various modes of production represented in the social formation and discerning the ways in which they combine. We have therefore to pay attention to three features: first of all we shall examine the Gyaman peasant communities, the members of which are essentially recruited from among the Kulango and are organized on the lineage model. Second, we come to the Abron, the wielders of political power, who demand various sorts of rent from these communities. Finally, there are the slaves, whose presence is revealed by both documents and investigation. We shall consider each of these aspects in turn.

First of all, let us look at the peasant communities. As we have just said, they are organized according to the lineage model. Among both the Kulango and the Abron, succession at this level is matrilineal. The inheritor of the wealth and social rank of Ego is his uterine brother or the eldest son of his eldest sister. On the other hand, residence for men is generally patrilocal. Ego lives with his father and moves to his mother's brother's compound [4] only when he succeeds him. Thus we are in the presence of so-called disharmonic societies: while the matri-lineages are dispersed, the residential unit, the compound (Abron: *efie*, Kulango: *bin*), is inhabited by a man, his brothers, and their children, who belong to different matrilineages. The women live apart; if they are from the same village as their husbands, they continue to reside with their mothers, which produces what Alland calls a system of duolocal or parallel residence (patrilocal for men and matrilocal for women) (Alland 1972: 69).

As well as being the residential unit, the compound is also the basic economic unit from the standpoint both of production and distribution. Members of a compound allocate their time between two categories of fields: those of the head of the compound and those of the various households that constitute the compound. The cultivation of the former must be given priority and all members of the household must take part in this work. The resultant produce is then consumed in collective meals prepared by the women. These daily meals bring together all the men of the compound around its head. The food harvested also serves as a form of reserve and insurance for times of need, i.e. drought, tiding-over difficult periods, famine, etc. Finally, the head of the compound may sell part of what is produced to provide for the non-alimentary needs of his dependants, thus acquiring livestock, arms and captives or increasing the patrimony of the compound. In addition, each household in the compound has its own plots, the food from which is consumed by the wives and children of the household head. The latter may also find that there is an excess of food and sell part of it for goods and supplies, which are then his personal property. We should note that women do not have their own fields. They do raise certain crops—gumbo, capsi-cums, sorrel, tomatoes, etc.—but these are secondary crops which they grow on the fields their husbands have prepared for planting yams. Finally, some handicrafts are also carried on within the bounds of the compound: the weaving of cotton, the preparation of shea butter or palm oil, etc. Such activities are subject to the same rules of allocation as are applied to agricultural labour.[5]

Furthermore, artisans in the strict sense of the term (blacksmiths, jewellers, carpenters, cobblers, basket-makers) are found in Kulango and Abron villages, but none of them are completely specialized. While they devote a greater proportion of time to their craft, they all possess and cultivate their own fields with the help of their close relatives (Tauxier 1921: 147).

Certain activities required more manpower than is available in an individual compound. Such is the case with house-building, collective fishing, and, above all, hunting. Cooperation in these is organized at the neighbourhood or village level or even between several villages. In the case of hut-building, the compound is assisted by neighbouring compounds and in turn helps them when the occasion arises. Thus cooperation here is part of a process of mutual aid staggered over time. In hunting and fishing all the people in a village and sometimes from several villages are mobilized, but cooperation remains sporadic. The fish and game caught are distributed among all the participants, but their association ceases with this act of distribution and is not institutionalized (Tauxier 1921: 145, 147).

This is a brief summary of the immediate relations of production and distribution that organize these peasant communities. Two relations play an important role here: the relation between men and women; and the relation between those whom we shall provisionally call the elders and the younger members of the community. As for the first, we offer the following comments: if, among both the Abron and the Kulango, women are undeniably dominated by men and have their labour exploited by men, then this domination is less pronounced, and exploitation less intense, than in other nearby lineage societies like the Dida or the Guro. First of all, there is a more equal sharing of tasks in the division of labour between the sexes. Of course, women are responsible for all the housework and the cultivation of secondary crops (maize, manioc, cotton, capsicums, gumbo, etc.), but in contrast to the situation among the Dida, for instance, men do most of the work involved in the cultivation of the staple crop. The planting, hoeing, and harvesting of yams falls to them; women engage only in the weeding. As for handicrafts, although the women spin cotton, it is the men who weave it and make the clothes. Furthermore, women may sell for profit what remains of the articles they have produced after having satisfied the needs of the household and the compound. Goods left by a woman go to her uterine sister, her daughter, or her sister's daughter, but never to her brother, husband, or son. Finally, while the heads of compounds are always men, women, especially elderly women, are regularly consulted and they exercise a discreet but considerable influence on decision-making. On the other hand, 'women's business' is settled by women and men only have their say in cases of serious conflict. On the whole, Abron and Kulango women enjoy a relative autonomy, which is further enhanced by the rule of parallel residence and the tendency toward village endogamy where the woman remains under the protection of her natal family. This relative autonomy reappears at the level of politics, as the position of Abron queens attests.

In order to understand the relations between elders and youths, we must re-examine the role played by the head of the compound. As we have seen, he organizes the work in the collective fields of the compound and distributes the produce from them. A portion of this is allocated for the immediate consumption of the men in the compound; here the head appears simply as the pivotal point in the mechanism of redistribution among the producers. But another portion is exchanged, whether for productive or reproductive goods (livestock, implements, arms), captives, or, finally, for prestige goods (jewellery, loin-cloths).

These various goods are thought of as the common patrimony which the head of the compound distinguishes from the personal goods he was able to acquire before acceding to his position as head. But the use and management of this patrimony are the prerogative of the heads of compounds. They consult the older people, but are not bound to follow their advice. While, as far as productive and reproductive goods are concerned, the compound head's power can be considered a power of function at the most (i.e. as labour organizer, he is simultaneously responsible for the acquisition, renewal, and allocation of the means of labour), this is not the case when it comes to his control over prestige goods. Once the immediate subsistence of the producers and their families is guaranteed, the accumulation of these goods appears as the motive and goal of all production. Indeed, these goods have no economic utility; they are simply the object of what could be called ostentatious hoarding. They form the treasures which are occasionally displayed (at feasts or funerals) and their value expresses the social rank of the homestead and its head. In the last analysis, there is a perfect correlation between the holding of prestige goods and the position of elder. All those, regardless of their age, who actually or potentially dispose of these goods (heads of compounds or their successors) are thought of as elders. Equally, all those who are excluded from the possession of these goods are considered youths. But, on the other hand, the only social function served by these goods is that of being the property of elders and providing the material manifestation of their hegemony. Thus the surplus labour of youths serves to produce the social symbols of their own dependence. On the whole, in so far as there is extortion of surplus labour, there is indeed exploitation, but such exploitation does not in and of itself contain its own goal. In the capitalist mode of production, the domination by the capitalist appears as a condition and a means for the exploitation of the worker. I would unhesitatingly say that the relation here between elders and youths is the opposite, since in the exploitation of the youth the goal is to produce the symbols of the elder's domination. We shall return later to the political implications that can be drawn from this statement.

In my opinion, the exploitation of youths by elders among the Kulango and the Abron is more effectively accomplished in this process of production and appropriation of prestige goods than through marriage exchanges and the prestations accompanying them. Of course, the elders, notably the heads of compounds, are in charge of negotiating the marriages between young people, and in this sense they do indeed control the demographic reproduction of society. Furthermore, marriage is preceded by the payment of brideprice, at least part of which is the product of the youth's labour. The brideprice, which is more often raised by the groom's father than by his mother's brother, is delivered not to the bride's mother's brother, but to her father, who moreover shares it with her mother. But at the end of the nineteenth

107

century, the rate of brideprice, lower among the Kulango than among
the Abron, was in both cases far less than in west Ivory Coast societies at the same period, especially if one considers their respective
wealth.[6]

This difference, which undoubtedly has to do with the matrilineal
character of Abron and Kulango society, means that the young Abron
bear a lesser burden in this respect than their Dida counterparts. On the
other hand, the goods comprising the Kulango or Abron brideprice are
not specialized goods. Among the Dida, anklets, which constitute the
essential part of the brideprice, never leave the circuit of matrimonial
exchanges once they have entered it. Their only function is to circulate
from one lineage to another in the opposite direction from women.
Among the Abron and the Kulango, on the contrary, brideprice
consists of a certain sum of money (cowries, gold-dust, or British
shillings), which does not remain in the matrimonial circuit, and products
like salt, which are consumed as soon as they are received. Goods of this
kind, of varied origin and utility, escape the control of the elders far
more easily than do the Dida anklets. Thus, we can ask ourselves if
brideprice plays the role of a marriage-regulating force among the
Abron as it does among the Dida. Without labouring this point, I shall
confine myself to the following remarks. First of all, the Abron, like all
the Akan peoples, show a preference for Ego to marry his matrilateral
cross-cousin. But on the other hand, when a man takes a wife from a
given compound and has several daughters by her, he will marry one of
them to a member of his wife's natal compound. 'This is done to replace
the mother,' declared Tauxier (1921: 321 n.). Now this restitution implies
that Ego marries his patrilateral cross-cousin. These two customs are
compatible only within the framework of marriage by exchange between
bilateral cross-cousins, which we know is an admitted and fairly
common practice among the Abron. It expresses at least a tendency
towards what Lévi-Strauss calls restricted exchange, which can only be
reinforced by the tendency towards village endogamy we have noted.
Now, in the case of restricted exchange, the mere application of the rule
is sufficient to ensure equilibrium in marriage exchanges, rendering the
intervention of a regulatory mechanism superfluous. If the latter is
nevertheless present, then it has other functions: sealing the agreement
between groups united by alliance, or remunerating, at least symbolic-
ally, the efforts of those who have brought up the wife. Whatever the
functions of brideprice among the Abron, the exploitation of youths
takes place directly and not indirectly through the elders' control over
goods intended for brideprice.

This specific situation of youths as a class is to some extent recognized
in the Abron political system. Indeed, in Abron, as in Ashanti or Brong
villages, one finds a person with the title of 'youngmen's chief' (*nkwankwaahene*) alongside the village chief. He is elected by the young and
organizes the collective work sessions to which the young people are

periodically summoned to perform such tasks in the public interest as the upkeep of the roads. He is the arbitrator of disputes among the young and can impose fines on those responsible. Furthermore, he is the young people's representative at the council of compound heads which assists the chief and intervenes on behalf of the young in all important matters. In fact, as Busia has shown, he is far more than the representative of a mere age-group, he can be considered as a sort of 'tribune of the people'; not only does he defend the interests of the young, but also more generally those of the 'ordinary citizens' (commoners) before the heads of the homesteads, the village and the higher-ranking chiefs. It is clearly significant that one and the same word (*nkwankwaa* or its synonym *mmerante*) should be used to designate both youths and commoners.

Confrontation between elders and youths therefore is first of all manifest in the controversies which can oppose the *nkwankwaahene* to the elders and village chiefs, but this explicitly official form is neither the sole nor the principal form in which it can be expressed. The following comment are taken from Alland's research on witchcraft among the Abron (Alland 1965: 495–502; 1972: 102–14). In addition to magicians who produce various amulets, one finds soul-eating witches (Abron: *baifo*; Kulango: *deresogo*). These witches can only attack members of their own family. If they want to assault a stranger, they must obtain the authorization of this stranger's family's *baifo*. Family should be understood here as bilateral kin. In contrast with the Ashanti, where a man only has to fear witches from within his own matrilineage, the witches who attack an Abron man may belong to either his paternal or maternal kin, since, as Alland says, an Ashanti only lives with his father temporarily, often joining his mother's brother's household at a very early age. On the other hand, among the Abron, as we have seen, avunculocal residence is the exception and generally a father holds a far more important place in his son's life than he does among the Ashanti, especially in matters of marriage. Thus, here witchcraft appears as a preferred form of conflict between near relatives. Now, what are the stakes and who are the protagonists in these disputes? Alland mentions that they occur over inheritance and principally oppose men. Stated explicitly: 'the greatest tensions develop between a man and his sons, a man and his sister's sons and a man and his cross-cousins'. Indeed, when Ego strictly follows the matrilineal rule of succession (and inheritance) and leaves nothing to his sons, he deprives them of the fruits of their labour. If, on the other hand, he gives them a part of his wealth during his lifetime, then his nephews are wronged. Finally, there is rivalry between Ego and his patrilateral cross-cousin over Ego's father's legacy, and between Ego and his matrilateral cross-cousin over the legacy of Ego's mother's brother. But these various confrontations are only aspects of a single fundamental contradiction.

We have seen that the surplus labour provided by Ego results in increasing the patrimony of the compound, but by virtue of the matrilineal rule of inheritance, this patrimony in fact belongs to Ego's father's matrilineage. On the death of Ego's father, it will therefore pass to Ego's patrilateral cross-cousin. Therefore it is really Ego's father's matrilineage which exploits his labour and appropriates the product of his surplus labour. It is this group which in confronting Ego constitutes the elders, if we define elders as we have previously done, i.e. not by their age, but by the control they exercise over prestige goods. Of course, sometimes Ego can find an ally within this camp in the person of his father, and this is why Alland is correct in suggesting the possibility of a conflict between a man and his sister's son. But this ally runs a grave risk of being disowned by his peers, and in any case for him to fall in with one or the other camp, the two camps must first of all exist. Finally, quarrels over inheritance, which according to Alland lie at the root of most witchcraft accusations, break out when Ego, with or without the support of his father, tries to appropriate the product of surplus labour which he had been constrained to carry out for the benefit of his father's matrilineage: in other words, when he attacks, if not the foundations, at least the effects, of the exploitation of which he is the victim.

Let us immediately prevent a possible misunderstanding. This exploitation is not the consequence of the dissonance between patrilocal residence and matrilineal descent, i.e. of the disharmonic nature of society. Pierre-Philippe Rey, to whom this whole analysis owes much, indeed saw that the disharmony only follows a determinate line of demarcation between the exploiters and the exploited, a line which in a patrilineal, patrilocal society would pass between the various generations within the patrilineage. This does not mean that the difference between harmonic and disharmonic societies is without consequence for social conflict: exploitation is more appreciable for those subjected to it in disharmonic societies than in harmonic ones. In a society in which residence and descent follow the same line, for instance the paternal, the young man thinks that by working for the elder he is also, in the long run, working for himself. He can hope to succeed his father one day and so gain possession of the prestige goods he helped to produce when he was young. But in a disharmonic society, where Ego works for his father and succeeds his maternal uncle, no relation can be established between the labour furnished and the wealth inherited. The youth can no longer consider the surplus labour required of him as a long-term investment. He is forced to see it as a gift bereft of any reciprocation. Here again, however, this difference should not be exaggerated. As we have seen, a Dida youth may hope to take his father's place one day. Likewise, an Abron youth may hope to succeed his mother's brother. In this sense, the harmonic or disharmonic nature of society only determines the rhythm with which the metamorphosis of youth into elder occurs—progressive in one case, taking the form of an abrupt mutation in the other. The fact of metamorphosis remains, despite the differences in rhythm.

This point should be emphasized as much on account of the many controversies it has created as for its importance for a correct understanding of the political effects of exploitation within the framework of a lineage society. In a patrilineal, patrilocal society, where the separation of youths from elders operates as a division between generations, the normal functioning of society calls for the transformation of youths into elders. In actual fact, not all youths will become elders; some will die before reaching that goal, others will be preceded by elder brothers throughout their lifetime; but all of them may legitimately think that they will one day cross the barrier. In a disharmonic society, the same peculiarity is found in another form. Of course, here youths and elders are not distinguished by their age. But if we come back to the case of the Abron, we see that while Ego is being exploited by his father's matrilineage, he also belongs to the matrilineage of his mother's brother, and in this position he exploits the labour of the latter's son. In one case, there is the hope of promotion, in the other the permanent ambiguity of class position, but the political effect is the same. The exploited class does not succeed in constituting itself as a political force capable of unified action at the level of the total society, and confrontations remain enclosed within the boundaries of local communities. The utilization of extorted surplus labour acts in the same way; we have seen that the main aim of exploitation is to affirm the elders' domination and to create the material symbols of this domination. But once these symbols are created and reproduced, exploitation has fulfilled its function. Here we do not find the tendency towards continuous intensification which is inherent in exploitation once its goal becomes the acquisition and accumulation of exchange-values.

Conflicts that develop in this context find a particularly adequate form of expression in the set of witchcraft beliefs and practices. Whether it is a case of discord between Ego and his father's matrilineage, or a dilemma in which Ego finds himself torn between the compound and matrilineage solidarity, these conflicts are the effect of contradictions affecting the very foundations of social organization. Now if these conflicts occur publicly, as in quarrels about witchcraft, then the form in which they are expressed prevents recognition of them for what they are. Indeed, they are explained as the nefarious influence of the soul-eaters. At the same time, it is the perversity of an individual and not the discord between structures that is assigned the blame. As a consequence, conflict does not extend beyond the individual's circle of close relatives. Furthermore, this perversity is represented as a supernatural phenomenon. I hope I may be forgiven repeating here the following comments made in my 1969 work on the Dida:

Kinship relations are the foundation of the social order and constitute what one might call the social nature. They furnish, as it were, the categories within which the society becomes conscious of itself. Conflicts between kin, in so far as they summon forth these categories, could not be thought or assimilated by the society without them: not only can they not be acknowledged, they are literally inexpressible and unthinkable. Conceiving of itself in kinship terms, society simultaneously excludes kinship problems from its field of vision. Kinship conflicts, shaking the very foundations of social nature, cannot be understood as natural phenomena, and society can only view them as the effect of supernatural powers. Finally, the representations which they offer are less concepts than illusions . . . On the whole, the society may block these conflicts, but it can never recognize them: only by changing fundamentally will it achieve this understanding (Terray 1969: 167).

In fact, by attributing conflicts to the supernatural, the Abron and Kulango simultaneously prevent themselves from grasping the causes of these conflicts: witches can be executed, but witchcraft cannot be suppressed; while giving themselves the possibility of living with their contradictions, at the same time they deny themselves the means of overcoming them. We can see the extent to which witchcraft beliefs and practices indeed constitute an ideology in the marxist sense of the word. On the one hand, they reflect social reality but, on the other, they act upon it. By giving contradictions an expression that prevents their clear recognition, witchcraft beliefs and practices contribute to their neutralization and thus to the maintenance of the *status quo*.

A final comment: here and there I have pointed to the presence of captives. But within the framework of the lineage mode of production, the existence of captives introduces no relations of production basically different from those that already exist. Upon arrival in a compound, a captive has no fields of his own: he works on the land of the compound head who in turn gives him all his food. Thus his position is no different from that of a free adolescent. Later, when his master gives him a wife (on the condition that he is well-behaved), he is given an individual plot, from which he will obtain his own and his family's sustenance, still working for his master in the remaining time. The latter may even allow him to do a little trading, in which case one-third of the profit will go to the master (Tauxier 1921: 328 n.). As we have seen, the young men of the compound are submitted to identical regulations. On the whole, the difference between the lot of the youths and that of the captives above all stems from the fact that the latter are given the dirtiest and most back-breaking tasks, and that they have no matrilineage which could defend them and give them the hope of changing their status. In this sense, captives *in this context* may equally be defined as the lowliest of the young and as perpetual youths. Here we have patriarchal or domestic slavery, which is little more than an extension of the lineage

112

system. The relatively benign character of this slave system was noted by Captain Benquey in 1904:

> For the Abron and above all for the Kulango agriculturalist, a slave is an assistant who enables him to increase the area he cultivates or who lessens the burden of heavy field work. The master himself works alongside his captives. A sort of intimacy which lessens the distinctions between them and renders the captive a servant rather than a slave grows out of their daily contact (Archives AOF, dossier K21).

Briefly summarized, these are the principal characteristics of the lineage mode of production among the Kulango and the Abron, as far as they can be reconstructed from oral accounts and written documents. We must now look at how it has been transformed through the action of other modes of production represented in the Abron social formation.

As far back as we can go in Abron history, we find traces of a political superstructure that cannot be related to the lineage mode of production. Before the Abron conquest, the Kulango were divided into a number of small independent chiefdoms, each encompassing about ten villages. The chief is appointed from within a 'princely' matrilineage by several homestead heads playing the role of grand electors. Thus the chief of Wolobidi is chosen by the village elders of Wolobidi and the neighbouring villages of Bosanye and Sogola. He can be both a political chief and the master of the soil, as is the case with the chief of Wolobidi. His power is of an essentially judicial nature. He is responsible for the administration of justice in his own village and for hearing appeals against sentences awarded by the village chiefs who are subordinate to him. Serious cases such as homicide are heard by him directly. But he exercises this power by conciliation and appeasement. The proceeds from fines, consisting of oxen and bags of salt, are destined to the 'worship of the earth'. In other respects, the chief has no specialized personnel and can mobilize only limited manpower (his own village) for his own benefit. Elephant tusks and the skins of slaughtered lions and panthers are delivered to him. Among the Nafana we also find chiefdoms, and the power of Nafana chiefs appears to have been greater than that of their Kulango counterparts before the invasion of the Abron. For instance, the Nafana chief of Bondoukou installed village chiefs who were under his authority, summoned villagers to work on his lands, and recruited servants from among them. In wartime, he levied a tax to pay for powder and one-third of the spoils were handed over to him. Finally, he took a commission on products sold in the Bondoukou market and claimed a quarter of every animal butchered in the town.

At the village level are two positions with distinct powers: village chief (*ango ise*) and master of the soil (*sako tese*), but a single individual may occupy both positions. The village chief, assisted by the eldest of the compound heads, adjudicates and can impose fines, which are used in the manner described above. Each year villagers come to do two days' work on his land. At the time of collective hunts, he has a right to a portion of the main parts of the game; at the time of the bush-fire festival, he receives two chickens from each compound head and a thigh of every chicken sacrificed. On the death of a compound head, he claims one of the deceased's captives or one of his children, whom he will bring up until his marriage. As for the master of the soil, he is responsible for making the specified expiatory and propitiatory sacrifices and takes his portion of the sacrificed animals and products. Furthermore, when a stranger comes to village territory prospecting for gold or gathering palm products, he must hand over a part of what he has collected to the master of the soil. Neither the village chief nor the master of the soil has any power over the division of land between the villagers. Within the limits of village-held land, the latter can clear and divide up hitherto uncultivated ground without asking anyone's permission (Folquet in Clozel and Villamur 1902: 351; Tauxier 1921: 167–9).

The Abron conquest began at the end of the seventeenth century and was not completed until the beginning of the latter half of the eighteenth century, when the Kulango chiefdoms of Wolobidi and Kano Nagare were defeated and destroyed. The Abron practised quiet infiltration as well as violent warfare in order to enslave the country. They also knew well how to profit from the heterogeneity and divisions among the resident populations. First they supported the Nafana against the Kulango, and later turned against these former allies. They confronted the Kulango principalities one at a time, the latter never succeeding in joining forces against the invader.

Once the conquest was over, those chiefs who were included in the kingdom retained of their previous powers only those relating to their role as master of the soil, or else they became mere village chiefs. As we shall see, most of their previous powers were transferred to the Abron chiefs, and the villages under their authority were henceforth under the direct jurisdiction of Abron chiefs. Thus the Kulango completely lost their relative political autonomy; their status was thenceforth identical to that of the Abron peasant communities in the south of the country.

How, then, was Abron hegemony expressed? As we have said, it had no consequences as far as the control and distribution of land were concerned. In some cases the Abron established themselves in zones which had hitherto been empty. Elsewhere, they respected the Kulango's prerogatives as the first inhabitants and masters of the soil. They asked the permission of Kulango *sako tese* to settle and cultivate unoccupied land. They paid the latter the specified fees for gathering palm products and prospecting for gold.[7] Only the king and Abron province chiefs can have gold extracted from where they please, not having to pay a fee (Benquey in Clozel and Villamur 1902: 208; Tauxier 1921: 337–8). Furthermore, in their social life the Abron have adopted the language of their subjects. Even today the king uses only Kulango in his everyday life. On the other hand, it seems that marriage between the Kulango and the Abron has never been forbidden. Yet the frequently contracted unions are between an Abron husband and a Kulango wife. The children of these unions, contrary to the matrilineal principle, are considered as Abron.

What, then, are the positive signs of Abron domination?

1 The right of deciding matters of war and peace belongs to the Abron chiefs alone. The Kulango owe military assistance to the Abron. They are divided among the various Abron army corps and take orders from the Abron.

2 The Kulango, like the Abron peasants for that matter, deliver the tail and tusks of slaughtered elephants, and lion and panther skins to the king or Abron province chiefs upon whom they depend (Tauxier op. cit.: 308–42). Ivory, at least, is the source of a profitable trade.

3 All gold nuggets taken out of the ground are delivered to the king and province chiefs (op. cit.: 337–8), who can furthermore sponsor gold-prospecting in their own respective territories, without having to hand over the usual proportion to Kulango chiefs.

4 Both Kulango and Abron peasants furnish the king and the Abron province chiefs with prestations in labour during the period when agricultural activity is most intense (when the yams are dug out of the ground). Each year villages are called in rotation for a day's work.

5 At the time of the yam festival, in which only the Abron participate, Kulango villages, and they alone, it seems, give the king and the Abron chiefs prestations in kind (yams, sheep, chickens, game), although the quantity is not excessive: six to a hundred yams and one to twelve sheep per village.

6 The Abron king and chiefs appropriate all twins and albinos born in their respective territories (Benquey in Clozel and Villamur 1902: 195; Tauxier 1921: 338–9). Likewise they can take girls they fancy as wives (Benquey in Clozel and Villamur 1902: 198–9; Nebout in Clozel 1906: 172–3).

7 Finally, in the area of law, minor offences (adultery, theft) are still tried by Kulango village chiefs, but appeals against their sentences are heard by Abron chiefs. Serious crimes (homicide, adultery with the wife of an important person) are brought directly before the Abron chiefs. As for the master of the soil, he can impose traditional sanctions corresponding to these offences, but these are nevertheless supplementary to the punishments meted out by the Abron courts.

The judicial process represents an important source of revenue for the king and the chiefs, several aspects of which should be underlined. In the first place, the king and chiefs (and through them the political authority) intervene directly in most witchcraft conflicts which, as we have seen, tear peasant communities apart. Indeed, they alone hold the poison which permits the discovery of witches. When a villager is suspected of evil practices, the village chief notifies the king or province chief to whom he is subordinate. The latter sends his spokesman who organizes the ordeal and administers the poison to the suspect. If he is guilty, he is immediately executed and both his property and at least one of his children are confiscated and handed over to the king or chief (Benquey in Clozel and Villamur 1902: 214–15; Tauxier 1921: 358 n.).

Except in the case of witchcraft offences and lese-majesty or high treason, which both call for the death penalty, the fine is the most frequent sanction imposed by the king or the chiefs. When one of the parties has taken the royal oath, recalling either a past defeat or a departed ancestor of the sovereign, he obliges the latter to bring the case before his court. The fine is then increased appreciably to compensate for the unpleasantness suffered by the sovereign. These fines are the famous 'customs' which also benefit the province chiefs (Tauxier 1921: 351). Finally, the winning party must demonstrate his gratitude to his judges by giving them gifts, the grandeur of which varies with the stakes of the trial and the rank of the contestants (Benquey in Clozel and Villamur 1902: 234). Now fines, customs, and gifts are all payable in gold-dust: in this way, the king and the chiefs are able to draw a sizeable portion of the gold amassed by ordinary citizens into their treasury.

If the condemned man is insolvent, he must give one of his dependants—his son or captive—as security. The dependant will remain in the service of the chief as long as the debt remains unpaid. Since the debt carries a high interest rate, it is not unusual for the debtor to remain permanently unable to free himself. Thus the chief acquires new captives at little cost, since if the 'security' dies, he must be replaced (Archives AOF, dossier K 21; Benquey in Clozel and Villamur 1902: 224, 234; Nebout in Clozel 1906: 172–173). But the confiscation of witches' children and the holding of pawns as security are not the only means available to the chief for increasing his store of captives. When an individual persists in his evil deeds and becomes debt-ridden, his close relatives, weary of having to pay heavy fines on his account, hand him over to the king or chief, who can either sell him abroad or retain him in their service (Benquey in Clozel and Villamur 1902: 224). Thus judicial procedures enable the king and the chiefs to accumulate gold and captives for themselves. We shall soon see the decisive role which wealth in these goods plays in the functioning of the Abron social formation.

8 Finally, Tauxier writes of levies on the village chiefs' and notables'

legacies which profit the king and chiefs. He seems to think that this is a true tax (Benquey, op. cit.: 211; Tauxier 1921. 338). In fact, even if the economic effects are similar, the intention is different. If the king or chief graces the funeral of one of his subjects with the presence of one of his servants or envoys, he must be thanked with gifts, which here again vary according to the rank of the deceased.

Compared to that of the Kulango, the lot of the far less numerous Nafana appears relatively privileged. Indeed, it was the Nafana who welcomed the Abron emigrants from Akwamu to Gyaman, and who helped them to put down the Kulango. They therefore profit from a sort of favoured status. Of course, here again the Abron chiefs retain a monopoly over gold nuggets and receive half of any ivory collected. But in war, the Nafana constitute a distinct army corps, belonging to the *adonten* (advance-guard). The Nafana chief of Bondoukou continues to fix the levies listed above. He 'commands' Bondoukou in the name of the king (his command is in most respects largely theoretical, given the position in the kingdom of the Dyula, who constitute a majority of the town's population). At the king's court the Nafana play the role of mediators: a guilty person who takes refuge with them is guaranteed immunity as long as he remains on their land. Finally, and most important, they cannot be fined.

Besides the kingdom itself, we must describe what one might call the Abron Empire, comprising the Nasian, Barabo, Bini, Bona, and Asikaso. These territories are inhabited by peoples of varied origin. Nasian is a Kulango principality; the chief there has retained the prerogatives of his counterparts before the Abron conquest. Barabo is governed by the Dyula from Korodugu who responded to the call of the *Gyamanhene* Kofi Sono. Bini, Bona, and Asikaso are Anyi chiefdoms. In theory Nasian, Barabo, and Bini are responsible to the Abron chief of Penango, Bona to the chief of Ankobia, and Asikaso directly to the king. In fact, the autonomy of these 'borderlands' is very great, but their submission is principally visible in two areas. The king or the Abron province chief concerned is the appeals judge for judicial decisions rendered by local chiefs, who themselves may be fined. In case of war, these territories owe military assistance to the Abron, but the latter neither intervene in the appointment of local chiefs nor collect tribute. Thus the Abron tutelage is not very oppressive. However, it should be noted that from then on the Nasian would long constitute a sort of reserve of captives.

Such are the various forms taken by Abron domination. Now we must try to state its scope, goals, and effects more clearly.

In the first place, this domination is explicitly founded on the use of force. Better organized and united, the Abron were able to conquer the Kulango, and never hesitate to recall the stages of this victory during the course of festivals and political and religious ceremonies. They do not seek, nor does it appear that they have ever sought, to conceal the fact that they rule the country by virtue of the right of conquest. As we have seen, they did not appropriate the lands supporting the Kulango. I have already cited the passage in which Marx indicates that when the direct producers possess their means of production and can therefore autonomously provide for their own needs, 'extra-economic reasons regardless of their nature' are required to constrain them to furnish surplus labour to benefit others. Purely and simply, the extra-economic reason in this case is that of being strongest.

Second, what exactly do the Abron expect from the various prestations which they demand of the peasant communities? Some of them (the delivery of lion and panther skins, the contributions at the yam festival) have a visible symbolic function: their goal is to demonstrate the Kulangos' subjugation and the Abrons' hegemony in a public and somewhat tangible manner. From others (the monopoly over gold nuggets, rights over ivory, the machinery of fines, confiscation, and pawning) the Abron aristocracy tends to accumulate not surplus or wealth of a general nature, but certain well-defined categories of goods, the significance of which will be shown later. But this aristocracy does not derive its immediate sustenance from the surplus labour of its subjects. In time of famine the Abron chiefs' servants may go and dig yams in Kulango fields, but this remains an exceptional practice. On the other hand, the aristocracy does not forbid the Kulango access to resources from which it derives a considerable amount of its wealth: the Kulango, like the Abron, may prospect for gold or organize trading expeditions. Moreover, when the Kulango fight beside the Abron, they share in the spoils. In these areas, as we shall see, the Abron aristocracy is assured of a dominant position, but it has not decreed formal measures restricting its subjects: it is a case of *de facto* supremacy rather than *de jure* monopoly. Then, as far as tribute itself is concerned, it appears relatively moderate when compared, for example, with that levied on Ashanti peasants at the same period. Indeed, to my knowledge, there are no equivalents among the Abron of many taxes collected in the Ashanti kingdom, such as the fees for right of passage demanded solely of Ashanti merchants returning from the coast (Bowdich 1819: 320; Wilson 1856: 177; Rattray 1929: 110–11); a tax of 20 per cent on gold used in making jewellery (Bowdich 1819: 320; Wilson 1856: 177); duties on the proceeds of the sale of captives to Fante merchants (Isert 1793: 250; Bowdich 1819: 320; Hutton 1821 [1832: 301]); or a levy of twenty-five nuts per load of kola taken to Salaga market (Rattray 1929: 110–11). Moreover, in contrast to the Abron, the Ashanti levied heavy duties payable in gold or captives on the kingdoms which they conquered. Bearing in mind that by way of tribute Kulango villages each year furnish the king or chiefs with a day's work and some yams, whereas the satellite states of Gyaman are not compelled to pay any rent, I think it will be agreed that the subjects of the kingdom enjoy a rather privileged status.

Of course, various factors explain this difference. For a hundred and thirty-five years, Gyaman had been dominated by the Ashanti, and forced to pay them annual tribute, which according to Bowdich could be as high as a hundred *peredwan* of gold, or a thousand pounds sterling (Bowdich 1819: 321 and Glossary, XI). Undoubtedly the Abron could hardly add their own demands to this already heavy burden. But this explanation is inadequate for, failing levies in gold, they could have imposed far heavier duties in labour or in kind on their subjects and vassals than those with which they were satisfied. In my view, their moderation has another origin. It was not primarily a material surplus product, whether in goods for consumption, production, or prestige which the Abron expected from the communities they dominated, but first and foremost military assistance. Thus the exploitation of Kulango peasants encounters a sort of ceiling: it ceases where it would risk compromising this military assistance. And this ceiling counters not only the direct and open forms of exploitation, but also its indirect and hidden forms, and particularly those connected with the exercise of judicial power: here we can recall the fate of *Gyamanhene* Adingra Kuma, who was conquered by *Asantehene* Osei Bonsu at the battle of the river Tain in 1818. Throughout his reign, Adingra showed himself severe and without compassion; he condemned many to death and slapped back-breaking fines on his subjects; he was renowned for his harshness and cruelty. But when he had to face the Ashanti in battle, a considerable number of his troops abandoned him and this defection was one of the major reasons for his defeat.

We can better understand the relatively peaceful character of co-existence between the Kulango peasants and their Abron masters after that incident. In the first place, the antagonism which opposed them was experienced and conceived of by both sides as antagonism between peoples rather than between classes. Of course, there are peasants of Abron origin, but they are few in number and concentrated in the south and east of the country, so that in Gyaman one can say that the peasantry to a large extent coincide with the Kulango and the aristocracy with the Abron. Now while it is true, as we have seen, that conquest extended over several years, it seems that afterwards the Kulango bore Abron hegemony without too much difficulty. Apart from the 1818 episode mentioned above, I know of only one instance of collective rebellion by the Kulango. After the 1818 disaster, the Nasian chiefdom tried to regain its independence. From the time he acceded to the throne, Adingra's successor, *Gyamanhene* Kofi Fofie, had to campaign to put down this uprising. Not long after the French had established themselves in Bondoukou, Captain Benquey wrote: 'The Ngoulango hate the Abron who have always oppressed and stolen from them unscrupulously. Thus the desire to regain their independence is still very strong among them' (Benquey in Clozel and Villamur 1902: 348). But this account is not entirely convincing, for the new occupants had every interest in dividing so as to rule, and in turning the Kulango against the Abron aristocracy. Of course, Kulango inertia may be at least partly explained by the decentralized and divided character of their social organization: we have seen that the Abron, upon their arrival, had destroyed all powers whose authority extended beyond village limits. But this inertia is also undoubtedly a product of the specific nature of Abron domination.

For in the last analysis this domination remained what Marx calls formal domination: it had not profoundly changed the mode of production which is subjected to it. Of course, the central role which the acquisition and accumulation of prestige goods plays in the lineage mode of production, without being the result of intervention by the Abron aristocracy, has perhaps been reinforced through their exemplary behaviour. Furthermore, we have seen how this aristocracy used the witchcraft conflicts through which the lineage system's own contradictions are expressed. That only leaves the relations of production, which remained unchanged: the Abron respected the land rights of the Kulango and did not try to impose their own customs and beliefs upon them. By various means they appropriated at least part of the surplus produced by the Kulango communities, but we have seen that this levy was itself limited by their concern to assure themselves of their subjects' assistance in military matters. To a certain extent, among the various factors that determined the relationship between the Kulango and the Abron, it was this concern which has been the decisive factor. We must therefore now explain it, but we shall only achieve an explanation by looking at the second mode of production represented in the Abron social formation, that which is founded on the exploitation of the labour of captives.

We mentioned earlier that the introduction of captives into peasant compounds did not fundamentally change the relations of production characteristic of the lineage mode of production. But the situation was different for the captives held by the Abron aristocracy or the Dyula merchants. With them we witness a new mode of production, the structures of which we shall attempt to delineate.[8]

First of all, where do captives generally come from? They may be Abron or Kulango, but in most cases they are of foreign origin: they are called *dunko* if they have been bought and *nnomum* if they have been captured in a raid or war.

We have seen how a free Abron or Kulango may be reduced to the status of a captive as a result of either his misbehaviour or the inability of his homestead head to pay the fines imposed upon him. But there are few 'indigenous' captives in the country. This is not because the sanction of putting people up for sale is rarely invoked, but because those who suffer this fate are immediately resold abroad owing to their bad reputation or to prevent them from being tempted to escape. Thus the vast majority of captives are foreigners, brought into the kingdom through trade or warfare.

Where do the Abron buy their captives? Mostly in Kong, but also in Salaga and Bondoukou itself. Captives offered at these markets come primarily from the north, from Grusi and Mossi territory. From the fragmentary information we have on the price of captives, we can conclude that until the end of the nineteenth century the purchase of captives is an expenditure comparable to the purchase of a horse, a pair of donkeys or oxen, or four loads of salt. But this price is subject to considerable variations over time. Indeed, the captive market is very sensitive to fluctuations in supply and demand. Should a war break out in the area, captives immediately abound, provoking a slump in the market price. Conversely, the cutting-off of trade routes or prolonged periods of peace result in a considerable increase in the price.

Given these uncertainties, the Abron could not rely on trade alone to assure themselves of a resource as essential to them as captives. Two other methods give them direct access to this resource: raids and war.

Raids are 'private' undertakings, the explicit aim of which is to hunt for captives. In principle every Abron may organize a raid. In fact, since the financing of raids (purchase of guns, powder, and ammunition) and the recruitment of participants are the duty of the organizer, only the king, province chiefs, and high-ranking notables have the necessary wealth to engage in such enterprises. In other respects raids are only carried out against well-defined regions: those which are incapable of countering them, given the permanent weakness of their political and military organization. Furthermore, the transformation of such and such a neighbouring zone into a reserve of captives and the prohibition against the establishment of a strong power and the importation of arms, is an established feature of the foreign policy of the great Akan states. If we are to believe the accounts of Binger and Braulot (Binger 1892, II: 194; Braulot 1893: 60), the Nasian long played this role for the Gyaman kingdom.

Wars, on the other hand, are 'affairs of state', since they can only be decided upon by the unanimous consent of the king and province chiefs. Contrary to appearances, I do not think that generally their explicit aim was the taking of captives. Of course captives constitute the most significant part of the spoils of war. In principle these spoils belong entirely to the king and province chiefs who sustained the essential expenses necessary for the preparation for the campaign. In fact partition is the rule, and if the Kulango or Abron peasants seem to participate in the aristocracy's military endeavours without balking, it is indeed because they also hope to receive their share. Prisoners taken in combat are equally divided between the warriors who captured them and the king or province chief exercising authority over these warriors. As for the women and children seized after victory, they belong to whoever captured them. Thus the king and the chiefs are indeed far from appropriating all the captives taken in war, but the greatest number of captives are attributed to them and can populate entire neighbourhoods in the principal villages. However, do the Abron engage in war *in order to* obtain captives? Generally I do not believe so. When asked about this, they give an answer similar to that which the *Asantehene* Osei Bonsu gave to Dupuis in 1820: 'I cannot make war to catch slaves in the bush like a thief. My ancestors never did so. But if I fight a king and kill him when he is insolent, then certainly I must have his gold; and his slaves and the people are mine too' (Dupuis 1824: 163). In fact, examination of the various wars carried out by the Abron in the course of their history reveals well-defined causes at the origin of most of them: the subjugation of neighbouring peoples, rebellion against the Ashanti tutelage, etc. The only exceptions are the warlike expeditions launched against the Djimini, Gyamala, and Tagwana after the 1818 disaster. It was indeed then a case of repopulating the devastated kingdom.

What is the status of captives acquired in this manner? We have seen that the captive can be considered a perpetual youth within the peasant compounds. It is a different matter in the compounds of the king or chiefs. It is not that the rules applied are different. Here also, captives may come to acquire a wife and a plot of land after a certain period of time, conditional upon good behaviour. But within the court their number is proportionately far greater: a single master may possess several dozen or even, in the case of the king, several hundred captives whose surveillance is entrusted to his sons or free dependants. He does not work with them; moreover most of them do not live with him. They are settled in camps located near the fields which they tend. Among the Dyula the distance seems even greater. Thus the system of permanently living together, which in peasant compounds creates paternalistic bonds between master and captives, disappears.

What functions do these captives take on in the kingdom's economy? First, it is they who cultivate the fields from which the Abron aristocracy draws its immediate subsistence. Before the colonial period, Abron chiefs and their close relatives no longer engaged in manual labour, but lived entirely from the agricultural labour of their captives, assisted occasionally by the inhabitants of neighbouring villages. Second, captives carry out most of the work connected with the extraction of gold, which is done in two ways among the Abron. By one method, gold, in dust form, is filtered from the alluvial soils deposited by streams running over auriferous terrain by means of a process analogous to the panning method used by individual gold prospectors in both nineteenth-century America and Australia. While men gather the gold-bearing sand, the panning itself is confined to women and captives. Every family head, whatever his rank or origin, be he Abron or Kulango, can freely try to obtain gold in this way, save that it entails paying a fee if the site

122

exploited is located beyond his village territory. As we have seen, only the king and the chiefs are exempt from this fee. But gold is also extracted from real mines or more exactly from pits, the average depth of which ranges from three to ten metres but may sink as far as twenty metres, if we are to believe Clozel's account (Clozel 1906: 53–4). Now, since the work at the bottom of these pits is both extremely back-breaking and dangerous (there are frequent landslides and the miner has little chance of escape), it is confined exclusively to captives. Several pits must be dug in order to find and exhaust a lode; since each of these exploitable pits mobilizes from three to six persons (one or two teams each consisting of a miner, a man responsible for taking the soil and blocks of quartz to the surface, and a panner) only those who have abundant servile man-power at their disposal can profitably engage in mining endeavours. This is why, although theoretically mining is open to everyone, it is in fact confined to kings, chiefs, and high-ranking notables. A further economic task that is largely the responsibility of captives is the trans-port of merchandise. Of course captives do not hold a monopoly on porterage; free men may carry for themselves or for others. But here again the king, chiefs, and notables rely principally on their captives to look after the transport of goods which they want to send to Kong, Salaga, or the coast.

Except for the time dedicated to agriculture, captive labour is largely utilized for long-distance exchange, the network of which, as we have seen, crosses Abron territory. This orientation is apparent in the case of porterage, but is equally true of gold. Indeed, how is the latter used? Nuggets are made *in situ* into ornaments and jewellery which go towards augmenting the value of the king's and chiefs' treasures. On the other hand, gold-dust is introduced into the circuit of long-distance trade and is by far the principal export of the kingdom. Directed towards Djenné, the Hausa, or the coast, gold-dust enables the Abron aristocracy to acquire in exchange Saharan salt, livestock, Bobo iron, captives, Kano fabric and leather, sea-salt, and lastly European trade goods such as cloth, alcohol, iron and copper rods, firearms, powder, and ammunition. Thus, on the one hand, it is this commercial traffic which enables the Abron aristocracy to realize a large part of the surplus labour and surplus product which it extorts from its captives. But, on the other hand, if the aristocracy plays a preponderant role in this traffic, and if the part they play far exceeds that of their subjects, it is principally because they have the greater number of captives.

But what in the last analysis do Abron chiefs expect from the exploita-tion of their captives? First, there are the immediate subsistence goods acquired through the agricultural labour of these captives. Second, there are luxury goods, salt, livestock, alcohol, and goods that contribute either to immediate production (iron) or to the reproduction of the whole of the social formation (captives, arms), which are all obtained in

123

exchange for exported gold. Lastly, there are the goods like loin-cloths, also acquired by exchange, or gold nuggets destined for ostentatious hoarding, which I see as the ultimate goal of all production. In any case, it is apparent that the goal of exploitation is not the accumulation of exchange-value, the realization of market profits. When Abron chiefs organize trading expeditions to Kong or the coast, it is not in order to obtain a greater profit in money (cowries or gold-dust), but to buy certain defined goods at a better price. In other words, use-value continues to govern the totality of the production of the Abron chiefs' captives, whether it is commercialized or not. This way exploitation still remains relatively moderate here.

The moderation in exploitation can be appreciated if we compare it to the exploitation suffered by the captives of the Dyula merchants. The latter also have abundant servile manpower at their disposal, which they employ in two different ways. First the product of the agricultural labour of captives settled in cultivator hamlets around the town of Bondoukou ensures the provisioning of the town and is sold at the market to caravans crossing the country seeking supplies. Second, this work-force also carries out transport tasks. But the Dyula are merchants and their activity is entirely directed toward the realization of market profits. Furthermore they treat their captives far more harshly than do the Abron chiefs. I have previously quoted the passage in which Benquey describes the relatively favourable conditions bestowed on captives by the Abron and above all the Kulango. Following this passage, Benquey writes:

> Among the Dioula, on the contrary, there is no contact between masters and captives. The latter, dispatched to cultivator villages, have but little to do with their masters. The Dioula man is above all else a merchant eager for gain, seeking to draw the greatest possible profit from everything that can be bought or sold. Now the slave is . . . an easy investment and the source of considerable profit. Therefore, to the Dioula merchant, the slave is a piece of merchandise to which he gives the same consideration he would an ox or sheep (Archives AOF, dossier K 21).

Even if this account paints a somewhat dismal picture, we shall in fact see that the Dyulas' captives clearly enjoy a less favourable position than do those of the Abron as far as protection and the situation of their children are concerned.

How do captives bear their lot? There are many indications suggesting that tension, which can in many cases become acute, exists between masters and captives. First of all we shall look at some of the sanctions provided for dealing with captives who show themselves 'lazy, unruly, or disobedient', terms obviously expressive of the masters' view of resistance by captives. On the other hand, the captive occasionally attempts to escape; of course, if he is originally from the north, he is hindered in the execution of his plan by the scars on his face, which immediately betray his origin and status in the eyes of free men. But when he takes part in a trading expedition as a porter, he may take advantage of the situation and seek to regain his freedom. Opportunities for escape greatly increased in 1874, when the English authorities of the Gold Coast Colony not only abolished slavery in the territory they controlled, but ruled that any captive, even of foreign origin, could enter a protest and obtain his freedom once he entered this territory. Thus in 1892 *Gyamanhene* Kwaku Agyeman complained to the British Captain Lang of having 'occasionally lost a slave in Cape Coast' (Report of Lang, 17 November 1892, PRO, CO Africa West n. 435). Besides, since the master is entirely responsible for his captive's actions, the latter can cause the former considerable difficulty by wilful misconduct. Of course, he risks severe punishment afterwards, but he can thereby avenge himself for the ill-treatment inflicted upon him, and this threat may temper his master's severity. Furthermore, captives from the north, especially the Gousi, are widely reputed to be dangerous sorcerers. In my view, all these features clearly reveal the reality of the antagonism between captives and their masters.

But beyond the individual defensive acts just described, can we speak of a collective and organized resistance by captives? As far as the Abron kingdom is concerned, the information available to me does not permit an answer to this question. But documents pertaining to the Ashanti kingdom suggest that the rulers of the region did not consider the possibility of a massive rebellion by captives as merely hypothetical. On the eve of the 1818 war between the Ashanti and the Abron, the *sannahene* (treasurer) reported to Hutchinson that 'many slaves had revolted and joining the Buntoko standard were to fight against [the Ashanti]'. He added that, in his opinion, 'there are too many slaves in the country' and that the Ashanti 'want to get rid of some of them: there might be a deal of trouble from them' (Hutchison in Bowdich 1819: 382). After the victory, the *Asantehene* Osei Bonsu justified the harsh treatment reserved for prisoners to Dupuis by saying: 'What can I do? Unless I kill or sell them, they'll grow strong and kill my people' (Dupuis 1824: 164).

This view perhaps explains the relatively ambiguous attitude of the Abron aristocracy towards its captives. In the first place, they maintain a whole repressive arsenal against them, the principal features of which can be listed. The captive who misbehaves is first of all open to various physical punishments: deprived of food, struck, put in shackles or iron collars (Tauxier 1921: 326 n.). If he continues misbehaving, he is resold in Wenchi or Odumasi. In the case of serious crimes, his master surrenders him to the king or province chief in authority, and he is sacrificed at the tomb or funeral of the first notable to die.

But in other respects, Abron institutions offer a whole series of means by which the individual slave may appreciably improve his lot. He can be condemned and put to death only by a royal court (Benquey in Clozel and Villamur 1902: 222; Tauxier 1921: 326 n.). A master who kills his captive in a moment of anger will have to pay the fine punishing all homicides, whoever the victim. An ill-treated slave can change masters by asking a free man of his choice to take him into his service; he will call for the death of this man if he refuses to accept the offer; and, finally, he will support his request by pronouncing one of the great oaths of the kingdom. In such a situation, the new master is bound to accept the offer and to compensate the former master. There are some places of refuge within Gyaman—Barabo (Tauxier 1921: 358 n.)—and persons entitled to play the role of intermediaries in the system of royal justice —the chiefs of Suma, Kwatwoma, the Tefuhene, and the imam of Bondoukou. Criminals, free men, or captives who succeed in finding refuge in these places or with these persons are assured of safety as long as they remain under their protection. While the existence of such remedies also bears witness to the reality of antagonism, it contributes to reducing the acuteness of such antagonism and to neutralizing the conflicts resulting from it. It should nevertheless be noted that the system of royal justice does not generally interfere with the internal affairs of the Dyula, except in those cases where the Dyula request such intervention. Hence the Dyulas' captives have less protection than those of the Abron.

The progressive amelioration of the captives' lot and above all of that of their descendants similarly limits the scope and intensity of confrontation between masters and captives. As we have said, after a certain period of time, the captive is given a wife and can thus start a family. With this gesture, the master is not seeking to ensure the 'natural' reproduction of his captives, since, as we shall see, the children of captives are not themselves captives. It is rather a case of his tying down the captive, of making him a part of the compound: escape is more difficult for a man burdened by a family than for an isolated individual. On the economic level, the captive who has shown himself worthy of confidence first receives a plot of land, and then permission to trade for himself, on condition that he turns over a part of his profits to his master. He can thus accumulate savings, which he manages freely. Some captives even succeed in amassing enough wealth to enable them to buy captives in their turn. On the whole, even though emancipation is unknown among the Abron, and only Abron or Akan captives may be bought back by their close relatives, the captive can appreciably better his situation during his lifetime. Some, but a very small minority, may even become unofficial although heeded councillors to the king and chiefs or may accede to the status of *kra*. The *kra*, who is as it were his master's double, leads the same life as the latter. He is supposed to divert to himself the dangers which threaten his master, and, given the closeness of their relationship, he may exercise a real influence on his master.

Nevertheless, the captive who has achieved some gains is never completely protected from a sudden change of fate. His belongings may be taken back from him, he may be separated from his wife, resold, and even if he has always behaved irreproachably, he risks being slaughtered at the funeral of his master or some notable. Such is the inescapable fate of even the *kra*, who must necessarily follow his double into the here-after. On the other hand, the descendants of captives (*dunko-ba*) are neither resold nor sacrificed, at least not unless they have committed some crime. But in this respect their status does not differ from that of freemen. Once they reach adulthood, they simultaneously receive a plot of land and the right to trade. In contrast to their parents, they can contract stable marriages. Back-breaking, dirty, or dangerous work is no longer imposed upon them (Archives AOF, dossier K 21; Tauxier 1921: 326 n.). This progressive assimilation of captives' descendants proceeds and accelerates as generations pass, so that finally the *dunko-ba* come to swell the manpower of peasant communities. Here again, however, the situation of the Dyulas' captives is different: even if their lot and that of their descendants improves with time, it never equals that of freemen. The position in the community of the descendants of cap-tives remains indelibly marked as inferior.

With the gradual emancipation of these descendants, we encounter one of the most salient contradictions of Abron society. We have seen that the Abron aristocracy draws its essential wealth from the exploita-tion of captive labour. As the productivity of this labour varies little, the aristocracy has every interest in maintaining and increasing captive manpower. Now, they forbid themselves the sure and effortless means of achieving this end: the simple 'natural' reproduction of those captives whom they already possess. To me the reason behind this attitude seems to be political in nature. The various forms taken by captives' resistance among the Abron have been enumerated above: this resistance would have undeniably been stronger had servile status been hereditary, for the captive class would then have had real continuity in time, and would have consequently been more capable of collective initiative and action. Upon their arrival in the country, captives coming from widely differing areas do not know one another, do not speak the same language, and do not share the same customs and beliefs. It is therefore difficult for them to unite among themselves. But if they had transmitted their status to their descendants, these factors of disunity would have disappeared by the following generation. Born in the same compound, subject to the same rules, the captives' children could have allied themselves against their masters far more easily than their parents. I do not think that the political and social structures of the Abron kingdom were sufficiently well organized successfully to confront a threat of this kind. The Abron aristocracy constitutes a small minority of the kingdom's population. They have no permanent army at their disposal, and the Abron state only consists of a rather loose confederation of provinces which retain a very considerable autonomy. For all these reasons, the high-ranking

Abron could not risk maintaining a class of true slaves at the very heart of the kingdom, slaves like those whose insurrection endangered the very existence of the Roman Republic. If the Dyula were bolder in this respect, it is undoubtedly both because the surveillance of their captives, who were concentrated around the towns, was easier and because their common adherence to Islam gave them greater cohesion.

However, the integration of captives' descendants into the society of freemen entails an important consequence. Unable to impose the same tasks on the *dunko-ba* as on their parents (agricultural labour for the master, extraction of gold, porterage) the Abron aristocracy is obliged to replenish its stock of captives every generation. Now, as we have seen, this reconstitution ultimately relies on the use of military force. Generally, the establishment of relations of servitude, the protection against possible uprisings, and the orderly reproduction of captives all depend upon strength in war. Thus we may simultaneously understand both the specific nature of the Abron state and the specific nature of the relationship that the mode of production based on the exploitation of slaves bears to the lineage mode of production within the social formation.

Indeed, in Gyaman, the dominant aristocracy is above all a military aristocracy. The state structure is modelled on that of the army, and the subdivisions of the former correspond to the corps of the latter. Each province occupies a determinate and always identical place on the battlefield. Bravery is the most esteemed of virtues and constitutes the surest means for a freeman of low station to gain the king's favour and to advance himself in the social hierarchy. For example, a valiant warrior may be given the functions of *safohene* (captain), which means that he is both a company commander in wartime and the administrator of ten or so villages during peacetime. The king and chiefs, who bear the expenses of equipping warriors, dedicate a considerable amount of their resources to buying arms and powder; and one of the most persistent orientations of Abron foreign policy is the search for free access to the ports where the Europeans unload guns and ammunition. Of course, the Abron thus attempt to secure the means of resisting Ashanti imperialism, but they also try to ensure *vis-à-vis* their northern and western neighbours an uncontested military superiority that would guarantee the success of their raids. On the ideological level, the exaltation of past victories and the seeking of support among the ancestors and supernatural powers with a view to future wars are the major aspects of all the state's ritual and religious activites.

We have shown above that the Abron aristocracy principally expects military assistance from its vassals and free subjects, and have thereby explained the relatively light tribute demanded of peasant communities and satellite principalities. Now, if the Abron aristocracy attaches such importance to this assistance, it is because it is the precondition of an orderly reproduction of the relations of servitude. All things considered, the aristocracy's need to ensure this reproduction being what it is, determines the volume of surplus extorted from the peasant community and the form of this extortion. We have distinguished in all two modes of production in the Abron social formation, one of a lineage and tributary character, the other slave. We now see that the functioning of the former is subordinated to the requirements for the reproduction of the social relations that constitute the latter. It can be concluded that the Abron social formation is dominated by this slave type of mode of production just described; the Abron social formation is organized around it. In this respect, this brief sketch of the nature of the Abron state confirms the results reached in our examination of the status of peasant communities. The relations of servitude are based on the use of force; and the nature of the state, like the status of the communities, is determined by the exigencies of this use of force.

The analysis of the development of the productive forces in the pre-colonial Abron kingdom, outlined at the beginning of this study, allowed us to predict such a conclusion. We then noted that, given the abundance of land and the simplicity of the instruments of production, labour-power was the principal factor in the labour process; that the efficiency of the labour process was a function of the volume and concentration of manpower and the scale of cooperation at work; and finally, that personal dependence was the preferred means for the control of men and hence for the extortion of surplus. Now, in the lineage mode of production, the youths and women certainly depend upon the elders, but the segmentary nature of the social organization reduces the number of labourers who can be brought together under a unitary control. Of course, there are various forms of association which permit the assembly of several elementary work groups, but such occasional cases of mobilization do not extend beyond rather narrow limits. In other respects, the relative autonomy retained by women and youths and the progressive emancipation of the latter are obstacles to the exploitation of which they are victims. These limitations and obstacles can be appreciably overcome through the establishment of servile relationships, the most complete and strictest form of personal dependence. In other words, on the basis of the existing productive forces, the mode of production based upon these servile relationships simultaneously allows the greatest productivity and the most highly developed exploitation. Consequently we can understand the reasons for its hegemony.

Until now we have principally seen the modes of production represented in the Abron social formation from the perspective of the dominated classes. In conclusion, I would like briefly to describe the status of the dominant class.

In reality, it is composed of two clearly distinct sections: the Abron aristocracy and the Dyula merchants. We have seen that the Abron aristocracy holds the monopoly of political power. In fact, the aristocracy is composed of all those who participate in the exercise of this power in one form or another: the king and the dignitaries surrounding him—the *okyeame* (spokesman), *gyasehene* (steward), *sannahene* (treasurer) and his servants, *asokwafo* (musicians), *akofranafo* (sword-bearers), *brafo* (executioners), messengers, etc.; the four province chiefs who have a smaller number of dignitaries and servants themselves; and the *safohene* (captains) each commanding five to ten villages in the name of the king or chiefs. We have already underlined the military nature of this aristocracy, and described its relationship to its subjects and captives. Two points remain to be examined. What are its internal structures, how is it organized? How does it distinguish itself from the dominated classes in everyday social life?

As far as the first question is concerned, given the strict correlation between membership in the aristocracy and the holding of political power, we can consider that the political system and the architecture of the Abron state, i.e. the arrangement and the equilibrium of the relations between the various holders of power, indeed constitutes the internal organization of the dominant class. Now, four prominent features are apparent:

(*a*) The territory of different provinces is not continuous. Each is made up of entangled enclaves. Nevertheless, the actual royal domain has the shape of a star, the points of which surround the disconnected elements of the other provinces. Given this arrangement of political space, attempts at secession become highly problematic.

(*b*) The provinces are very largely autonomous. The king does not intervene in the nomination of their chiefs, and the latter exercise most of the prerogatives which the king exercises in his domain. In the judicial sphere, sentences delivered by province chiefs may theoretically be brought for appeal before the king, but the latter usually upholds his subordinates' decisions. Finally, the principal political decisions (entering a war, concluding an alliance) must be made by unanimous agreement.

(*c*) The rules of succession to the throne, which establish a system of rotation and alternation between the numerous levels of various segments of the royal matrilineage, enlarge the foundations of the dynasty by interesting a great number of possible pretenders in the integrity and prosperity of the kingdom. These rules allow conflict over succession to be contained within the single segment which is in the position of successor. They also ensure the continuity of the kingdom's policies: any sovereign who abuses his power or tries to be too original would lay his close relatives open to reprisals by his successor and risk having his work nullified by the latter. In fact, the study of the kingdom's foreign policy and its principal orientations (the struggle against Ashanti tutelage, the alliance with Kong) demonstrates that this policy has been maintained by all successive kings, regardless of their segment of origin. Furthermore, the conflicts which we can reconstruct do not oppose one segment to another: the antagonists are equally recruited from the various segments. It should be noted that the same principles of rotation and alternation also apply to both province chiefs and the great dignitaries of the kingdom, and thus that the whole aristocracy is step by step permanently implicated in the functioning of the system.

(*d*) The *safohene* obtain their title in return for military or financial services rendered to the king or chiefs, and can transmit their title to their descendants. The holders of ultimate power face the particular problem of preventing the development of a hierarchy of wealthy men parallel to the political hierarchy. Wealth beyond a certain limit must be placed in the service of power, and its possessor must be integrated into the political hierarchy, or else lay himself open to fines or witchcraft trials entailing the confiscation of his goods.

The effect if not the goal of these provisions is to assure the Abron aristocracy of this minimal cohesiveness without which it could not succeed in maintaining its hegemony, given its minority status. But there is the other side of the coin: immobility. The political structure of the kingdom, constructed during the mid-eighteenth century, was not to be modified again and its foreign policy remained unchanged. The Abron did not succeed in establishing a real administrative authority in the interior, like the one the Ashanti were to organize and which was initiated during the reign of Osei Kwadio (see Wilks 1966: 216 ff.). In fact, their political system remained deeply marked by its lineage and segmentary origins; moreover, the relationships between the constituent members were thought of in terms of kinship: a certain chief is the 'son' of the king, a certain dignitary is considered his 'nephew'. While all this entails flexibility, it also implies paralysis.

How does this aristocracy distinguish itself from the dominated classes at the level of social life? Undoubtedly through the influence of a sort of distance effect, it seems to me that we have a tendency to underestimate the breadth of distances separating classes at the level of lifestyle and standard of living. In the first place, members of the aristocracy do not work with their hands. They benefit from richer and more abundant food: while they eat yams and meat, captives must often content themselves with manioc and dried fish. Similarly, the former use crockery imported from Europe, while the latter use gourds and wooden or earthen bowls. The aristocratic residences are more spacious, more solidly constructed, and contain more furniture (chairs, tables, cushions, etc.). The king, chiefs, and their close relatives sleep in beds, while the peasants and captives lie on mats. The aristocrats travel on palanquins carried by their servants. Social differences are also manifest at the level of clothing and ornaments. For the great, there are sumptuous loincloths, silks, diadems of gold thread, sandals encrusted with gold, rings, bracelets, gold and pearl necklaces, and richly decorated gold canopies; for the peasants and captives there are brief sheaths of beaten bark, rough cotton goods, and glass-ware. A strict form of etiquette obtains in interviews between inferiors and superiors. The former only present themselves to the latter with their shoulders uncovered and their feet bare, and only address them through the recognized mediating spokesman.

In conclusion, let us examine the Dyula communities. We shall not dwell on their internal organization, which is relatively well known today (see Benquey in Clozel and Villamur 1902: 287 ff.; Tauxier 1921: 227 ff.; Marty 1922: 217 ff.). We shall simply describe their relations with the Abron aristocracy, which are far more relations of alliance than of subjection. Of course, the Dyula are under the authority of the king, who intervenes as the ultimate arbitrator of conflicts among them. Owing the king military assistance in wartime, the Dyula of Bondoukou constitute a special corps of the advance guard while those from Barabo are members of the Penango province troops. However, they have many privileges. The imam of Bondoukou is the mediator at the court of the king: *de facto*, if not *de jure* the Dyula are not burdened with fines and they cannot be sacrificed at the funerals of important persons. Above all, the Dyula play an active role in the political affairs of the kingdom. The imam of Bondoukou sits as a titled member of the council of the king and chiefs; furthermore, many *karamoko* are councillors or suppliers of *safi* (amulets) at the courts of the *Gyamanhene* and province chiefs, bringing their hosts 'supernatural aid', which is essential in war and against drought, epidemics, and so on. This assistance is repaid by gifts of gold-dust and warrants the Dyulas' exemption from fines. However, their influence is limited in two ways. Any Abron who converts to Islam is simultaneously excluded from all political office, since he can no longer carry out the ritual tasks inherent in these offices. Second, the capitals of the kingdom and those of the provinces are not, nor have they ever been, in Bondoukou.

Describing the relationship which unites them with the Dyula, the Abron say, 'The Dyula are the king's wives', which among the Akan expresses a certain degree of subordination, but principally a strict conplementarity. We have already encountered the complementary nature of this relationship at the economic level: thanks to the Dyula merchants the Abron aristocracy is able to 'realize' the surplus product extorted from its captives on external markets. Conversely, through the maintenance of order in their territory, guaranteeing the free circulation of caravans, the Abron aristocracy contributes to the regular flow of commerce and thus to the enrichment of the Dyula. Economic interdependence is expressed at the political level by close cooperation which was to overcome all the difficulties imposed on the Abron kingdom and even the Samorian invasion. Given all these reasons, one might concede that the Dyula are indeed members of the dominant class, but they are not the deciding factor. For, with the exception of the cultivator hamlets which they established around Bondoukou, the Dyula confined themselves to distribution and circulation and did not intervene in the domain of production. This is why, despite their presence, the kingdom's economy did not become a market economy, but remained dominated by use-value until the dawn of the colonial era.

I will add only a few concluding remarks to the preceding commentary. In confining oneself to the economic infrastructure, one can easily recognize the existence of relations of exploitation and, consequently, of classes in the Abron kingdom. But if the analysis of classes led only to this sort of result, it would not be worthy of further interest. Its aim must be far wider: it must account for the specific forms which the class antagonism discovered takes in each mode of production, and also for the limits of such antagonism. For in the case of the Abron kingdom, for example, the difficulty does not lie in identifying the presence of classes, but in understanding why their opposition was not transformed into widespread and open conflict. Two sets of explanation of this problem have been offered: at the economic level, use-value continues to dominate production and therefore exploitation tends to remain constant; at the political level, the concrete social groups through which classes are realized or embodied have neither the cohesion nor the permanence to ensure the appearance of a truly collective consciousness. In other respects, the nature of these groups has the effect of hiding the reality of classes. This is even the case with captives, where the opposition between indigenous people and foreigners continues to a certain extent to mask the opposition between exploiters and exploited. Of course, these explanations are only hypotheses which must be verified, enriched, and completed. I would be satisfied if I had at least been able to demonstrate the necessity of advancing them. For, by using the idea of classes to understand pre-capitalist social formations, we inevitably reduce the distance separating them from the capitalist formation. But marxist analysis cannot be reduced to the locating of similarities. Equally and above all it will prove itself when it is able to restore these particularities, these specific differences, which give each social formation under consideration a 'singular essence'.

Notes

1 Today I would be far less categorical on this matter, as is evident from the pages that follow.

2 Their names appear in the literature in a considerable variety of forms; those used here follow D. Westermann and M. A. Bryan's *Languages of West Africa* (London: Dawsons, 1970) (Ed.).

3 Freeman to Chief Medical Officer, 22 June 1889 (PRO, CO Africa West 354). This estimate coincides with what we know of the area encompassed by the kingdom and of its borders at the end of the nineteenth century. At the same period Ewart spoke of 1600 square miles (Ewart to Colonial Office, 24 October 1889 (PRO Africa West 354)), which is certainly too low an estimate. Binger, on the other hand, mentions the figure of 50,000 square kilometres, or double the actual figure, perhaps in the hope of magnifying the importance of the protectorate treaty which Treich-Laplene made with Gyaman (Binger 1892, Vol. II: 173).

4 The French terms *cour* and *ménage* have been rendered as 'compound' and 'household' respectively (Ed.).

5 For the Kulango, see Folquet in Clozel and Villamur (1902: 359), Tauxier (1921: 135, 140, 150, 157–8, 168); for the Abron, see Benquey in Clozel and Villamur (1902: 208), Tauxier (1921: 304–10, 320n.).

6 According to Folquet (in Clozel and Villamur 1902: 353–4), brideprice among the Kulango consisted of twelve chickens, twelve kola nuts, and six thousand cowries valued at 'around sixteen francs' at that time. Tauxier gives the following list: four chickens, a loin-cloth, a pair of pants worn by women (*bila*), a little salt and maize flour. He concludes: 'Together it couldn't be worth more than fifteen francs' (Tauxier 1921: 161). According to Benquey, brideprice among the Abron consisted of two loin-cloths, a piece of material for making a *bila*, 'a sack of salt (about 37.50 francs) . . . 28.75 francs in cash' (Benquey in Clozel and Villamur 1902: 196). The various items listed by Tauxier, who was relying on information given him by a representative of *Gyamanhene* Tan Date, i.e. a loin-cloth, a piece of material for a *bila*, half a sack of salt, several sums of money, were valued by him at slightly more than forty francs at that time. At the same period, brideprice among the Dida consisted of an ox, a rifle, two large loin-cloths, and a certain number of anklets varying according to the region: forty packets or one hundred and sixty francs in the south; from ten to fifteen packets or sixty francs in the north (Terray 1969: 205–6).

7 Folquet (in Clozel and Villamur 1902: 358–9), Benquey (in Clozel and Villamur 1902: 208), Benquey (in Gouvernement Général de l'AOF 1906: 174), Tauxier (1921: 308), Alland (1972: 104).

8 I shall confine myself here to a brief résumé of the data I presented in 'La captivité dans le royaume abron du Gyaman', my contribution to the collection on West African slavery which is being prepared by Claude Meillassoux.

References

ALLAND, A. 1965. Abron Witchcraft and Social Structure. *Cahiers d'études africaines* 5 (4): 495–502.
— 1972. *The Human Imperative*. New York: Columbia University Press.
ALTHUSSER, L. and BALIBAR, E. 1972. *Reading 'Capital'*. London: New Left Books.
BINGER, L. 1892. *Du Niger au Golfe de Guinée*. 2 vols. Paris: Hachette.
BOWDICH, T. 1966 (1819). *A Mission from Cape Coast Castle to Ashantee*. 3rd edn, London: Murray.

BRAULOT, CAP. 1893. *Rapport de mission*. Archives FOM, Côte d'Ivoire 3 (3).
BUKHARIN, N. 1969. *Historical Materialism*. Ann Arbor: University of Michigan Press.
BUSIA, K. 1968 (1951). *The Position of the Chief in the Modern Political System of Ashanti*. 2nd edn, London: Oxford University Press.
CLOZEL, F. J. 1906. *Dix ans à la Côte d'Ivoire*. Paris: Challamel.
CLOZEL, F. J. and VILLAMUR, R. 1902. *Les coutumes indigènes de la Côte d'Ivoire*.
DUPUIS, J. 1967 (1824). *Journal of Residence in Ashantee*. 2nd edn, London: Cass.
ENGELS, F. 1969 (1878). *Anti-Dühring*. London: Lawrence & Wishart.
— 1972 (1884). *The Origin of the Family, Private Property and the State*. London: Lawrence & Wishart.
GOUVERNEMENT GÉNÉRAL DE L'AOF. 1906. *La Côte d'Ivoire*. Notices publiées à l'occasion de l'exposition coloniale de Marseille. Paris: Imprimerie Crete.
HUTTON, W. 1821. *Voyage to Africa*. French translation cited: *Nouveau voyage en Afrique*. Paris: Imprimerie de Chassaignon, 1832.
ISERT, P. 1793. *Nouveau voyage en Guinée et dans les îles caraibes*. Paris: Maradan.
JOSEPH, G. 1915. Villes d'Afrique: Bondoukou. Bulletin du Comité de l'Afrique française.
LENIN, V. I. 1971 (1919). A Great Beginning. *Selected Works*, Vol. III: 219–42. Moscow: Progress Publishers.
MARTY, P. 1922. *Études sur l'Islam en Côte d'Ivoire*. Paris: E. Leroux.
MARX, K. 1967 (1867). *Capital*, Vol. I. Trans from the 3rd German edition by S. Moore and F. Engels.
— (1894). *Capital*, Vol. III. 3 vols. New York: International Publishers.
— 1973 (1857–8). *Grundrisse*. Harmondsworth: Penguin Books with New Left Review.
MARX, K. and ENGELS, F. 1965. *Marx–Engels: Selected Correspondence*. Moscow: Progress Publishers (1955).
— 1969. *Selected Works*, Vol. I. Moscow: Progress Publishers.
MEILLASSOUX, C. 1964. *Anthropologie économique des Gouro de Côte d'Ivoire*. Paris: Mouton.
POULANTZAS, N. 1972. *Political Power and Social Classes*. London: New Left Books.
RATTRAY, R. S. 1969 (1929). *Ashanti Law and Constitution*. 2nd edn, Oxford: Clarendon Press.
REY, P.-P. 1971. *Colonialisme, néocolonialisme, et transition au capitalisme*. Paris: Maspéro.
TAUXIER, L. 1921. *Le Noir de Bondoukou*. Paris: Leroux.
TERRAY, E. 1969. L'organisation sociale des Dida. *Annales* de l'Université d'Abidjan, series F **1** (2).
— 1972 (1969). *Marxism and 'Primitive' Societies*. New York: Monthly Review Press.
WILKS, I. 1966. Aspects of Bureaucratization in Ashanti in the Nineteenth Century. *Journal of African History* **3** (2).
WILSON, J. L. 1856. *Western Africa*. New York: Harper.

Joel Kahn

Economic Scale and the Cycle of Petty Commodity Production in West Sumatra

In a now famous passage from *The Eighteenth Brumaire*, Marx wrote:

> The small-holding peasants form a vast mass, the members of which
> live in similar conditions but without entering into manifold relations
> with one another. Their mode of production isolates them from one
> another instead of bringing them into mutual intercourse ... In so far
> as millions of families live under economic conditions of existence
> that separates their mode of life, their interests, their culture from
> those of other classes, and puts them in hostile opposition to the latter
> they form a class. In so far as there is merely local interconnection
> among those small-holding peasants, and the identity of their interests
> begets no community, no national bond, and no political organisation
> among them they do not form a class (1951: 302–3).

In summarizing a number of studies of peasant societies, Peter Lloyd
concludes generally that these societies are characterized by the 'social
isolation of the individual family and the intensity of competition
between families. Co-operation is minimal' (1971: 40).[1] Rather than
rushing to the conclusion that this is generally true of peasant societies,
however, anthropologists would be wise to take a lead from Alavi who,
in commenting on Marx's statement, writes: 'It would be a mistake to
read into this passage a statement of some universal attributes of
peasants ... That statement, it should be noted, was made specifically
with reference to the French peasantry and in the particular context of
their role at a moment of crisis in French history' (Alavi 1973: 26).

In this paper I propose to investigate this problem of the scale of social
organization with particular reference to material derived from fieldwork in a peasant village in West Sumatra.[2] I will also attempt to analyse
the material in a broader historical framework in order to show how a
particular mode of production produces a cyclical development of the
productive forces, so that in some periods productive units are small in
scale, while at others the scale of productive groups increases. While
Swift, in discussing a Malay village in Jelebu, writes that 'the small scale
of organization is the most striking feature of the peasant economy'
(1965: 26), I shall rather suggest that scale varies according to a par-

ticular set of historical conditions. The cyclical movement is in part the result of a set of relations of production, but it is also the result of inter-action with other modes of production in the Indonesian social for-mation.

Finally, the usefulness of this model [3] will be tested with reference to the development of the productive forces in one sector of production, blacksmithing, and at the same time an alternative to Swift's explana-tion of underdevelopment in West Sumatra will be offered.[4]

I

My field research was carried out among the Minangkabau in the Indo-nesian province of West Sumatra. In this section of the paper I will concentrate on a single township (*nagari*) in the highland district of Agam. It is here that the production of steel goods for the province is concentrated, in the *nagari* of Sawah Lawas. Sawah Lawas is located on the edge of a highland plateau physically and socially centred on the market and administrative town of Bukit Tinggi. Founded by the Dutch, on the site of an old *nagari*, Bukit Tinggi remains the market centre for the whole densely populated plateau area.

Sawah Lawas itself is reached by a partly paved road, along which small buses pass at frequent intervals, especially on market days. The trip takes about twenty minutes, allowing for frequent stops.

The township is divided for administrative purposes into five sections (*kampuang*) each with a headman appointed by the township mayor. The largest of these sections has a resident population of about 3,000 and it is here that the blacksmithing industry is concentrated. The largest male occupational group are pedlars and small traders who live outside the township itself,[5] but who return periodically. Of the fully resident working males, from 60 to 70 per cent earn their living pri-marily from the production of steel goods for the market. Apart from traders living in the township, there are a number of other occupational groups including carpenters, seamstresses (most young women sew clothes to sell in Bukit Tinggi), farmers, and both active and retired government employees.

The section of Sawah Lawas must import much of its food from out-side. The 150 hectares of irrigated riceland within its boundaries are divided into small plots, most of which are farmed for subsistence only. However, subsistence cultivation provides the average family with rice for only about two months out of each year. Thus other sources of income are essential in order to provide cash for the purchase of both rice and other necessary commodities.

Blacksmithing fulfils this need for most men. The smiths turn out the axes, sickles, hoes, ploughs, machetes, knives, and other implements used in the kitchens and fields throughout the area. Indeed, they are marketed throughout the island of Sumatra.

Techniques vary slightly with the type of goods being produced. All the work is related to the forging and finishing of scrap steel into steel goods for the market. Forging is done in a small workshop, the *apa basi*, which is usually a small thatched hut with walls of bamboo slats and a pounded earth floor. The steel is heated in a coal fire on an open hearth which is kept at the correct temperature by the use of a pair of hand-operated piston bellows.

A duct leads from the bottom of the bellows to a point in the hearth just underneath the coal fire. The red-hot steel is removed from the fire and forged on an anvil, usually by two men who do the heavy sledge work required, and a third who wields a smaller hammer.

After the implements have been roughly forged they are tempered in water and, when necessary, filed and polished in order to make the shapes uniform and give them a sharp edge.

Most of the *apa* concentrate on a single type of steelware. The workers in each workshop also tend to be specialists. Thus we have: the *nangkodoh* or head smith, who directs the activities of forging and is also the entrepreneur in that he finances the *apa*, buys the raw materials, and sells the finished goods (it is he who uses the smaller hammers, and holds the implements on the anvil in a pair of tongs); the *tukang tapo* who handles the heavy sledgehammer; the *tukang ambuih* who operates the bellows; and the *tukang kikia* who files the partly completed goods after they have been forged.

It is difficult to compute accurately the investment required for an *apa*. Smiths usually make many of the tools—tongs, sledgehammers, and smaller hammers—themselves. The building itself costs very little: bamboo, its major component, is inexpensive, and often simply taken from family land. The only real investment of any scale is the anvil, which may cost anywhere between Rp. 25,000 and Rp. 50,000.[6] Other tools, such as vices and files, are also purchased. Suffice it to say here that the general level of investment is indicated by the price of the anvil, which far exceeds the combined cost of all other instruments of labour.

The cost of raw materials required in forging is much greater. For example, a *nangkodoh* working full time to produce axes may spend about Rp. 25,000 on scrap steel and Rp. 7,000 on coal in a single month. These are the main raw materials, although smiths need periodically to buy supplies of files, sandpaper, oil, wood for handles, packaging materials, and metal dies with which they impress their own trademarks on the finished goods. The market in these secondary raw materials is relatively stable, but all smiths with whom I talked expressed anxiety over the flow of the basic raw materials, coal and scrap steel, either because they were not always available when needed, or because sometimes when they were available at a reasonable price the smith did not have the cash to buy. The erratic rising of prices combined with periods of shortage and sharp short-term price fluctuation, make the supply of raw materials an obstacle to profitable blacksmithing.

The goods are generally sold by the *nangkodoh* to one of the twenty-five-odd traders in steel goods in the Bukit Tinggi market. These merchants, mostly Sawah Lawas men as well, range from the roving street pedlar to the owners of small shops with large investments in steelware of around Rp. 2,000,000. In Bukit Tinggi the goods are then sold either to customers in the market area who come in from surrounding villages on market days, or to travelling pedlars who take the goods to other markets in West Sumatra or to other parts of the island.

Relations with the merchants tend to last over long periods of time, but the pattern is very different from that described for other parts of Southeast Asia. Merchants in steelware rarely advance credit to the smiths, nor do they have any hand in the operation of the *apa*. Loans are sometimes made, but they are rarely of any real significance. On the contrary, the extension of credit in effect runs in the other direction with the merchant accepting goods partly on a consignment basis, and paying the smiths only as he sells them.

The composition of the productive work unit varies with the type of goods being produced because of the variety of techniques. Hoes (*pangkuah*) are in general made by a group of four people: one *nangkodoh* or head smith; two *tukang tapo* or sledgers; and one *tukang ambuih* who operates the bellows. The forging of hoes, of all goods produced in Sawah Lawas, requires the most heavy sledge work. While some filing and finishing is necessary, this can usually be done by one or both of the *tukang tapo* at those times during the day when the *nangkodoh* only is needed for forging.

Axes, like hoes, need little filing and thus only rarely do we find a full-time filer (*tukang kikia*) in an axe-maker's forge. The work group is generally the same as that for hoes. Machetes and sickles can be made by only two people working together, although occasionally we find a third worker who does some sledging and some filing and finishing.

Knives are the most common Sawah Lawas product. One person can make knives alone by buying forged blanks, and filing and adding handles and paint himself. Alternatively, a larger group can be assembled to work together doing both the forging and finishing.

If we compare the productivity of smithing in Sawah Lawas to the capitalist production of similar goods, the low level of the former is obvious. This is true not just for smithing in West Sumatra but for most forms of rural production. Low productivity here stems from a number of aspects of productive forces, including: the general duplication of tasks related directly to production or ancillary to it; the atomistic nature of the productive units; the inability of the *nangkodoh* to stockpile raw materials; and, most important, the low productivity of labour, the result of the low technological level of smithing in Sawah Lawas.

Although the number of *apa* in operation at any one time varies, it was reported by the mayor at one stage that about 80 *apa* had registered by paying a small tax. It is quite likely that this is an accurate figure because the man responsible for collecting the tax was a highly motivated official who had recently worked as a blacksmith himself. The rest of the smiths in the township are men engaged on their own in the production of knives, and other smaller goods, who work in small outhouses not classified as *apa*. During the period of research there were no units of production larger than those described above. Thus no more than four or five cooperated to make hoes or axes, and no more than three to make machetes or sickles. Each *apa* was financed separately by the *nangkodoh*, who bought raw materials, hired labour, and marketed finished goods as an individual unit. Rarely was more than one such unit housed under the same roof, and even when this was so the individual *apa* was entirely independent of the other. External financing of the *apa* through bank loans or merchant's capital was nonexistent.

The most recent attempt to form a cooperative, just to buy scrap steel from the pooled resources of its members, was a failure. It attracted fewer than thirty members, who invested Rp. 1,000 each. This money was insufficient and the cooperative never really got started. Although there have been several attempts to revive it since its founding in 1968, all have so far failed because there has been no further interest in pooling resources.

The small scale of economic activity means that there is a lack of cooperation above the level of the *apa*. This means, for example, that each *apa* markets its finished products individually. Marketing takes place once or twice a week. To take his goods to market the *nangkodoh* has to close down the *apa* for at least one half of the day, and thus often a full day's forging is lost every week, simply because the task of marketing is carried out by many more people than are in fact necessary. Other duplication exists for similar reasons.

Because there is no pooling of resources to buy raw materials the individual *nangkodoh* has to buy coal and steel frequently. However, because of the erratic nature of the market in coal and steel, the *apa* are frequently forced to shut down, either because no coal or steel is available, or because that which is available is being sold at too high a price. Furthermore, because the *apa* depends on the cooperation of a small number of people, the temporary loss of one worker often means that work cannot be carried out.

While the loss of work time and thus productivity through the lack of cooperation is significant, it is the low productivity of labour which is the most significant cause of overall underproductivity. This is the result of the relatively low level of technology.

The *apa* units are clearly labour-intensive. The techniques of production, as they have been described, are both crude and unproductive. The quality of steelware compares unfavourably with that of imported, machine-made tools. The strength of steel in the finished products, for example, is poor both because of the low quality of the raw materials

141

and because forging in the open air and tempering in water are extremely undependable ways of regulating and fixing carbon content.

The lack of machinery means that individual goods demand a far higher amount of labour-time than do similar goods produced by capital-intensive techniques, even when we allow for the extra costs of capital-intensive production.

A picture of the productivity of the *apa* emerges when we look at *Table 1*, which presents material derived from a number of productivity surveys carried out in the field.

Table 1
Productivity of a sample of forges which produce axes (apa kapak) *over a period of one month*

product	number of apa	total number of workers	total production	total hours	man hours	production per man hours
small axe	2	9	920	357	3206	·29 axes
axe— 2-pound	2	8	300	227	1816	·17 axes

I have limited the data here to the productivity of those *apa* surveyed which produced axes only, the hours represent the total hours spent in the forge over a period of one month. The figures show that on average a productive unit of four people turning out a small carpenter's axe can produce just over one axe per hour, a low rate by any standards. The figures for the production of hoes, sickles, knives, etc., are comparably low.

We must now turn to the nature of the productive relationships in smithing, to look at the social organization of production. The social allocation of the smiths' labour-time in some ways resembles the organization of capitalist enterprises, although there are some important differences.

The *nangkodoh* is both the organizer of production and a participant in the work group. It is he who owns the means of production. While in Minangkabau irrigated riceland is still embedded in the complex matri-lineal kinship system, the blacksmith's forge, the labour-power of the workers, and the raw materials are purchased as commodities by the *nangkodoh*. In spite of a tendency to deny its existence in Sawah Lawas, the smiths are clearly involved in wage-labour. Typically, the *nangkodoh* divides the price of all completed goods into two equal parts. One half is set aside for raw materials, the other half for wages. Wages are paid twice a week, and the proportion allotted for labour is divided into a number of equal parts. If, for example, there are four people in the work group, including the *nangkodoh*, then the share for wages is divided into five equal parts. Each worker receives an equal share, and the remaining share is reserved 'for the *apa*'. Thus while it may appear that the *nangkodoh* receives the same rate as anyone else, in fact the extra share is often appropriated by him for his own use. This is the result of the fact that the share 'for the *apa*' is generally more than enough to cover depreciation on investments for which it is intended. Because of the fact that he is the owner of the means of production, the *nangkodoh* is able to extract a small surplus. The main relation of production is then between the *nangkodoh* and the workers, the owners of the means of production and the non-owners.

In spite of this, the *nangkodoh* is not significantly better paid than are the other workers in the work group. This, and the existence of a surplus appropriated by the *nangkodoh*, are reflected in *Table 2*.

Table 2
Return to labour and to the entrepreneur

(a) Average monthly returns to *nangkodoh* (from a sample of five *apa*)	= Rp. 7,600
to wage worker	= Rp. 4,400
(b) Average hourly returns to *nangkodoh*	= Rp. 62·6 (about 6 new pence)
to knife-maker, working alone	= Rp. 51·0 (about 5 new pence)
to *tukang tapo* (a wage worker)	= Rp. 32·1 (about 3 new pence)

This form of ownership, as a social relation between entrepreneur and wage worker, is given recognition in the ideology of property relationships. Some property in Sawah Lawas is classified as *harto pusako* or ancestral property. This includes, most importantly, rice-land, house plots, and houses. *Harto pusako* is controlled to some extent by the matrilineal segment, rights of alienation are limited by corporate ownership, and the property is inherited through the female line. However, a second form of property has become important in Minangkabau, the so-called *harto pantjarian* or earned property.[7] This is property which an individual acquires during his or her lifetime, and in most cases it is inherited from father to son or mother to daughter. There are fewer limits to rights of alienation of *harto pantjarian*. The most important type of *harto pantjarian* consists of small shops and trade goods, most of which have been acquired by migrants outside the village. However, the implements of small industry such as blacksmithing are always considered to be *harto pantjarian* as well, and pass from a man to his son.

The reproduction of this social relationship may rest outside the actual production process. It seems, for example, that access to land, either through his wife or through his family of origin, is important if a man is to become a *nangkodoh* as opposed to a wage worker. In some cases kin ties, most frequently the relation between father and son, become a relation of production. A survey of rights to land in Sawah Lawas shows that *nangkodoh* have, on average, more land rights than do

143

individuals working alone who, in turn, have more than wage workers. In those few cases of landless *nangkodoh*, it is usually true that they have been able to become entrepreneurs only by drawing on the labour of sons. This is possible, however, only at certain stages in the developmental cycle of the family and on the whole *nangkodoh* prefer, if possible, to hire either non-kin or distant kin to work in their *apa*.

As it has been described, the smithing industry seems to present us with a form of paradox. On the one hand, we have a form of commodity production with wage-labour and the individual ownership of the means of production. On the other, we find that techniques and the technical organization of labour are at a relatively primitive level. A similar form of productive organization in the West has produced a continuous revolution at the level of productive forces, whereas in this case such a revolution has not taken place. It is thus important to understand why *nangkodoh* have not been able to increase their profits either by increasing the size of productive units, or by increasing productivity through the development of new technologies, or the adaptation of techniques already in existence, many of which are known to the Sawah Lawas smiths.

It has already been shown that the *nangkodoh* is paid only slightly more than are his workers, the result in part of the small scale of organization. Moreover, it is the *nangkodoh* who runs the risks when goods are given to the merchants on consignment, for the workers are paid regardless of this fact. Finally, the time spent by the *nangkodoh* in the management of the *apa*, as distinct from the time actually working with it, is not insignificant. The result is that in order for the *nangkodoh* to make enough of a return he must be both entrepreneur *and* participant in the work group, a fact clearly recognized by all the smiths with whom I discussed the matter. In the production of hoes, for example, four workers are needed, including the *nangkodoh*. If he were to increase the size of the work group, in order to increase his surplus, it would affect productive capacity only if he were to increase it by four and buy a second anvil. Given the cost of financing the second group, the increased risk, and the fact that the *nangkodoh* cannot work in both groups at the same time, such expansion is clearly an unprofitable concern. It would become profitable only if the *nangkodoh* were to reduce the share allotted for labour. If he did this, under present circumstances, he would not be able to find workers, who would remain free to choose to work with his competitors. There is simply no incentive to make this sort of change.

Cooperatives, which are often proposed as a way of solving this dilemma, come up against the contradiction themselves, since they must inevitably sell at a higher price than that charged by the small, independent competitors. While the failure of cooperatives in Sawah Lawas has been attributed by the people and by government agencies to mismanagement, and peasant conservatism, the structural constraints alone are enough to discourage their formation.

Small-scale technological improvements are ruled out for the same reasons. Most smiths, for example, are aware that the use of oil instead of water for tempering would improve the quality of the steel. However, small-scale improvements such as these serve not to increase productivity, but to increase costs. In spite of the fact that finished goods are of a slightly higher quality, consumers are unwilling to pay the higher price. The explanation lies not in the lack of technical knowledge, but apparently in the market itself.

Large-scale improvements might, in the long run, increase productivity and thus reduce costs of production. While the production of steel goods is perhaps exceptional in this respect it is nevertheless generally true that investments at such a level are extremely high in relation to the incomes of producers. It is quite clear that, even if all the Sawah Lawas smiths were to pool their resources, they could not even make a down payment on the type of machinery necessary to produce more cheaply than they could using present methods. Capital accumulation of this scale clearly requires an initial period in which a large number of workers can be exploited by a single entrepreneur. As we have already seen, this form of exploitation is ruled out, given the present price structure, and the nature of labour in West Sumatra. Rey and Dupré (1973) have argued that in West Africa such dislocation required direct political measures on the part of colonial governments, political measures which the Indonesian government, at least now, is not prepared to take because of their inevitable unpopularity.

The lack of external investment in local industry may, it seems, be attributed to the same thing. The unprofitability of the industry, caused by the small size of work groups, simply does not attract capital, even when it is acquired in other spheres of economic activity under present circumstances. Thus, in spite of the fact that smithing is a labour-intensive industry, it is the lack of available labour which prevents large-scale capital investment, since capital needs labour in order to produce a surplus. What local capital there is can be more profitably invested in other sectors, or more frequently as merchant capital in areas undergoing local depressions for a variety of reasons.[8]

The underproductivity of smithing, then, seems to be the result of two main factors. First, it results from the absence of a labour force which can be exploited to yield a high level of capital accumulation. Second, it seems to be the result of the market price that smiths can charge for their completed goods. I shall return to these points below. Suffice it to say here that the market price seems to be determined by the price of imported goods, which are sold at prices between ten and fifteen per cent higher than domestically produced goods. The low level of return to the smiths is, then, in part a result of integration into a world economy in which production is, in general, more productive. In this sense smithing can be seen as a sector of world steelware production, and low returns are the direct result of the fact that average or socially necessary labour-time is lower in this production overall than it is in Sawah Lawas. As Marx pointed out in the opening pages of *Capital*:

> Some people might think that if the value of a commodity is determined by the quantity of labour spent on it, the more idle and unskilful the labourer [or, we might add, the less productive the labour] the more valuable would his commodity be, because more time would be required in its production. The labour, however, that forms the substance of value, is homogeneous human labour, expenditure of one uniform labour-power. The total labour-power of society, which is embodied in the sum total of the values of all commodities produced by that society, counts here as one homogeneous mass of human labour-power, composed though it be of innumerable individual units. Each of these units is the same as any other, so far as it has the character of the average labour-power of society, and takes effect as such; that is, so far as it requires for producing a commodity, no more time is needed on an average, no more than is socially necessary (Marx 1973, Vol. I: 39).

In the case of smithing in Sawah Lawas, the boundaries of the society have expanded across national borders. In spite of the fact that smithing is carried on outside the capitalist mode of production, as I shall argue below, it remains true that value is, in a sense, determined by capitalist production outside of Indonesia itself.

It is thus evident that an analysis of smithing in Sawah Lawas must take account of the nature of the relation of the industry to economic structures external to the township. However, I shall argue in the second section of this paper that the system is best seen not as an interaction between separate structures, the one affecting the other only marginally, at the level of market forces. On the contrary, the wider, macro-structure must be analysed as a collection of the structures which together give it its peculiar dynamic. If this is true it is no longer possible to consider territorial divisions as the basic units for analysis. Rather, it is more rewarding to use a more abstract concept, the concept of a mode of production, to analyse the social system which we have been describing.

II

Godelier (1972, 1974), Terray (1972), and others have attempted to refine Marx's concept of a mode of production so that it might be used to analyse societies that are predominantly non-capitalist. The difference in their approach from that of some earlier marxists is that they use the mode of production to refer not only to what had been called an infrastructure. Rather, they suggest that a mode of production is made up of a number of different elements or functions. Althusser, for example, describes the different 'instances' of any mode of production: the economic base, the juro-political and ideological instance.

The approach also differs from that of the more traditional interpreters of Marx in the way it rejects the idea that all the other instances are merely reflections of the economic base. Godelier particularly emphasizes that kinship relations, for example, can actually become the social relations of production, and not merely a reflection at the level of ideology of the economic. Economic relations, then, are not relations between people and things, but relations between people with a material element or implication.[9] These relations might, at the same time, be superstructural relations, thus making the layer-cake approach to social structures an untenable one.

The brilliance of Marx's analysis of capitalism lies in the way he locates its dynamic in the interaction of two structures, the structure of productive forces and the structure of the relations of production. Godelier describes this relation as a contradiction: '[T]he fundamental contradiction of the capitalist mode of production . . . consists in the contradiction between the development and socialization of the productive forces and the private ownership of the means of production' (1972: 78). To oversimplify, it could be said that capitalism is characterized by a social relation between classes which allows one class, the one which 'possesses' capital, to exploit a second class. Capital is then itself a social relation of production. This social relation contains a tendency towards a development of the forces of production, a result of the inherent need to expand the rate of exploitation. At the origin of capitalism this dynamic combined with a revolution of productive forces to produce the capitalist mode of production. In the later phases of capitalism, however, Marx suggested that the contradiction would become evident in periodic crises in the capitalist countries.[10]

An analogous process can be seen in the history of West Sumatra. A new set of productive relations seems to have emerged at the turn of the century, as a result of the impact of colonial rule. However, the forces of production have not been revolutionized, but rather have a cyclical movement which allows us to distinguish between the capitalist mode of production and what I shall call the petty commodity mode of production.[11] I propose to analyse here the evolution of this mode of production, and to attempt to find the cause for this cycle in the relation between petty commodity production and two other modes of production which affect it, the capitalist mode of production and a form of lineage production which is largely restricted to the cultivation of irrigated rice.

By intervening in an internal war, the Dutch were able to establish direct political control in the area of West Sumatra known as the Padang Highlands by 1837.[12] The main interest at this time was in the cultivation of coffee for the world export market. In 1847 West Sumatra became one of the only places outside Java where the so-called Culture

147

System, or system of forced cultivation, was established by the Dutch. In Java, sugar was cultivated by peasant labour on village riceland. Villages were required to set aside a fixed proportion of riceland for sugar, and to provide labour to cultivate the sugar. The sugar was then processed in Dutch- or Chinese-owned mills and exported in the Dutch sector of the economy. By this system the Dutch hoped to disrupt village organization as little as possible while still extracting a surplus in the form of an exportable commodity (Geertz 1963a).[13]

In West Sumatra the system of forced cultivation was quite different. In 1847 a law was passed which made it compulsory in the highland area for every able-bodied man to cultivate a fixed number of coffee trees.[14] The coffee was then sold to the government monopoly at a fixed price. The system met with some success, at least in the mid-nineteenth century, in increasing coffee production. However, by the end of the century, pressures were mounting to abolish forced cultivation. Thus in 1908 the system was replaced in West Sumatra by a tax on income. Forced cultivation was lifted, artificial monopoly prices were abolished, and government surplus was now extracted through a tax.

The period from 1908 to the mid 1920s is described in some detail by Schrieke, a Dutch sociologist who was commissioned by the colonial government to investigate the causes of the communist uprisings of 1926–7 (see Schrieke 1955–7; Benda and McVey 1960). The period saw a shift of economic activity from the central areas of the Minangkabau heartland to the southern part of the province which had not been affected by the Culture System. The economic boom which followed was most strongly felt not in the Padang Highlands but to the south in Korintji and the areas bordering on Djambi. Changes in the economic structures in these areas tended to produce accompanying changes in the central area, which produced commodities to be consumed in these districts, provided labour for these areas, and was the source of a growing population of petty traders who served the producers in the south.

The reasons for the shift are not entirely clear. There are a number of factors which seem to have been important. Forced cultivation in the Padang Highlands tended to reduce the amount of land available for the growing of commercial crops. Huitema (1935: 51) suggests that soils were quickly exhausted owing to the pressure to use available land when it should have been left fallow. Population increases were in all likelihood also greater in the areas affected by the Culture System. The outlying districts, on the other hand, were sparsely populated, with a high proportion of land for commercial crop cultivation, at least partly a result of their exclusion from the Culture System. The disease of coffee trees must have hit the highland areas hardest, and replanting of disease-resistant strains after 1900 was greatest in the south.

It is for these reasons interesting to note that after the end of forced cultivation the amount of coffee grown in the Padang Highlands declined, while those areas which had not been subject to the Culture System, such as Muaro Bungo, Djambi, Korintji, and Bangko, experienced sudden increases in production.

While forced coffee cultivation contributed to some extent to economic changes in the villages, its influence seems to have been to lay the groundwork for more far-reaching changes in the early decades of this century. In this period certain changes took place which led to a liberation of the productive relations, i.e. which allowed for the emergence of pure commodity production.

Prior to the tax of 1908, the Dutch had made it a policy to preserve the subsistence base of the colonized economy, and thus also the traditional kinship systems which played a part in the organization of production. In Java, as we have already seen, the aims of the sugar cultivation were to preserve a land-owning peasantry which acted as a seasonal labour force through political compulsion. In West Sumatra a series of restrictions were imposed which served to prevent rice being bought and sold. In both cases the aim was to preserve the relationship to the land of all the peasants in order to prevent complete destruction of the precapitalist forms of organization, and thus to prevent the emergence of a rural proletariat which would cause political disturbances. To quote from Schrieke (1955–7: 97–8):

> In this way the natural development of a district whose latent possibilities had long before pointed to the evolution of an exchange economy was impeded by an administration whose sincere aim—at least in its rice policy—was to maintain law and order. Care had to be taken to see that in every *negeri* as much paddy as possible was stored and as little as possible exported and sold. For a population amply supplied with food meant a contented and peaceful population. A former Padang Highlands commissioner ('resident') was even of the opinion that the *kinchirs*, those ingenious native rice hulling mills driven by a water wheel, were harmful, since they made it easy for the paddy to be processed into granular rice, for which the export demand was greatest. This civil servant thought that if the population were forced to stamp rice by hand, it would be more inclined to limit stamping to the quantity required for its own consumption.

The restrictions on the export of rice, and the efforts to keep rice out of local markets, were lifted in 1912. While restrictions on the alienation of lineage riceland were not abandoned, the availability of rice as a commodity allowed for a division of labour not possible before 1912. The periodic depressions in the rice-producing areas, combined with the need for a cash income in order to pay the tax, served to create a labour force. The rebellions in the highlands after the imposition of the tax are evidence of the hardship that accompanied the demand for a cash income.

Schrieke cites evidence of the use of wage-labour prior to 1920 in

149

rubber-tapping, in the clearing of coffee gardens, and even in some rice-growing areas. Similarly, he points out that land was, in this period, also entering the commodity market. In some areas the overlapping rights of the matrilineal kin groups were relaxed, but also land which was not terraced for irrigated rice cultivation was bought and sold as individual property (*harto pantjarian*).

Finally, it seems to be the case that the period following the imposition of the tax led to the formation of a class of entrepreneurs and traders who were able to take advantage of the new markets for land, labour, and export commodities. Sarekat Islam, a Muslim modernist movement which pressed for a form of freedom and independence in the face of Dutch rule, found a good deal of support in West Sumatra in the early years of this century (Wertheim 1959).[15] The period 1910–20 was marked by the emergent conflict between the modernists and the traditionalists in the province, known respectively as the Kaum Muda (the young family or group) and the Kaum Tua (the old family).

We now have the conditions for commodity production: land and labour entering the market, as well as a growing group of entrepreneurs with sufficient assets and land to employ wage-labour. This was primarily in the export sector, but it seems that some goods for domestic consumption, such as steelware from Sawah Lawas, were also produced in this way. The evidence suggests that the entrepreneurial units were able to develop freely before 1920. The price of rice remained stable or rose slowly, while world commodity prices increased, thus making it possible for entrepreneurs to pay subsistence wages and still generate a profit from the surplus. This growth in the size of productive units, a change in the forces of production facilitated by the new relations of production, represents the first part of the cycle of petty commodity production.

In about 1923 there was a major crisis, in that the price of rice rose rapidly (Schrieke 1955–7), while world commodity prices stagnated. Although we have no good evidence on the effects in the petty commodity sector, it seems likely that there was a squeeze on entrepreneurs and workers alike. Entrepreneurs could not raise wages without vastly reducing profit margins. In the capitalist sector this was quite clearly the case. The Dutch railroads, for example, were forced to lay off a number of their workers in West Sumatra in 1923. The crisis then led to a breakdown of the larger-scale units and a return to atomized production, the other half of the cycle.

Crisis is then the result of rising rice prices. It is interesting to speculate on the possible causes of this. It seems likely in this case that rice prices rose as a direct result of the growth of petty commodity forces of production. Migration from rice-producing areas, even today, produces something of a labour crisis in those areas. The migrants tend to be the young, especially young men. The people left behind to cultivate rice and to keep irrigation systems and earthworks in good repair are the less efficient producers, particularly the old men and women who cannot find work as migrants. After a number of years of this loss of the community's labour-power, the relative inefficiency of labour, and the gradual deterioration of the paddy fields means that the production of the same amount of rice demands more labour; thus the value of rice increases and so does its price. Because rice is still produced largely on lineage land, rice production is not transformed and does not become like the other forms of commodity production.

To summarize: a rise in world commodity prices leads to an increase in the scale of production and size of productive units in the commodity sector. Labour is then absorbed into this sector. The loss of labour in the rice-producing sector results in a loss of efficiency and thus an increase in the price of rice. The increase in the price of rice, the basic staple food, causes a squeeze in the commodity sector. As contrasted to the case of the development of capitalism, the relations of production in agriculture are not broken by the effects of the new forces of production. This seems to be the result of the limited potential for growth of petty commodity production, caused by overspecialization in relation to world demands, the limits set by world price structures, and, most important, the lack of a labour force with no alternative but to accept starvation wages.

The cycle of productive forces also causes crises which lead to large-scale political disturbances. It could be argued that the crisis of 1923 eventually led to the communist uprisings of 1926–7.[16] The cycle, however, also produces crises at its downswing, i.e. when the productive units are smallest. This can best be seen for the period just after national independence in 1950.

In this period production was largely atomized as a result of political and economic turbulence of the years between 1927 and 1950. Indonesia had lost most of her prewar export markets. Estate production declined, while smallholder production increased. All the evidence for West Sumatra suggests a general economic decline which meant a return to small-scale, atomized production. Only the production of rice rose in this period. The cycle was now reversed, the situation was the opposite of that before 1923.[17]

Between 1954 and 1956 rice prices again rose sharply, as they had in the early 1920s. As before, this produced an economic crisis in the province.

Why did the price of rice rise this time? Again, the relationship between petty commodity production and the production of rice in the lineage sector should be investigated.

Geertz points out that a feature of wet-rice cultivation is that a single holding can be made to increase its yield by a margin equal to the subsistence needs of each extra labourer.[18] Thus if three people work a paddy field and produce enough for their own subsistence, then the labour of a fourth person will produce enough extra yield for his own subsistence. While it is clearly true that productivity increases with increasing labour intensivity, Geertz has, I think, exaggerated the effect. As more and more people are absorbed by a fixed amount of rice land it seems likely that marginal productivity will decrease. This means that more labour is now used to produce the same amount of rice as more and more people are absorbed into rice production.

This seems to have been the case in the 1950s, at least in West Sumatra. In the period between 1950 and 1954 rice production rose, as more people returned to farming from the petty commodity sector. This increase in production was achieved without any overall increase in the amount of land under cultivation, a fact which supports Geertz's analysis. Between 1954 and 1956, however, prices rose sharply, probably because the increased labour absorbed from the declining commodity sector was no longer producing equal marginal yields. Since, however, land is controlled by the family, these returning migrants were given access to land in spite of the declining productivity. The result, again, is a crisis in the commodity sector, although this time the squeeze occurs on the downswing of the cycle. The different political movements of the period between 1956 and 1958 must be understood in terms of this cycle.

III

I have argued that an analysis of production in any village in West Sumatra must take into account the fact that the village economy can be understood only with reference to the development of a particular form of production which I have called petty commodity production. In examining the cycle of commodity production in West Sumatra, I have further argued that the nature of the relationship to capitalism, on the one hand,[19] and to a form of lineage production, on the other, must be clearly understood in order that the dynamic of commodity production can be accurately described. In the final section of this paper I will return to blacksmithing in Sawah Lawas in order to test the usefulness of this approach to the problems of development of the smithing industry.

It is quite commonly assumed that the scale of economic organization is crucial to the development of the economy. Banfield, for example, writes that the '[l]ack of . . . association is a very important limiting factor in the way of economic development in most of the world. Except as people can create and maintain corporate organization, they cannot have a modern economy' (Banfield and Banfield 1958: 7). In his analysis of the Javanese town of Modjokuto, Geertz has written of the task of an entrepreneurial class, if they are to achieve 'take-off', that 'from an individualistic, marvelously intricate trading pattern they must move to a systematically yet simple organized firm-based "business" pattern dedicated to long-term economic ends' (Geertz 1963b: 48). Geertz goes on to point out that what he calls the 'lumpiness problem' may form an obstacle to development in Indonesia, when he suggests that there is 'some question as to whether a large-scale industrial structure can any longer rise directly out of a trade and small manufacturing pattern' (ibid.: 79). Having pointed out from his study of a Malay village that the 'small scale of organization is the most striking feature of the peasant economy', Swift (1965) suggests that the obstacles to development of larger-scale organization are the main obstacles to development.

It is, however, when they attempt to explain the small scale of economic activity that these writers run into difficulties. Banfield's thesis that it is amoral familism which is the main obstacle to economic expansion is well known. Swift lists among those features of Malay society which prevent large-scale organization: the weakness of traditional groupings and value attitudes 'such as fatalism, the short run orientation, the reluctance to alter an arrangement which is satisfactorily meeting minimum consumption needs' (1965: 170). In a brief analysis of West Sumatra, 'Minangkabau and Modernization' (1971), Swift returns to the theme of individual motivation. He argues that other Sumatran groups, like the Batak, have succeeded by 'using their patrilineal groupings in their adjustment to the modern situation and apparently being prepared to sublimate individual competition to group advantage to some extent. I suggest that the intense competitiveness of the Minangkabau is such that success as part of a group is not satisfying for the personality and cultural drives involved. I see the genius of the Minangkabau as most suited to a quick perception and grasping of short term opportunity, best exemplified in the world of petty trading' (ibid.: 265). Individualism is then put forward as an explanation. Swift goes on to suggest that '[f]rom the general viewpoint of economic development . . . We can derive some confirmation of the importance of an achievement orientation in successful modernization, with a less clear rider on the dangers of too much competitive individualism' (ibid.: 267).

Let us compare this sort of explanation with the structural explanation offered above, with reference to the blacksmithing industry in Sawah Lawas. While material on prewar economic organization in the township is hard to come by, the theory suggests that we might expect to find an expansion of the units of production in specific periods of time. In fact, in the late 1950s and early 1960s four enterprises were set up in Sawah Lawas which incorporated almost all the smaller *apa* units into larger enterprises of the manufacture-type.

The largest of these depended on a guaranteed market in the North Sumatran city of Medan. The entrepreneur sold his products to a government trading company. There was one large workshop in the township, with six work groups, but there were also ties with some fifteen other such groups producing hoes and axes. These all produced goods on order for the entrepreneur, who in turn financed the running of all the work. He bought raw materials, paid each group a piecework wage, and also arranged to provide members with cheap food and clothing at certain times of the year.

The head of the enterprise was not originally a smith, but a local merchant who, through influential contacts in Bukit Tinggi, managed to arrange a bank loan of some Rp. 2,000,000. He invested the money in tools and raw materials for about twenty workshops and the balance was kept to ensure that the smiths working for him were paid regularly. The business experienced a final decline around 1965.

The general pattern for all the enterprises is quite similar. The explanation seems to lie in the decline of imports into Indonesia, including the import of steel tools, after the regional rebellions of 1958. Wages, as in the 1920s, lagged behind price rises because the price of rice did not rise as fast as the prices of other commodities. Those with money to invest, and with access to the newly opened markets for domestically produced commodities, were able to bring together into a single enterprise a large number of workers. This in turn allowed the entrepreneurs to increase their profits. In fact, one of the entrepreneurs invested in medium-range technology which allows him to continue operations today. Again, a sharp rise in the price of rice led to a squeeze, and, with the exception of the machine shop, all the enterprises failed.

It was also in this period that domestic industry in West Sumatra experienced its greatest period of growth.[20] The most striking example was the building of a number of heavily capitalized cloth factories in Padang, the provincial capital, and in some highland towns. Since 1965 all these industries have experienced a decline, and during the period of my research there were no cloth factories operating anywhere near full productive capacity.

By assuming that the atomistic nature of economics in some peasant societies is fixed and unchanging writers such as Swift would be hard put to explain the changes that have been described here. In tracing this small-scale organization to Minangkabau ideology at a moment in time, Swift fails to account for the cycle. While his description of ideology may have been accurate, alone it cannot constitute an explanation. The arguments concerning cultural obstacles to economic change seem to call for the kind of criticism levelled by Marx and Engels against the Young Hegelians in their book *The German Ideology*:

> In direct contrast to German philosophy which descends from heaven to earth, here we ascend from earth to heaven. That is to say, we do not set out from what men say, imagine, conceive, nor from men as narrated, thought of, imagined, conceived, in order to arrive at men in the flesh. We set out from real, active men, and on the basis of their real life-process we demonstrate the development of the ideological reflexes and echoes of this life-process . . . Morality, religion, metaphysics, all the rest of ideology and their corresponding forms of consciousness, thus no longer retain the semblance of independence.

They have no history, no development; but men, developing their material production and their material intercourse, alter, along with this real existence, their thinking and the products of their thinking (Marx and Engels 1970: 47).

While in this critique of idealism the authors may have overemphasized the material basis of their theory, they nonetheless demonstrate the radical break made by the developing methodology of historical materialism, and the poverty inherent in empiricism when faced with history.

In this article I have attempted to develop a model to deal with the methodological and theoretical problems arising in the study of peasant villages that have been incorporated into a national and international society. I have attempted, in constructing a mode of production for West Sumatra, to look at the interaction of a set of productive forces and an emergent structure of productive relations. The main difference between local commodity production and capitalism seems to lie in the cyclical movement of productive forces in the former, as opposed to the revolutionary development of capitalist forces of production. This movement can be seen to be the result of a complex interaction of three separate modes of production: a lineage mode of production, petty commodity production, and capitalism. Because of the unique dynamic of petty commodity production, the nature and the causes of crises differ from the periodic crises of capitalism, although the former may arise from the latter. Finally, this has led to a reinterpretation of the problem of the scale of organization in Minangkabau society which attempts to account for changes in scale, and thus to trace other historical changes to these changes.

In this sense, then, the paper only begins to deal with the problems. It is proposed as a different and, it is hoped, more useful way of looking at Minangkabau society.

Notes

1 Lloyd (1971: 40). For similar conclusions, see Foster (1960) and Rubel *et al.* (1968).

2 Fieldwork was carried out in Sumatera Barat between December 1970 and July 1972. It was financed by a research grant from the London-Cornell Project for Southeast Asia Studies, and sponsored in Indonesia by the Indonesian Academy of Sciences. The writer would like to take this opportunity to thank Dr M. Bloch, Professor A. E. Kahn, Mr Clive Kessler, and members of the editorial collective of *Critique of Anthropology* for reading various drafts of the paper and offering many helpful suggestions.

3 In the main I have drawn on the works of Godelier (1972) and Balibar (1972) for the formulation of the relation between productive forces and the relations of production.

4 In a short paper on Minangkabau, Swift (1971) has presented a brief analysis of the economy and the special economic abilities of the Minangkabau as an ethnic group. His formulations will be presented in the last section of this paper.

5 The Minangkabau are famous throughout Indonesia for a particular form of temporary migration (*marantau*). Work on this pattern is being carried out by Mochtar Naim (see Naim 1971). For more general information on Minangkabau, see Josselin de Jong (1961) and Bachtiar (1967).

6 The exchange rate at the time of research was approximately 1000 rupiah (abbreviated Rp. 1000) to the pound.

7 For an analysis of property law in Minangkabau, see Josselin de Jong (op. cit.) and Naim (1968).

8 A temporary boom in clove prices in 1972 led to relatively large investments by outsiders in clove-producing areas. The investors 'bought' the clove trees temporarily for the time of the harvest. The buyers harvested the cloves and sold them for prices between three and four times the price paid to the owners.

9 This approach has found its way into British social anthropology, particularly in analyses of land tenure. See, for example, Gluckman (1965).

10 This analysis is most developed in *Capital*, Vol. III, with the discussion of value and price.

11 For some of Marx's observations on this form of production, see Marx (1973, Vol. I, Pt. IV). Since this article went to press the author has revised his position considerably; see Kahn (1974).

12 The so-called Padri Wars have received some attention in the literature (see Cuisinier 1959).

13 Geertz (1963a) devotes a small section of this book to a comparison of the effects of the Culture System in Java and West Sumatra. While the study claims to be an ecological one, it should be noted that the main difference between coffee and sugar cultivation was in the organization of production. In Java it was carried out within the framework of large enterprises, in Sumatra by individual planters.

14 The material used here on coffee cultivation is derived largely from Ples (1878) and Huitema (1935). Ples was a government-appointed inspector sent to West Sumatra in 1875 to investigate the state of coffee cultivation. See also Parels (1944); Kooreman (1900); Lulofs (1912); and Kielstra (1886). A review of some of the literature was carried out by Cramer (1957).

15 For an interesting analysis of the origins of the Kaum Muda–Kaum Tua conflict see Abdullah (1971, esp. Ch. 2).

16 It is not my intention to make this argument in detail here, since it is the subject of another article in preparation. The best information on the communist uprisings of 1926–7 is found in the writings of Schrieke (op. cit.) and Benda and McVey (op. cit.).

17 Analyses of the Indonesian economy in the decade after independence are found in Glassburner (1971) and Mackie (1967). Available statistics are published by the Indonesian Biro Pusat Statistik as statistical abstracts.

18 This is one of the basic postulates of *Agricultural Involution* (Geertz 1963a).

19 Frank (1965, 1969) argues that it is in fact development (by which he means the development of capitalism) that creates underdevelopment, and that economic structures in the Third World can be understood only by reference to capitalist integration. He has written: 'Underdevelopment far from being due to any supposed "isolation" of the world's people from the modern capitalist expansion . . . is the result of the integral incorporation of these people into the fully integrated but contradictory capitalist system which has long since embraced them all' (1969: 224).

20 This tends to confirm at least one aspect of Frank's analysis concerning the stagnation that may be produced by capitalist integration. He writes: 'It is also significant . . . that the satellites have managed such temporary spurts in development as they have had, during wars or depressions in the metropolis, which momentarily weakened or lessened its domination over the life of the satellites' (1965: 12). Hoogvelt and Child (1973), in an interesting analysis of the effects of sanctions on the Rhodesian economy, have come to a similar conclusion, i.e. that relative isolation from world capitalism leads to capitalist development in the satellites. LeClau (1971) has, however, warned against assuming that capitalist integration necessarily produces capitalism, a point I have stressed in this paper.

References

ABDULLAH, T. 1971. *Schools and Politics: the Kaum Muda Movement in West Sumatra*. Ithaca, NY: Cornell University Modern Indonesia Project, monograph series.

ALAVI, H. 1973. Peasant Classes and Primordial Loyalties. *Journal of Peasant Studies* 1 (1).

BACHTIAR, H. 1967. Negeri Taram. In Koentjaraningrat (ed.), *Villages in Indonesia*. Ithaca, NY.: Cornell University Press.

BALIBAR, E. 1972. The Basic Concepts of Historical Materialism. In L. Althusser and E. Balibar, *Reading 'Capital'*. London: New Left Books.

BANFIELD, E. C. and BANFIELD, L. F. 1958. *The Moral Basis of a Backward Society*. Glencoe, Ill.: Free Press.

BENDA, H. J. and MCVEY, R. T. (eds.) 1960. *The Communist Uprisings of 1926-7 in Indonesia: Key Documents*. Ithaca, NY: Cornell University Modern Indonesia Project, translation series.

CRAMER, P. J. S. 1957. *A Review of Literature on Coffee Research in Indonesia*. Turnalba, Costa Rica: Inter-American Institute of Agricultural Studies.

CUISINIER, J. 1959. La guerre des Padri. *Archives de sociologie des religions* 4.

FOSTER, G. 1960. Impersonal Relations in Peasant Society. *Human Organization* 19 (4).

FRANK, A. G. 1965. *Capitalism and Underdevelopment in Latin America*. New York: Monthly Review Press.

— 1969. *Latin America: Underdevelopment or Revolution*. New York: Monthly Review Press.

GEERTZ, C. 1963a. *Agricultural Involution*. Berkeley: University of California Press.

— 1963b. *Peddlers and Princes*. Chicago: University of Chicago Press.

GLASSBURNER, B. (ed.) 1971. *The Economy of Indonesia*. Ithaca, NY: Cornell University Press.

GLUCKMAN, M. 1965. *The Ideas in Barotse Jurisprudence*. New Haven: Yale University Press.

Joel Kahn

GODELIER, M. 1972. *Rationality and Irrationality in Economics*. London: New Left Books.
— 1974. On One Definition of a Social Formation. *Critique of Anthropology* (1): 63–73.
HOOGVELT, A. M. M., and CHILD, D. 1973. Rhodesia: Economic Blockade and Development. *Monthly Review* **25** (5).
HUITEMA, W. F. 1935. De Bevolkingskoffiecultuur op Sumatra. Wageningen: H. Veenman en Zonen.
JOSSELIN DE JONG, P. E. DE 1961. *Minangkabau and Negri Sembilan*. Leiden: Ijdo.
KAHN, J. 1974. Imperialism and the Reproduction of Capitalism: Towards a Definition of the Indonesian Social Formation. *Critique of Anthropology* (2).
KIELSTRA, E. B. 1886. De Koffiecultuur ter Westkust van Sumatra. *De Indische Gids* **11**.
KOOREMAN, P. J. 1900. De Gouvernements Koffiecultuur ter Sumatra's Westkust. *De Indische Gids* **1**.
LECLAU, E. 1971. Feudalism and Capitalism in Latin America. *New Left Review* (67).
LLOYD, P. C. 1971. *Classes, Crises and Coups*. London: MacGibbon and Kee.
LULOFS, C. 1912. Eenige Cijfers omtrent de Volkskoffie Cultuur ter Sumatra's Westkust. *Tijdschrift voor het Binnelandsch Bestuur* (42).
MACKIE, J. A. C. 1967. *Problems of the Indonesian Inflation*. Ithaca, NY: Cornell University Modern Indonesia Project, monograph series.
MARX K. 1951 (1851–2). *The Eighteenth Brumaire of Louis Bonaparte*. In Marx-Engels *Selected Works*, Vol. I. Moscow: Foreign Languages Publishing House.
— 1973 (1867–). *Capital*, Vols. I, II, and III. New York: International Publishers.
MARX, K. and ENGELS, F. 1970 (1846). *The German Ideology*. London: Lawrence and Wishart.
NAIM, M. (ed.) 1968. *Menggali Hukium Tanah dan Hukum Waris*. Minangkabau, Padang: Center for Minangkabau Studies.
— 1971. Merantau: Reasons and Effects of Minangkabau Voluntary Migration. Paper presented to 28th International Congress of Orientalists, Canberra, January 1971. Reprinted by Center for Minangkabau Studies, Padang.
PARELS, B. H. 1944. Bevolkingskoffiecultuur. In C. J. J. van Hall and C. van de Koppel (eds.), *De Langbouw in de Indische Archipel*. 'S-Gravenhage: W. van Hoeve.
PLES, D. 1878. *De Koffij-Cultuur op Sumatra's Westkust*. Batavia: Ogilvie.
REY, P.-P. and DUPRÉ, G. 1973. Reflections on the Pertinence of a Theory of the History of Exchange. *Economy and Society* **2** (2).
RUBEL, A. J., KUPFERER, H. J., *et al.* 1968. Perspectives on the Atomistic-type Society. *Human Organization* **27** (3)
SCHRIEKE, B. J. O. 1955–7. *Indonesian Sociological Studies*. The Hague: van Hoeve.
SWIFT, M. G. 1965. *Malay Peasant Society in Jelebu*. LSE Monographs on Social Anthropology. London: Athlone Press.
— 1971. Minangkabau and Modernization. In H. R. Hiatt and C. Jayawardena (eds.), *Anthropology in Oceania*. Sydney: Angus and Robertson.
TERRAY, E. 1972. *Marxism and 'Primitive' Societies*. New York: Monthly Review Press.
WERTHEIM, W. F. 1959. *Indonesian Society in Transition*. The Hague and Bandung: van Hoeve.

DOMINANCE DETERMINATION AND EVOLUTION

Jonathan Friedman

Tribes, States, and Transformations
Translated by the author

INTRODUCTION

The Kachin of Upper Burma have gained a great deal of renown among
anthropologists since the publication of Leach's *Political Systems of
Highland Burma*. Although they were already receiving some attention
from Granet, Lévi-Strauss, and others interested in the development of
kinship systems, it is not until Leach that we get a clear documentation
of the apparent oscillation between 'egalitarian' and ranked or even
stratified social forms. It is not my intention here to discuss Leach's
work in detail, since that would require a separate treatment which
would be somewhat peripheral to the purpose of this analysis. Rather,
using material from Leach and others, I shall attempt to present the
Kachin in terms of a larger theoretical model in which what appears as
oscillation is but part of a multilinear development generated by a
specific structure of social reproduction, and the evolution of 'Asiatic'
states as well as devolution towards more permanently 'egalitarian'
big-man societies both result from the underlying properties of a single
tribal system.

GENERAL MODEL

The goal of the following analysis is to account for a number of societies
distributed in space in terms of a model of social reproduction which
distributes them in time. Much emphasis has been laid by structuralists
and functionalists alike on the distinction between synchrony and
diachrony. For a great number of anthropologists, history is little more
than a stream of events, somehow outside of social structure, and
usually opposed to it. Even for evolutionists, the social forms that
characterize the major stages such as band, tribe, and state are assumed
to be institutional forms whose properties are fixed with respect to time.
Evolution is thus reduced to something that occurs between stages,
rather than presented as the outcome of processes that are inherent in
the social forms themselves. Lévi-Strauss is perhaps the only anthropologist who has dealt systematically with social variation, and he must

certainly be credited with having gone beyond the simple empiricism of his predecessors in order to arrive at the deeper structures which might generate such variation. But he has assumed that anthropologists, working as they do with ethnographic material, are restricted to variation in space, whereas historians can deal only with variation in time. In effect, structuralist models do reveal the family relations among a number of different social forms, but they do not account for the mechanisms that produce the variants. The marxist approach must transcend the false dichotomy between synchrony and diachrony by making the object of analysis the system of social reproduction, a system whose properties can be defined only with respect to time. These are precisely the properties to which Marx refers when he speaks of the 'laws of motion' of society. In such an approach, history is incorporated into the field of analysis rather than being separated from it. The 'stream of events' ceases to exist as an autonomous phenomenon. It is, on the contrary, something that can be derived from the properties of the system of social reproduction itself.

Structures of social reproduction are not of the same order as institutional structures. A kinship structure can easily be described without reference to time. It is only when we consider its reproduction that we are forced to account for another kind of relation, that which links kinship to production and distribution, which determines its function with respect to other institutions as well as to techno-environmental conditions. In order to deal with this latter set of intersystemic relations, we must necessarily take the entire social formation into account, for it is only from its internal properties that we can generate the system of transformations which is manifested in the actual historical and geographical distribution of observable societies.

The social formation includes several distinguishable functional levels:

1 Forces of production—including here, for the sake of simplicity, the exploited ecological niches; in other words, the totality of the technical conditions of reproduction.
2 Social relations of production—the set of social (i.e. non-technical) relations which determine the internal rationality of the economy, the specific use to be made of the means of production and the distribution of total social labour-time and product.
3 Superstructure—ideological and political structures whose contents may be derived from, and whose functions must be defined in terms of, the existent relations of production and conditions of reproduction. In *Capital*, Marx attempts to demonstrate the way in which profit, interest, and rent are second-order ideological categories derived from the division of surplus value according to capitalist relations of production.

We must stress here that the above categories are functional and not cultural. It is absolutely necessary not to confuse the levels of functioning of a social formation with the cultural institutions that take on those functions. What appears as 'religion' in terms of a number of inherent cultural characteristics might function as superstructure in one society and as relations of production in another. This is not to deny, of course, that the internal structure of the 'institution' determines its behaviour. It is only to distinguish it from the structure of material reproduction of which it is a part, its specific causality depending on the place which it occupies in that structure. Money-capital has the same internal properties whether it is restricted to children's games or dominates the process of production, but its material effects are vastly different.

The levels of the social formation are integrated in a single structure of reproduction which can be represented in the following way (*Figure 1*):

Figure 1 Model of Social Reproduction

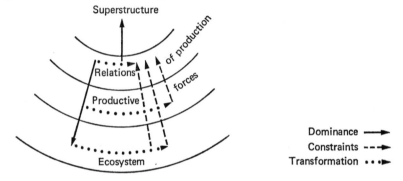

Superstructure

Relations

of production

Productive

forces

Ecosystem

Dominance ⟶
Constraints --⟶
Transformation ••⟶

Each of the above levels can be characterized by what has been called relative autonomy. This is not a question, as for some Althusserians, of partial functional independence, but rather one of the autonomy of internal structural properties (Friedman 1971). Unlike a number of materialists, we do not suppose that the different levels of a social formation emerge one from another (Harris 1968; Meillassoux 1972). On the contrary, the variation and development of the subsystems depend directly on their internal structures and their intrasystemic contradictions. But the realization of these internal tendencies depends in turn on the intersystemic relations that link the subsystems. These relations are of two types: from the ecosystem up is a hierarchy of constraints which determines the limits of functional compatibility between levels, hence of their internal variation. This is essentially a negative determination, since it determines what can not occur but not what must occur. We stress, however, that it is the internal properties of the various subsystems which determine the constraints of the larger whole, in that they define the set of possible relations which can unite those systems in the process of reproduction. Thus functional compatibility depends ultimately on the structures which must be combined

163

in the social formation. If the technical conditions of production are determinant 'in the last instance' it is because the structure of the productive forces sets the outer limits on the variation and development of all the other levels.

Working in the opposite direction, the relations of production dominate the entire functioning of the larger system, defining the specificity of the mode of production and its developmental tendencies. Intersystemic contradictions appear when the dominant relations of production cause several subsystems to reach their limits of functional compatibility.

Determination and dominance are assumed here to be structurally independent. Relations of production are not caused by the constraints of the productive forces. They can only be said to be fully determined where there exist necessary and sufficient constraints, i.e. where no other set of social relations could operate the process of social reproduction. This would appear never to be the case, however, and it has certainly never been demonstrated, though often implied. Similarly, we must reject, as a variant of mechanical materialism, the notion propounded by Balibar and others of 'structural causality' where,

> In different structures, the economy is determinant in that it determines which of the instances of the social structure occupies the dominant position (Balibar in Althusser and Balibar 1968, II: 110; my translation).

Here, again, while admitting the existence of a 'relatively autonomous' dominant structure, it is assumed that the material aspect of social relations of production (material flows) determines the social form which it will take, so that dominance becomes but a secondarily derived aspect of determination. While technological determinism is rejected, material flows, instead of being organized by social relations of production, appear as independent and determinant of those social relations. This seems an excessive attempt at reification of the material level, in the purely physical sense, as opposed to other levels of social life. The position adopted here is that *social relations are material relations if they dominate the process of material production and reproduction and that they owe their origin not to that which they dominate but to the social properties of the previous system of reproduction as a whole.*

While it is necessary to separate dominance from determination when considering the genesis of the levels of the social formation, this does not deny the simultaneity of their presence in the process of reproduction. From the point of view of the *functioning* of the social formation, constraints are always present in reproduction—to the extent that the properties of the forces of production, for example a production function, are felt in the spheres of accumulation and distribution of social product, more generally, to the extent that certain functions must be fulfilled by the existing institutional structures if they are to reproduce

164

themselves successfully. In the example we shall discuss, the manner in which a given social system uses its techno-environment profoundly alters its own conditions of reproduction by causing the emergence of a new set of constraints which are incompatible with the dominant social relations of production, and which therefore imply a transformation of the mode of production. Conversely, in other conditions of production, the internal dynamic of the social economy leads to the evolution of a new mode of production (class–state formation) without any major change in the technological base, or where such change is largely the outcome of the reorganization and intensification of existing productive forces, a process dominated by evolving relations of production. In the following analysis, we shall see, beginning with a single set of productive relations, how the interplay of internal variation, structural dominance, and intersystemic contradiction generates a multilinear evolution of the social formation.

SPECIFIC MODEL

Our point of departure is the Kachin of the Triangle region of Upper Burma. This is the region of lowest population density (5–6/mi^2), the highest percentage of primary forest, and greatest soil fertility.[1] Beginning with these optimal conditions of production, we shall attempt to show how the functioning of a specific social system generates several different types of transformation in time. The environment which determines the conditions of production is not simply a limiting factor. It is also a variable subject to change as the result of human activity, a part of the production process as well as a determinant. As such, the transformations that occur include significant changes in the conditions of production themselves.

TECHNOLOGY AND ECOLOGY

The Kachin are swidden agriculturalists whose principal crop is dry rice, which they cultivate on mountain slopes. Given the conditions of abundant rainfall and rich soils, swiddening yields a considerable annual surplus with a minimum labour input. This form of technology, however, has certain very critical properties with respect to the local ecology. In order to maintain high productivity it is absolutely necessary to maintain the soil fertility, the latter depending largely on the ratio of years of cultivation to years of fallow. The normal cultivation/fallow cycle is in the range 1/14 to 1/20, the upper limit being 1/12. If fallow is shortened to under twelve years the optimal conditions for reforestation are no longer operant. Beyond this threshold, fertility and labour productivity progressively decrease. More labour is required, owing especially to the increased need for weeding, which becomes the most time-consuming activity in the labour process. There may be less

165

organic matter to burn, the soil is more exposed to erosion, and output per acre is generally much lower. This lower limit for fallowing defines an upper limit for demographic density, since, in order to maintain the 1/12 ratio, any working population must have at its disposal thirteen times more arable land than it uses in one season.

A given technology in given environmental conditions constitutes a techno-ecological system whose internal properties impose a certain number of constraints on the functioning of the productive relations by determining the outer limits of technical reproduction of a population at a given level of productivity. The technology, however, is quite neutral with respect to the process of reproduction, and it is the relations of production themselves which determine the way a population will behave towards its own limit conditions.

In fact, one of the transformations we shall discuss consists precisely in violating the optimal limits of forest regeneration, resulting in ecological degradation, a gradual succession to secondary forest and grassland. Leach's so-called 'ecological zones' (Leach 1964: 22–8) are not natural zones but rather the result of the progressive over-intensification of a basically extensive technology, a phenomenon which is more closely linked to increasing population density than to any other factor. While rainfall is perhaps lower in the eastern regions of the Kachin Hills, though not significantly so (80–100″/yr as opposed to 100–150″/yr—both are areas of rapid regrowth), the cultivation/fallow cycle is everywhere below optimal conditions, ranging from 1/10 to 2/10, 2/8, and worse. This appears to be due directly to population densities that are three to five times greater than in the Triangle region (reports of land shortage are frequent in these areas). With increasing degradation there are a number of more or less elaborate adaptations which occur. The extensive use of nitrogen-fixing bean crops is widespread among the eastern Kachin. Among all groups except the Triangle Kachin, the hoe is an indispensable item for working the increasingly difficult soil. We often find some kind of crop rotation, with beans and less demanding grains such as millet and job's tears replacing rice. Among the Chin we find the most elaborate system of rotation in the area, with cycles of 4/30, 5/40, 6/18, etc., in which peas play an important role in maintaining fertility. The Chin, as opposed to other groups, can still get fairly good per-acre yields, but at a much increased labour cost. Irrigated terracing, which occurs among the Angami Naga and some eastern Kachin, may be an adaptation to extreme land shortage in areas of steep slopes, where dry terracing used to prevent soil runoff could easily be transformed into irrigation in the presence of high rainfalls. As it does permit high settlement density, it might occur where there is a great deal of intervillage warfare, although this is by no means necessary. In any case, irrigation is not to be thought of as a technological innovation but as the most extreme form of intensification. While yields per acre are again fairly good, though much lower than in ideal swiddening conditions, the labour productivity is very low and there is little possibility of rapidly expanding the cultivated area. This is in contradiction to the demands of the kind of tribal economy we shall describe, and groups which do use terracing revert to swidden cultivation wherever possible.

The ecological degradation and consequent technological modifications described above are the outcome of the dominance of a particular set of social relations, but they in turn cause a radical transformation of those relations.

RELATIONS OF PRODUCTION

Leach has shown how Kachin society seems to oscillate between two political forms, one 'egalitarian' (*gumlao*) without any sort of chiefship, where the largest political unit is the village, and the other, hierarchical (*gumsa*), characterized by the existence of large domains headed by hereditary chiefs and their aristocratic relatives.[2] For the purposes of this argument we shall begin with the system at its structural origin point (*gumlao*) in order to outline its laws of development towards centralized hierarchy as well as the contradictions that cause its breakdown.

PRODUCTION UNITS AND LOCAL LINEAGES

While the household is the smallest unit of consumption and cooperation, the local lineage (minor lineage) is the main unit of appropriation and exchange. This patrilineal, patrilocal group contains four or five households linked by a single altar dedicated to a common ancestor. Several such local lineages form a hamlet (*kahtawng*), which usually clears a single field. This in turn is divided into smaller lineage plots. A number of tasks such as clearing, burning, and maintaining footpaths are communal activities, but actual cultivation and appropriation is a local lineage affair. Several hamlets of ten or more houses (not more than thirty) form a village cluster (*mare*) which in *gumlao* polity delimits the universe within which most alliances are contracted and in *gumsa* society becomes a political domain headed by a chief (*duwa*). Demographic growth leads directly to territorial expansion, a continuous dispersion of the population, which more or less maintains density at a level permitting forest regeneration and high efficiency of agricultural exploitation. One might perhaps speak of an optimal settlement size which would enable most villagers to have their fields within easy reach. One might even be tempted to see the hamlet or lineage as a necessarily determined unit of cooperation. While one can certainly speak of theoretical optima for settlement size with regard to specific tasks, it would be a serious mistake to assume that cooperative units were technologically determined. This is the kind of error made by a number of marxists (Terray 1969; Meillassoux 1972), who confuse the fact of

167

cooperation with the social form that it takes.[3a] Clearing, burning, and cultivation are all necessary tasks, but the nature of the groups that perform them is not technologically determined. Among the Lamet, a group of only three or four households will clear and burn a field. Among the Naga, a village of several hundred households may perform the task. Further, local lineage appropriation is not the outcome of technological necessity but is a socially determined phenomenon. The larger cooperative group and the village cluster within which most exchanges take place might perhaps be linked to the long-term needs of social reproduction, especially if success in agriculture were variable over time. But, even if this were the case, I would argue that the modality of these longer-term relations, e.g. alliance, exchange, feasting, is predicated on the existence of separate *socially defined units of appropriation*, so that the argument for technological necessity is to a large extent vitiated. In the last analysis, all that can be claimed is a technological necessity for some form of distribution and cooperation, but we cannot tell from the forces of production what this form will be. In any case, the relations within the larger group are quite variable and are clearly dominated by factors other than the technological needs of long-term cooperation. Alliances can be restricted to the village or extended into a much larger region, and distributive feasts are not attempts to overcome variable productivity, which does not appear to pose a problem in this kind of techno-ecology, but essential elements in the political economy of the tribal system, whose existence can only be explained historically, with reference to the preceding mode of production.

What emerges, then, is that a number of necessary technical activities are organized socially rather than the social organization being determined by those activities.

The members of a hamlet or village cluster all believe in a common descent from a single distant ancestor–founder, who is simultaneously the territorial spirit. Higher levels of lineage segmentation are poorly defined in *gumlao* society. But in spite of this lack of genealogical precision which, moreover, allows for the manipulation of kinship relations, the local lineage ancestors, territorial spirits, celestial spirits, and the highest deity (*ga nat*) are all linked in a single segmentary structure which, as we shall see, is instrumental in the evolution of *gumsa* hierarchies.

EXCHANGE AND THE ARTICULATION OF ALLIANCE
AND DESCENT

The Kachin are one of the classic examples of a society practising generalized exchange. As detailed analyses by Lévi-Strauss and Leach of this aspect of Kachin society already exist, we shall restrict ourselves to a number of points that are necessary for our discussion.

Generalized exchange can be defined minimally by a proscription against taking a wife from either the same patrilineage or from wife-taking lineages, i.e. a negation of endogamy and restricted or patri-lateral exchange. This leaves a man the possibility of either renewing alliances to former wife-givers and wife-takers or establishing new alliances. The former case is equivalent to matrilateral cross-cousin mar-riage, but the latter defines the same kind of global structure in which all lineages are linked in one or more circles of wife-givers (*mayu*) and wife-takers (*dama*). The only difference is in the degree to which the same alliance circles are reproduced over the generations. As such, we might speak of a more or less open system depending on the percentage of new alliances over time. Open systems are closely correlated with political and economic expansion, where the population included in the circles expands and where there is consequently a multiplication of new lineage segments (Lehman 1963: 97).

Demographic growth has the effect of translating lineage segmenta-tion into local segmentation. As the local lineage has a depth of only three or four generations, all segments which are beyond this narrowly circumscribed sphere are lost through genealogical amnesia. This effect is greatly reinforced by the high rate of emigration, which is linked to the dispersed settlement pattern. As a result, the local lineage contains but a few households at any one time. Segmentation tends, thus, to become fission, which in turn has a significant effect on the alliance structure, since the local lineage remains the only stable unit of exogamy. The articulation of lineage fissioning and generalized exchange produces a situation in which kin are continually transformed into potential allies. And, as the alliance relation is the dominant politico-economic relation in this society, as *mayu/dama* is the form of ranking,[3b] the structural preconditions of extensive hierarchization are well established.

The principal internal or intrasystemic contradiction of generalized exchange is the incompatibility between the transitivity of indebtedness, and thus of relative rank, implied by the asymmetrical relation and the closure of the marriage circle, which implies that the lowest-ranked group can become wife-giver to the highest.

$$\begin{cases} A \to B \to C \to \dots N \to A \\ A > B > C \quad \dots N > A \end{cases}$$

While this contradiction is always latent, it is not necessarily realized. In *gumlao* society, differences of rank do not exist at the lineage level. There is, perhaps, a kind of ritual superiority of a MB or WF with respect to his ZS or son-in-law, but this applies only to individual rela-tives and is not transitive. Further, and this is more important, small marriage circles of five or six lineages tend to maintain a single low brideprice for all groups, reinforcing equality through a strict control over exchange-values.

However, the very structure of generalized exchange allows for the kind of differentiation that would be blocked in a system of restricted

169

exchange. The unilaterality of the circulation of women defines the structural necessity of exchange goods that circulate in the opposite direction. The existence of such prestige goods (*hpaga*) permits the possibility of a valuation of women, of an alliance, or of the lineage itself, all of which is expressed in the variation of brideprice. But the motive force behind the rise and fall of brideprice can only be found outside the sphere of circulation.

DISTRIBUTIVE FEASTS AND THE POLITICAL ECONOMY OF THE LOCAL LINEAGE

While generalized exchange is the structural basis for the development of ranking, it does not furnish us with necessary and sufficient conditions for such a development. There is, however, another institution, the community feast (*manao*), which links production directly to social differentiation.

A local lineage that produces a substantial surplus can prepare a feast for the entire community. Buffalo (*mithan*) are sacrificed and their meat distributed along with a number of rice dishes and a great deal of rice beer. These *manao*, in which the host represents the entire community before the spirits of fertility and prosperity, greatly increase his prestige. The capacity to produce a large surplus demonstrates the importance and influence of lineage ancestors with the higher spirits who appear as the source of all prosperity and wealth. Prestige so

Figure 2 Political Economy of the Local Lineage

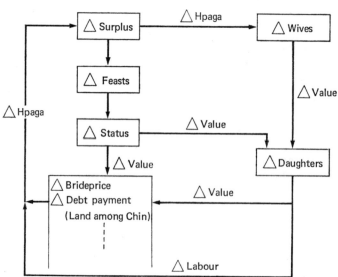

Value refers to an implicit transfer of status as opposed
to real transactions (hpaga, labour)

attained is converted into relative rank in the matrimonial circuit. By raising the 'social value' of the lineage, the value of its daughters is also raised, and they can, thereafter, only be married at higher prices. In this way, surplus that is converted into prestige generates affinal ranking. Matrimonial exchange and distributive feasts are thus linked in a single process of social reproduction.

Figure 2 represents a positive feedback system in which the accumulation of prestige is converted into increasing rank differentiation and a simultaneous growth of absolute surplus, which amplifies the same cycle of accumulation. Lineage surplus enters directly into two circuits. First, it is used to acquire wives in a political strategy whose twofold function is the validation of status and the increase in the size of the local work-force, hence the surplus available for feasting.

$$\text{surplus} \longrightarrow \text{wives} \longrightarrow \left\{ \begin{array}{c} \text{children} \\ + \\ \triangle\,\text{children} \end{array} \right\} \longrightarrow \left\{ \begin{array}{c} \text{surplus} \\ + \\ \triangle\,\text{surplus} \end{array} \right\}$$

Second, it is converted, by means of community feast-giving, into prestige, which is then transformed into higher relative rank through the marriage of lineage daughters.

$$\text{surplus} \longrightarrow \text{prestige} \longrightarrow \text{rank} \longrightarrow \left\{ \begin{array}{c} \text{prestations} \\ + \\ \triangle\,\text{prestations} \end{array} \right\} \longrightarrow \left\{ \begin{array}{c} \text{surplus} \\ + \\ \triangle\,\text{surplus} \end{array} \right\}$$

The functioning of this system transforms the egalitarian marriage circles into a political and economic hierarchy of wife-givers and wife-takers. The end-product is not, of course, a simple transitive ordering but, rather, a regrouping of lineages into more or less closed circles of allies capable of paying a similar brideprice, i.e. a spiral of ranking, where at each level there are a number of lineages of approximately equal status. The *mayu/dama* hierarchy is generated by the differential accumulation of prestige, which depends in the last instance on the production of lineage surplus. But this resultant structure does not suffice to account for the nature of *gumsa* polity. We have still to explain the institutional form taken by lineage ranking: the hereditary chiefs, the aristocracy which surrounds them (elder brother lineages), and the commoners. In order to understand the passage from relative *mayu/dama* ranking to chiefdoms we must analyse the segmentary structure that links local lineages to one another in a network extending from ancestors to the supernatural world of territorial and celestial spirits (*Figure 3*).

RELIGION, 'PROPERTY', AND THE FORMATION OF DOMAINS

In the course of *gumsa* evolution, higher segmentary levels become more clearly defined to the extent that they begin to assume important

171

Figure 3 Spirit-Ancestor Hierarchy

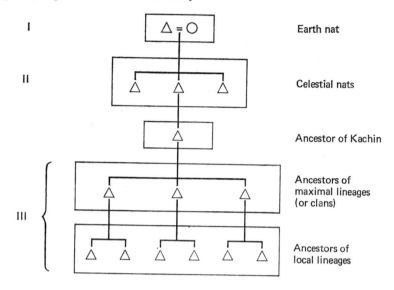

political functions. The principal levels, however, remain invariant throughout *gumsa/gumlao* oscillation.

All the lineages of a single territory are integrated in a series of increasingly inclusive segments in such a way that lineage and local segmentation always coincide and where local marriages can always be defined as endogamous in terms of higher genealogical levels.

The spirits (*nats*) are, in effect, no more than distant ancestors, but they posses 'imaginary' functions that are critical for social reproduction and are the condition foɪ the appearance of a new social relation. The supernature projection of the lineage structure is not, contrary to Leach (1964: 264), a simple reflection of a more concrete social reality. It is an integral part of that reality. The ancestor of the local group is the spirit who controls the welfare of his descendants and it is only through this spirit that one can approach the more powerful deities that are the source of all prosperity and fertility.

Community feasts are religious feasts whosc dual function is the distribution of surplus/accumulation of prestige and the propitiation of higher spirits in order to increase the wealth and prosperity of the entire group. We might best characterize this as a religion of productivity in which the real work process is inverted in its immediate appearance. Surplus is represented not as the product of surplus labour, but as the 'work of the gods'.

Now, if we place the model of lineage political economy in this more complete structural context we can, I think, deduce a series of logical steps whereby surplus is eventually converted into the absolute superiority of a hereditary chief.

1 A wealthy lineage head, A, who can afford to give great feasts to the entire village can only do so because he has good harvests.
2 But the way in which one gets such harvests is by sacrificing to the local and celestial spirits. That is, wealth is not the product of labour and control over others' labour but the 'work of the gods'.
3 Thus, if A is successful, it must be because he has more influence with the spirits.
4 But 'influence' can only be the result of a closer genealogical relationship.
5 Therefore, A must be more closely related to the local spirits, which is where the chain of supernatural communication begins.
6 The claim that A's lineage is the same as that of the local spirit, and that his ancestor is therefore the territorial deity, is perfectly natural.

Thus, the internal logic of the fetishized representation of the work process determines the form taken by political development. A chiefly lineage is simply one that succeeds in inserting itself at a higher segmentary level of the community's genealogical structure.

Figure 4 Religion and Political Transformation

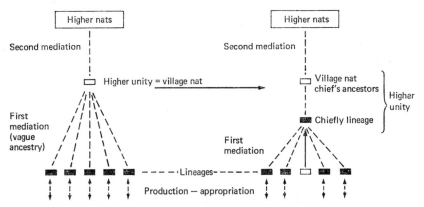

The chiefly lineage is, by definition, descended from the founder ancestor. It is therefore the lineage of the territorial spirit (*mung nat*) that ensures the continued prosperity of the entire group. This development, which takes place within a single structure, is clearly manifested in the transformation of community ritual. Among all Kachin there are three main communal spirits: the territorial spirit (*mung nat*); the chief celestial spirit (*madai nat*—or some other representative of this group); the supreme earth/sky spirit (*ga/shadip*—the male half, the *ga nat*, is dominant in ritual). Although in both *gumlao* and *gumsa* societies every household has altars to its own ancestors, control over communal spirits is not identically distributed in the two political forms.

173

	gumlao	gumsa
mung nat	*numshang*	chief's house
madai nat	*numshang*	chief's house
ga nat	*numshang*	*numshang*

numshang =
         communal altar

Among *gumlao* Kachin, all community ritual is held at the village altar. Among *gumsa* Kachin, two of the major spirits have been moved to the chief's house. But since the *mung nat* is the chief's direct ancestor and *madai* a distant relative, it is quite natural that their altars belong to him. Furthermore, he is, following again the logic of his segmentary position, the only member of the community who can make offerings to the *ga nat*, although he may give special dispensation to other wealthy aristocrats. His monopoly over the communal spirits assures his position as a necessary mediator between the community as a whole and the imaginary powers that control its survival. We stress, however, that the structure of the chiefdom is already present in the relation between the community and the territorial spirit. A formerly reflexive ideological relation, that of the community to itself mediated by the founder ancestor spirit, becomes a new socio-economic relation when a living lineage begins to occupy the previously 'empty category' defined by the imaginary segmentary locus at which all ancestral lines meet.

It would be quite wrong to characterize *gumsa* society as feudal. Lineage property does, of course, exist, but this only pertains to moveables such as prestige goods (*hpaga*) used in the numerous debt and bridewealth transactions. One of the principal *hpaga* items is cattle, which are accumulated in brideprice and slaughtered in distributive feasts as part of the cycle of conversion of surplus into prestige.[4]

Land, however, is strictly communal. It never enters the circulation sphere and so cannot be accumulated like other goods. The fact that groups immigrating to the domain of another chief often become wife-takers to residents and receive land to cultivate does not alter the state of affairs, since what is 'transferred' is a right to use communal land just like members of the 'original' resident group and not private control over specific plots. This is very unlike the situation among the Chin, where land titles commonly circulate and can be accumulated in brideprice and debt payments. Among the Kachin there is but one 'land title' defined in terms of a single common founder–ancestor. A chief owes his sovereignty not to the ownership of land but to his descent from the *mung nat*. As such, he represents the 'higher unity' of the community in a way that closely resembles the notion elaborated by Marx in his discussion of the 'Asiatic mode of production', where for tribes, as for states, this 'unity' might be 'expressed in the person of the despot or in that imaginary tribal entity which is the god' (Marx 1968b: 438, my translation).

174

The relations of production we have discussed are articulated in a unified structure that can be represented as in *Figure 5*.

Figure 5 Articulation of Relations of Production

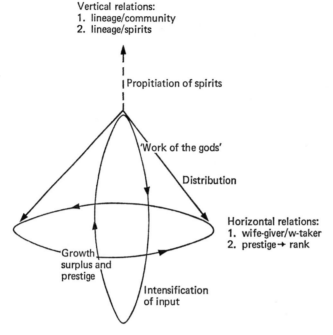

Religious feasts, the segmentary structure, the relation chief/community might all be designated as vertical, as opposed to the horizontal alliance and exchange relations. The close interdependence of the two structures is clearly revealed in the evolution of *gumsa* forms.

vertical: feast→prestige
horizontal: prestige→affinal rank
vertical: affinal rank→segmentary rank

This last transformation is decisive in that it determines the specific form of the *gumsa* domain. In the emergence of the chiefdom the *mayu/dama* relation is RE-presented simultaneously as an elder/younger relation between lineage ancestors.[5] In this way, relative affinal ranking is converted into absolute social age with respect to a common ancestor. This process generates a necessary 'after the fact' endogamy since local lineages united by marriage are immediately included, by definition, in a higher-order segment. As the territorial spirit is also the community founder, the chiefly lineage which is descended from it is by definition the senior lineage in the domain, and all other affinal ranks can be re-designated in terms of segmentary distance from this line, i.e. in terms of the genealogical proximity of local lineage ancestors to the *mung nat*. This accounts for the fact that aristocratic wife-takers to the chiefly

175

lineage are simultaneously classed as sibling lineages (elB lines where succession is by ultimogeniture—see note 5). What we have, in effect, is the development of a conical clan where lineages linked by marriage have an absolute rank position determined by their genealogical distance from the chiefly line (*Figure 6*).

Figure 6 Formation of the Conical Clan

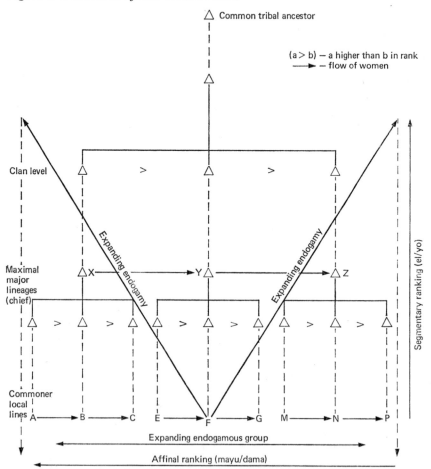

In this chart, two kinds of rank are represented simultaneously. Affinal rank, shown horizontally, is transformed into segmentary rank for lineage ancestors. But ancestors are not simply a time-depth phenomenon. They can be taken to represent 'older', and therefore, senior branches. Structurally, age-ranking and affinal ranking are equivalent since they are generated in the same genealogical space. While, for example, X, Y, or Z appears as the parent to three sibling lineages, it is in fact a senior branch to them. It is not merely an ancestor, but a living local lineage having affinal relations with other lineages of the same 'age-rank' (corresponds to Leach's rank-class). The transforming of affinal rank into segmentary rank implies that local lineage exogamy will always define a larger endogamous group at a higher genealogical level, which is by definition a higher level of social rank. In this way, the formation of a domain entails the formation of conical clan structure.

176

The evolution of the conical clan varies with the degree of hier-archization and only appears to be a well-established form in the Triangle zone and in Assam, where there were large *gumsa* domains and a certain development of class stratification. The conical tendency, however, is always present and has only escaped the attention of certain anthropologists because of an excessive empiricism that would treat the conical clan as a fixed institution while ignoring the internal processes

Figure 7 Gumsa Domain: Structure and Marriage Relations

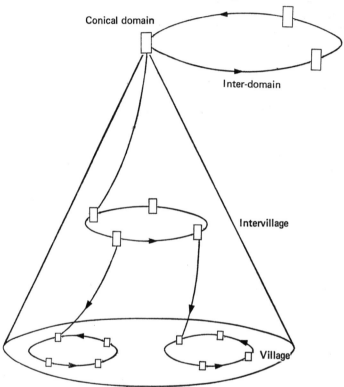

by which it is generated. Fried (1957), for example, who categorically opposes the conical to the egalitarian clan, is forced to relegate the mechanisms of the former's evolution to factors external to kinship structure. Leach, on the other hand, seems to ignore the existence of conical formations because of the rigid distinction he makes between the local lineage, which is a concrete entity, and the higher orders of the segmentary structure, which appear as mere 'ideological' projections. We have tried to show, contrary to these authors, that the formation of the conical clan is a logically implied aspect of the evolution of chief-doms. The fact that the territorial spirit is also the community founder already defines a necessary endogamy among the included local lineages, though this may remain a purely ideological phenomenon in *gumlao*

177

society. When, however, a chiefly lineage comes to occupy that key position, the segmentary structure which was formerly latent in the supernatural realm redefines the rank relations between all local groups. As the ancestral hierarchy is also the hierarchy of territorial spirits, the political segmentation of the conical clan is identical with local and lineage segmentation. This isomorphism is not an institutional fact. Territorial spirits only exist *for* communities. They do not float about in a supernatural ether, waiting to be called upon when the need arises. The fact, however, that political communities, no matter what their size, trace their ancestral lines back to a territorial spirit implies that expanding chiefdoms will have the same structure at all levels. The smallest local units will possess spirits who are in turn the descendants of higher spirits representing more inclusive areas.

Gumsa domains result from the extension of the above-described processes to increasingly larger territories (*Figure 7*). Every domain must have, by definition, a single paramount chief below whom there are aristocrats who rule smaller domains, village clusters, or single hamlets. All levels are linked by the matrilateral and segmentary ties that characterize the Kachin conical clan. It must be remembered, however, that while the conical clan is the form that finally emerges in *gumsa* evolution, the alliance structure is the dominant relation in so far as it is the means by which hierarchy is established in the first place.

ECONOMIC FLOWS

All material flows in Kachin society are channelled through the vertical and horizontal structures that constitute the relations of production.

A chief, once established, receives tribute and corvée from his dependants. This follows directly from the logic of his position. In *gumlao* society a certain amount of surplus is used in community sacrifices to the territorial spirit, but the latter, as a relatively easily satiated ancestor, has a low cost of maintenance. We find an analogous situation in *gumsa* society, except that the cost now includes the living descendants of that spirit, who have a necessary imaginary role in communicating with their ancestors, who ensure the economic reproduction of the society. Tribute consists in a small but historically variable proportion of the annual crop, much of which is returned in the great *manao* feasts. It is not surprising in this respect that the chief's house is referred to as the 'paddy store' (*htingsan*). We note here that feasts are no longer distributive activities but have become entirely redistributive. Corvée amounts to the cultivation of the chief's greatly expanded fields as a *communal duty* indistinguishable ideologically from other communal tasks such as the clearing of the village field and maintenance of footpaths. The output of this labour is similarly channelled back into redistributive feasts. A certain portion of the surplus obtained in tribute and corvée is used by the chief in matrimonial exchanges and it appears that chiefly marriages were very elaborate affairs indeed (Scott and Hardiman 1900, Pt I, Vol. I: 415). The tribute/corvée relation is clearly expressed, both ideologically and materially, in the obligation of all members of the domain to send to the chief the hind quarter of any animal hunted or sacrificed in 'his territory', and all such paramount chiefs are referred to as 'thigh-eating' chiefs.

Chiefly surplus is supplemented in a very important way by the output of slaves. The latter are produced by capture and by internal indebtedness—mechanisms to which we shall return in the next section. Slaves invariably belong to the paramount chief, although an aristocrat may often possess several. They are either internal (*tinung mayam*) or external (*ngong mayam*) slaves. The former live in the chief's house and are to all practical purposes equivalent to other members of his family. He pays their very low brideprice, but is entitled to all of the surplus they produce. In this they are similar to permanent children. External slaves have their own households and may be settled in other villages and are in most respects like low-status commoners, except that they pay a heavier tribute, which includes half the brideprice received for daughters, numerous first fruits, and every alternate calf born. This relation is surely an incipient form of class structure, and it is conceivable that it might develop not only as a result of capture, but also when villagers become heavily indebted to their chiefs.

Horizontal flows consist primarily of exchanges between allies. Matrimonial prestations are prolonged over many years and vary in size according to the rank of the lineages involved. Conversely, rank may vary according to the wealth of the lineage and its ability to meet a given price level. We note, however, that what appears at the local level as a horizontal flow may well turn out to be vertical from the per-

Figure 8 Economic Flows in the Gumsa System

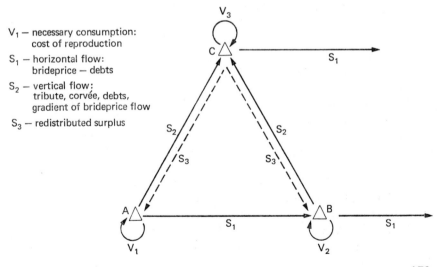

V_1 — necessary consumption:
    cost of reproduction

S_1 — horizontal flow:
    brideprice — debts

S_2 — vertical flow:
    tribute, corvée, debts,
    gradient of brideprice flow

S_3 — redistributed surplus

spective of the global structure. We refer to the gradient of brideprice as the degree to which bridewealth flows upward to nodal points in the hierarchy rather than remaining at the same rank level. This depends on the percentage of hypogamous marriages and the brideprice differential between ranks. When we consider the total affinal network, we may find that local horizontal flows serve ultimately to increase the rate of accumulation in the chiefly lineage.

Figure 8 summarizes the principal flows in *gumsa* hierarchies. The two most significant ratios are S_1/S_2 which measures the degree of hierarchization, i.e. the relative weight of vertical as opposed to horizontal flows, and S_2/S_3 which measures the degree of reciprocity in the redistributive sector. The evolution of the *gumsa* system entails an increase in both of these ratios, that is, a growing control by chiefs over the total social surplus.

$$\left. \begin{array}{l} S_t\!\!-\!\!\begin{array}{l}\text{total}\\\text{surplus}\end{array} \quad \dfrac{d^2S_2}{dS_1^2}>0 \\[2em] S_c\!\!-\!\!\begin{array}{l}\text{surplus}\\\text{controlled}\\\text{by chief}\end{array} \dfrac{d^2S_2}{dS_3^2}>0 \end{array} \right\} \implies \dfrac{d^2S_c}{dS_1^2}>0$$

EXPANSION AND CONTRADICTION

The functioning of the Kachin economy generates two types of growth: (1) Political expansion and growing internal differentiation tend to develop in the direction of a state–class formation. (2) This process is accompanied by a rapid demographic and territorial growth (*Figure 9*). We begin here with the latter development as it determines the limiting material conditions of political evolution in the Kachin Hills.

We have shown how the Kachin economy is based on an increasing or even accelerating demand for surplus, which is utilized to accumulate prestige and an increasing control over labour and material flows. The demand for surplus creates a demand for labour. Large families have a high positive value—not that *relative* surplus will be higher—it may in fact be lower if the ratio of consumers to workers increases, but since prestige depends on the accumulation of *absolute* surplus, the larger the group of dependants the more powerful their leader. In the initial stages of prestige-building, the number of wives and children is evidently a crucial factor, but through the positive feedback processes of the economy this is supplemented, if not largely replaced, by the prestations of dependent wife-takers and debt-slaves. The hunger for labour power is expressed in the capture of large numbers of inhabitants from surrounding areas, most of whom become the slaves of chiefs. The latter may have houses as much as a hundred yards in length.

As a result of such mechanisms, local population tends to grow quite rapidly. But the constraints of the technology dictate that in order to preserve the rate of productivity, territorial expansion must at least compensate for demographic growth, i.e. in order to prevent increasing density. With a fallow cycle of 1/12, territorial expansion must be at least thirteen times faster than the rate of increase in the labour force.

Figure 9 External Expansion and Contradiction

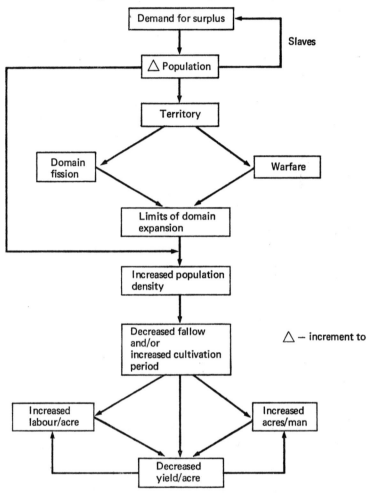

This constraint has some problematic implications for the political hierarchy. Assuming that a domain did expand territorially in accordance with the necessity of maintaining productivity, the political area would soon become so large that a noble installed in a peripheral region might easily accumulate his own dependent following. Such an individual could then enter into competition with the paramount chief and liberate himself from the latter's domination. In effect, the *gumsa* system is not economically centralized enough to prevent this kind of domain fission, which tends, consequently, to set an internal limit to

181

political expansion. Furthermore, the simultaneous growth of several groups must inevitably lead to their collision, followed by serious conflicts or warfare which would certainly block or slow down the rate of territorial expansion. But then, the demand for surplus, which goes on unchanged inside the domain which has ceased to occupy new lands, will necessarily bring increasing density followed by shorter fallows and/or longer periods of continuous cultivation, ecological degradation, and finally lower productivity per unit of labour and land.

Figure 10 Production and Consumption Functions in Swidden Agriculture and their Interrelation

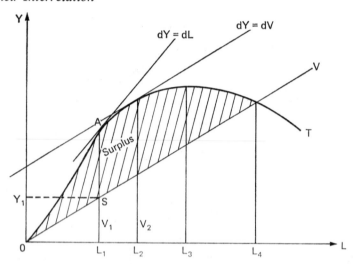

Figure 10 represents the main features of the situation described above and defines the material limits of functioning of the *gumsa* system.[6] The production function *T* represents the input/output ratio in conditions of progressive intensification. *V* is the necessary cost of social reproduction expressed in terms of consumption and is a linear function that follows directly from the rate of population growth. The combination of the two functions determines the variation in surplus over time—surplus that can be represented either as potential surplus labour time, $Y_1 S = 0L_1$, or as materialized surplus product SA.

The critical inflection points define four distinct regions of the graph. In the zone $0L_1$ yield increases at an accelerating rate so that every additional input of labour produces a still greater surplus output ($dY/dL > 0$, $dS/dY > 0$, $d^2S/dY^2 > 0$). After L_1 yield and therefore surplus continue to grow, but now at a decelerating rate ($d^2S/dY^2 < 0$) until we reach L_2, when surplus, though not yield, begins to decrease absolutely ($dS/dY < 0$, $dY/dL > 0$), since output now grows more slowly than necessary consumption. Finally, at L_3 total yield also begins to fall ($dY/dL < 0$) and at L_4 we arrive at the limit conditions for

182

material reproduction of the population irrespective of other social factors.

The properties of the above graph can be said to define a hierarchy of constraints which determine the limit conditions of technical reproduction of the social system. It can be represented as follows (*Figure 11*):

Figure 11 Hierarchy of Constraints of Production

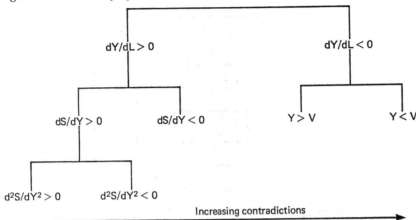

While these are indeed material constraints, they are not determined solely by the technology, but by the totality of the conditions of production constituted by the combination of technology, environment, and demography. The production function defines the set of all input/output ratios along the axis of progressive ecological degradation, but the latter is brought about by increasing population density, which is itself determined by the relations of production. This is a clear case where we can distinguish inter- from intra-systemic properties. While intensification brought about by the economic system does not alter the internal properties of the techno-ecology, it does determine the manner in which they will be manifested. We must now consider the way in which the constraints of the productive forces are articulated with the internal structure of the relations of production.

The overleaf schema (*Figure 12*) depicts the process of internal political-economic expansion of the *gumsa* domain.

The increasing demand for surplus leads, via the cycle Feasts→ Affinal rank→Brideprice→Feasts, to an inflation of all prestige goods (*hpaga*) and all prestations including brideprice and indemnity payments, which in their turn threaten every level of the social structure with increasing indebtedness. A given social rank implies the ability to meet all the exchange obligations of that rank. A noble lineage that does not have the resources to participate in the aristocratic alliance network eventually becomes a commoner lineage. A commoner, however, who becomes insolvent completely drops out of the kinship structure and becomes a debt-slave. If he cannot afford to pay his brideprice and other obligations he loses his political and economic independence and is transferred to the chief's house. The latter pays his brideprice but is entitled to all of his surplus. This transfer amounts to an increase in the size of the chief's 'family' work-force and serves to further his power of

Figure 12 Internal Expansion of the Gumsa Domain and its Contradictions

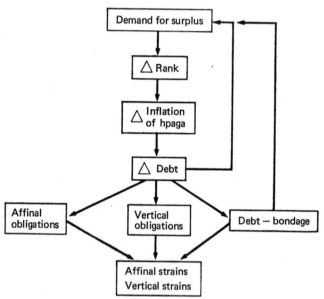

accumulation. While slave lineages can become commoners again after several generations, the obligations and debts generated by the functioning of the economy can only amplify the rate of extortion as well as the social inferiority of poorer lineages. The chief progressively gains control over the total surplus of the group, and his position is continually reinforced by his growing capacity to convert surplus into prestige and therefore to impose new obligations upon his subordinates.

H—*hpaga* value
S_0—demand for surplus
D—debt
t—time

==>—implies

$$1)\ \frac{dH}{dt} > 0 ==> \frac{dS_0}{dt} > 0$$

$$2)\ \frac{dS_0}{dt} > 0 ==> \frac{dD}{dt} > 0$$

$$3)\ \frac{dD}{dt} > 0 ==> \frac{d^2S_2}{dS_1^2} > 0$$

Rank differentiation linked to debt inflation causes an increasing verticalization of economic flows. But this hierarchization has objective limits determined by the production function, more specifically by the rate of surplus. In order for economic relations to continue functioning over time, it is necessary that:

184

$$\frac{dS}{dt} > \frac{dD}{dt}$$

that is, the technology must be capable of furnishing a real output corresponding to the accelerating demand. It is here that the very structure of the relations of production causes them to come into contradiction with the productive forces. All local lineages in a *gumsa* system are connected, from the highest to lowest, by a transitive *mayu/dama* network. As such, any increase in prestige at the top implies an increase in brideprice and other obligations at all levels. The rate of inflation of *hpaga* depends largely on the rate of accumulation by chiefs, one which is far greater than the average. As the chief has at his disposal a growing percentage of the total available surplus labour, by extortion as well as by the accumulation of slaves, he can easily counter the falling rate of *relative* surplus by increasing his accumulation of *absolute* surplus, i.e. at a rate faster than the deceleration of productivity. But this merely makes matters worse, since inflation goes on rampantly while most lineages are running into increasing difficulty in meeting their obligations.

$$\frac{d^2S_c}{dS^2} > 0 \Longrightarrow \frac{d^2D}{dS^2} > 0$$

The above inequalities show how the chief accumulates an increasing portion of the total social surplus [7] which, metamorphosed into higher inflation rates, entails a multiplication of debts at a rate faster than the real surplus required to meet them. This contradiction should emerge at the point where the rate of indebtedness begins to diverge from the rate of surplus (L_1 on the graph, *Figure 10*), i.e. where increasing obligations become incompatible with decreasing means of payment.

$$t\text{---time} \quad \begin{cases} \dfrac{d^2S}{dL^2} < 0 \\[2mm] \dfrac{d^2S}{dY^2} < 0 \end{cases} \longleftrightarrow \left\{ \dfrac{d^2D}{dt^2} > 0 \right\}$$

The situation should begin to become critical at the point where the chief starts to accumulate an increasing portion of a decreasing surplus, so that there is no possibility of meeting debt payments (L_2 on graph). This contradiction between forces and relations of production is manifested at the level of the social relations (the only 'lived' level) as a strain between all debtors and creditors, affines in the horizontal structure, and superordinate and subordinate chiefs and their dependants in the vertical structure. It is significant that the Kachin word for 'debt', *hka*, is also the word for 'feud'.

The material relations in the *gumsa* imply, further, that petty aristocrats, indebted village chiefs for example, are likely to be the focal

185

points of discontent since it is they who have the most to lose. For while they have high rank, they are economically equivalent to commoners, obliged to cultivate their own fields with few or no slaves and largely unaided by their dependants. They are surely the first to feel the exorbitant inflation imposed from above, since they are in constant danger of losing their rank.

In *Political Systems of Highland Burma*, Leach documented the existence of a long-term oscillation between *gumsa* and *gumlao* poles. At a certain stage in *gumsa* development *gumlao* revolts occur which destroy the political hierarchy, reinstating a more egalitarian organization. This is all quite predictable in terms of the model presented above. The return to *gumlao* consists in a general devaluation of *hpaga* values and of all *hka*, therefore the suppression of social rank. This is superficially similar to a capitalist depression. But since surplus is converted into relative rank and not capital, it all becomes a question of the devaluation of social status and not of property values. The *gumsa/gumlao* cycle is thus a social and not a business cycle. The egalitarian state resulting from the collapse of *gumsa* polity is similarly quite transitory, for while lineage rank is equalized in *gumlao* revolts the underlying mechanisms which generate hierarchy are left quite intact.

The restoration of *gumlao* organization brings with it the possibility of regeneration, not only of the *gumsa* structure, but also of the necessary techno-ecological conditions that are its basis. Political breakdown is accompanied by a redispersal of the population that permits the regrowth of primary forest without which the high productivity necessary for political development would be unavailable.

In sum, the dynamic of the Kachin system might be envisaged as an evolution towards increasing hierarchy and state-formation which comes into contradiction with its own material constraints of reproduction but which, by means of *gumlao* revolts, succeeds in re-establishing the conditions for a renewed evolution. As the material conditions of production are determinant in the last instance, we must now consider the multilinear effects generated by the same structure when these conditions are transformed.

DEVOLUTION

The notion of devolution here is not meant to refer to a simple reverse kind of evolution. Rather, it is the structural transformation that occurs when a social formation reproduces itself in continually deteriorating conditions of production. The structures that emerge are quite unlike those of *gumlao* society, although in both cases there is an absence of political hierarchy.

Long Cycles and Short Cycles
We shall refer to the kind of variation which occurs in *gumsa/gumlao*

oscillation as a short cycle. Its reproduction depends upon the long-run maintenance of the conditions of production, demographic density, and soil fertility. In the Triangle region, overall density has in fact been held at a very low level. While during *gumsa* periods there is certainly a tendency for increased demographic density within any one political domain with resultant overintensification leading to a partial degradation of the environment, the combination of continuous emigration with the dispersion which occurs in the aftermath of *gumlao* revolts re-establishes the conditions in which forest and the initial level of fertility can be regenerated. Thus, it is only where long-term territorial expansion is possible that the short cycle can be maintained. While this is the case in the Triangle itself, to the northeast, east, and southeast, Shan states and other tribes (Lolo, Lisu) with higher densities constitute both a political and a demographic barrier to Kachin territorial growth. In these areas there is a serious build-up of population. Density increases several fold (15–30/mi²) and the environment is progressively degraded as one moves east, changing from secondary forest into extensive grassland.

Diminishing yields necessarily weaken *gumsa* structures, which depend on the availability of a growing surplus. In this region (Leach's zones B and C, in Leach 1964: 23) the only chiefdoms are those which are able to exploit trade routes and valley Shan populations by taking a regular tribute. The political hierarchies are much less stable here and there are only *gumrawng*, 'boastful', chiefs who compete, like big-men, for political power as opposed to the *gumchying*, paramount, chiefs of the Triangle. In the northeast, where there are neither Shans nor trade routes to exploit, all groups are more or less permanently 'egalitarian' and there is no evidence of any supralocal organization.

Where the average demographic density of a large region increases it provokes considerable changes in the techno-ecological base and the emergence of new constraints of reproduction which in turn bring about a radical transformation of the social structure. This second kind of development is not oscillatory but unidirectional, and the transformations generated in this process of devolution are distributed on a 'long cycle'.

In the graph (*Figure 13*) the short cycles have the long cycle as their 'envelope' curve, the latter being tangent to all of the former. Short cycles thus represent the variation that occurs owing to political-economic constraints operating within the technological limits defined by the long cycle. At any point along the graph of increasing density and real ecological degradation, there is the possibility of fluctuation similar to that which occurs in *gumsa/gumlao* cycles. The reversibility of the short cycle, however, is continually displaced along the irreversible long cycle so that the very nature of the political and social variation must be quite different at different points on the envelope curve.

Population pressure leads to territorial competition and the multiplication of wars and feuds (Scott and Hardiman 1900, Pt I, Vol. I: 367). This in turn leads to the formation of larger villages; first, due to the slowdown of the fission process, a direct result of land shortage and, second, for reasons of military security. In the Triangle, maximum village size is about thirty houses. In the eastern trade route area it may be as high as eighty houses and farther north, where there are no trade routes, there are villages of one hundred and twenty-five houses. This new concentration of population brings about a topological trans-formation of the former structures. The formation of *gumsa* domains depends on the continual fissioning of the local lineage, its dispersal

Figure 13 The Long Cycle

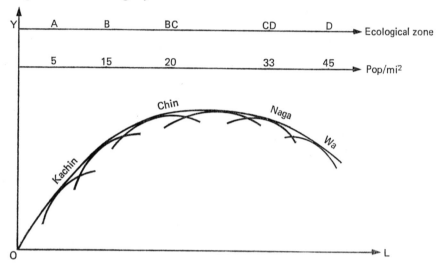

A. Primary forest predominates
B. Secondary forest predominates
C. Lighter secondary forest, scrub grassland
D. Grassland predominates

over a wide area, and a well-developed genealogical amnesia so that non-local lineages are more or less severed from the parental group and become potential affines in an expanding *mayu/dama* network. Where territorial expansion is blocked this process can no longer function. The local lineage becomes a much larger segmentary clan of the type that we find among the Chin. The rule of exogamy is necessarily extended to the larger group, since the genealogical network linking the minimal segments has become a matter of demonstrable descent reinforced by the fact of co-residence.

Furthermore, as it is no longer possible to send off one's siblings to found new settlements, it becomes necessary to divide up the existing land. Inheritance of land in Kachin systems is merely the effect of inheritance of segmentary position, by either ultimo- or primo-geniture. Differential shares are inconceivable where all land is communal by

188

definition and represented by a single lineage, descendant of the territorial spirit. As we pass now from Kachin to Chin and Naga groups,
inheritance becomes increasingly democratic, but this individualization
of rights is simultaneously the creation of a social relation to land
which did not exist in the Kachin system. For as land becomes divided
into inheritable titles it enters into the same category as other moveable
goods. We witness here the emergence of lineage landed property
which is negotiable like other forms of lineage property and which can
be transferred and even accumulated in brideprice and other interlineage transactions. As land becomes negotiable it enters into the horizontal exchange structure, thus destroying the entire basis of the
'Asiatic' Kachin structure, where land was indivisible. An important
verification of this is the existence in the Northern Chin Hills (Zahao,
Siyin) of societies where there appears to be a conflict between chiefs
who attempt to maintain control over all land, as a right attached to
their position, and the growing negotiability of individual titles which
are apparently accumulated by wealthy 'big-men'. This is a clear expression of the growing contradiction between the collapsing vertical
structure and the increasingly dominant horizontal structure. It should
be noted that these most northern Chin have a relatively low density
compared to the Central and Southern Chin, and their villages are much
smaller, although large by Kachin standards (Zahao villages average
less than 100 houses; Central Chin villages often have between 100 and
200 houses and there are some with 250).

Decreasing productivity makes interlineage hierarchization a problematic affair. Large conical domains with their paramount chiefs and
great redistributive feasts disappear, replaced by a more competitive
economy in which all available surplus is channelled into the horizontal
circuits. Village feasts expressing the relation between chief, community,
and powerful ancestors become 'feasts of merit' among Chin and Naga,
the locus of competition between affines, potlatches whose function is to
maintain or to raise relative rank with respect to allies as well as to the
greatly increased number of kin who can never become inferior wife-
takers.

The impossibility of converting lineage segmentation into local segmentation, the swelling of the exogamous unit, and the democratization
of inheritance all combine to break the cycle whereby affinal rank is
transformed into conical rank by destroying the relation between
lineage hierarchy, ancestors, and territorial spirits. As there is no longer
any continuity between local spirits and the higher supernatural powers,
there can be no position equivalent to a *gumsa* chief, direct descendant
of the territorial deity. On the contrary, the individualization of land
titles and their absorption into the horizontal structure that now
dominates the process of reproduction permits a new kind of hierarchization which might be described as pre-feudal. Surplus continues
to be converted into prestige and inflated brideprice for daughters, but

189

now land titles are often transferred in these as well as in debt payments, thus creating the possibility for the development of a landed aristocracy (*Figure 14*).

Figure 14 Transformation of the Cycle of Hierarchization

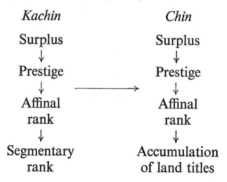

Among the Chin, a rather intricate agricultural adaptation including elaborate cycles of crop rotation has maintained a fairly good rate of productivity in intensified conditions so that an aristocracy has been able to develop on the basis of land-title accumulation. A small number of dominant lineages often own the majority or even the totality of a village's land. Ranking among such aristocrats, however, is always in a state of flux. The competition between allies is ferocious and brideprice inflation is very rapid. 'Chiefs' receive a small token rent from their wife-taker dependants, some of whom may also help to cultivate the former's fields, which must be quite large in order to provide the kind of surplus necessary for the 'feasts of merit'.[8]

In any case, this secondary development of hierarchy is considerably weakened by diminishing returns and the general degradation of the conditions of production, which continues in spite of the elaborate technology. When we move on to the Naga, the clan begins to counter the political independence of the minimal exchange unit, making internal differentiation more difficult. Among the Chin, the clan may act as a unit of exogamy but it has few political and economic functions. The rules of inheritance, however, which divide property somewhat unequally among all brothers, tend to spread land titles among a wide range of collateral lines after several generations, and there is some evidence that this is meant to prevent the accumulation of land control in any one branch of the maximal lineage or clan (Stevenson 1968: 68). Among the Naga, the power of the wider group of kinsmen increases. The number of obligations owed to collaterals multiplies and the control over land becomes a direct concern of the clan elders—among many groups, all land not in use reverts immediately to the clan as a whole for reallocation. Inheritance is often egalitarian in the extreme, undivided for a generation before being distributed equally among

190

Figure 15 Topological Transformation Kachin–Chin

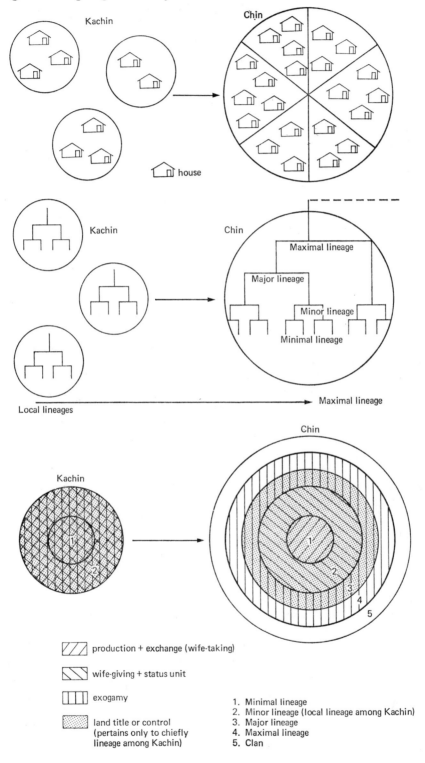

house

Kachin

Chin

Kachin

Chin

Maximal lineage

Major lineage

Minor lineage

Minimal lineage

Local lineages

Maximal lineage

Chin

Kachin

1
2
3
4
5

production + exchange (wife-taking)

wife-giving + status unit

exogamy

land title or control
(pertains only to chiefly
lineage among Kachin)

1. Minimal lineage
2. Minor lineage (local lineage among Kachin)
3. Major lineage
4. Maximal lineage
5. Clan

grandsons. The clan, of course, is also the relevant defence unit in feuds and disputes, which arise quite frequently.

The collapse of local lineage political economy, which is completely stifled by the growing dominance of the clan, diminishes the importance of generalized exchange. At maximal lineage and clan levels restricted exchange begins to predominate and exogamy is often extended to the clan group which occupies a village section. There are many cases of village moieties, and among all Naga groups there appears to be a mixture of dualist and asymmetric structures.

We can, nevertheless, detect a short cycle among the Naga. Where territorial expansion is possible the independent political economy of the local lineage assumes its former importance. Matrilateral exchange and accumulation of land titles, and therefore of dependants, occur among the Sema Naga, and chieftaincy does develop at the village level. However, the power of a chief depends on his ability to send off his sons to found new villages. Thus, the political hierarchy which, in any case, never extends beyond the village level disappears as soon as territorial expansion is blocked.[9] Given the high demographic density in the region as a whole, it is evident that expansion can only take place through intertribal warfare. Both the Sema and the Lhota only appear to have reached a stage of internal political development as a result of their expulsion of the Ao Naga (Sema villages average 100 houses, Lhota 250, and Ao 500 [Allen 1905; Hutton 1921a: 34]). Even so, as density continues to grow, wars become more frequent and their results more deceiving for the internal economies of the groups involved. In most areas, hereditary chiefs are entirely replaced by big-men or by clan elders. Individuals can still gain prestige through feasts of merit, but it is impossible to convert this into lineage rank because such feasts are isolated from the alliance network and the ancestral hierarchy. Furthermore, labour productivity is too low to permit the acceleration of surplus necessary to interlineage competition. Among the majority of Naga groups big-men have prestige but little power. Among the Ao in particular, political functions are all transferred to the village council of elders. Here, competition leads only to a kind of unstable and negative egalitarianism.

The devolution of the system is most evident among the Eastern Angami Naga (Fürer-Haimendorf and Mills 1936). Here every village has a *tevo*, supposed descendant of the sacred founder, mediator between the community and the supernatural, thus, structurally equivalent to a Kachin chief (*duwa*), representative of the higher unity of the group. In practice, however, the *tevo* is quite the contrary. He is formally excluded from all fertility and prosperity rituals. He is absolutely forbidden to give to or receive (especially food) from villagers. All sexual relations are prohibited during his first four years in office. He is subject to a whole series of ritual prohibitions, all of which are meant to ensure social reproduction.[10] As such, the *tevo* appears as a symmetric inversion of the Kachin *duwa*. For the latter, all positive acts of generosity imply increased prosperity while, for the former, the prohibition of such acts permits survival. Here, political equality is founded upon the ritual negation of everything that led the society to destroy its own conditions of production.

The long cycle leads, finally, to the Wa. Here density reaches its absolute limits and forest is entirely replaced by grassland. Villages are even larger than among the Naga, averaging between 500 and 700 houses surrounded by heavy ramparts. War is a daily condition of life and famines are quite frequent. There are apparently war chiefs whose power, however, is strictly limited to military leadership. Here, as among the Naga, headhunting is of prime importance, but for the Wa it becomes a well-institutionalized sport with its own special season, just before spring sowing. As among the Naga, it is assumed that the larger the number of captured heads, the better the crop will be. It is significant that, among the Kachin, individuals who might normally be killed by Naga and Wa are captured as slaves. Some Kuki-Chin groups that headhunt explain the captured trophy as a sign that the warrior will possess slaves in the afterworld, i.e. slaves are forsaken in this world in order that they might serve in the next. Among both the Naga and Wa, but especially the latter, headhunting is directly linked to survival, and human heads replace the buffalo-head trophies of the Kachin as a sign of prestige. Similarly, with respect to horizontal exchange, a man who fails to take a sufficient number of heads will have great difficulty in finding a wife. All of these transformations depict Wa society as a kind of morbid inversion of everything Kachin.

In many Wa villages there are large circular barrows, some of which have a circumference of four hundred feet. These are similar in form to the Naga 'sitting Circles' where founder ancestors are supposedly buried and which serve as ceremonial centres, perhaps for the dancing that occurs at great feasts. Kachin *manao* also make use of large circular dance floors. The Wa, in any case, are unaware of the origin of these circles, which have fallen into disuse. It is said, however, that the great stones (similar to those which are hauled to the village during Naga feasts of merit) which are strewn about in no particular order in these circles have their origin in the distant past when giant Wa ancestors, after doing battle, rested, their blood falling in great drops, which turned to stone.

> It is the custom for passers-by to lay a leaf or stone on one of the stones, at the same time *wishing for money, cattle, paddy and the repayment of debts* (Draye, n.d. in Harvey 1933: 14).

EVOLUTION: TOWARDS THE 'ASIATIC' STATE

We limit ourselves here to a number of suggestions concerning the kinds of structural transformation that might occur in *gumsa* evolution if it were to continue beyond the limits set by hill swidden technology.

Whereas the devolutionary process described above is characterized by the disappearance of vertical relations and the increasing dominance of the horizontal, the evolution towards state formation implies on the contrary a growing dominance of vertical relations. A *gumsa* chief participates in two relations at once. As representative of the higher unity of the community, he receives tribute and corvée. An important part of this wealth is used in redistributive feasts which, owing to his genealogical relation to the spirits, ensure growth and prosperity for the whole community. A chief, however, must also redistribute in order to guarantee his superiority through 'generosity'. This latter relation is dominated by the horizontal structure in which exchange determines relative rank, the chief being at once a 'father' but primarily a wife-giver to his dependants. In the formation of conical domains, the vertical structure tends to become dominant. Rank no longer depends on generosity but is defined in terms of absolute segmentary position. If the power of a Kachin chief remains ambiguous owing to the conjunction of horizontal and vertical attributes, the progressive hierarchization of the system will tend to reinforce his absolute status as direct descendant of the gods, as opposed to his relative rank as a wife- and feast-giver.

We have seen how the internal logic linking surplus production to genealogical proximity to the gods serves to convert big-man status into chieftaincy. We can suggest here that any significant increase in relative, but especially absolute, surplus would merely accentuate this kind of development to a point where vertical relations were everywhere predominant. This could result from a simple move to the fertile plains of Assam or from the successful intensification that might occur in lowland riverine irrigation. Both would cause an enormous boost in absolute surplus due to greatly increased carrying capacity, even though relative surplus might remain unchanged when compared to the best swidden conditions. Kachin groups that descended into the plains of Assam did in fact develop into small class-structured states (Butler 1847: 126; Hannay 1847: 44; Leach 1946: 481).

Where verticalization becomes absolute, all political rank is automatically determined by genealogical distance from the chiefly line. The conical structure, once firmly anchored in the heavens, inverts the whole function of exchange. Since lineage rank is now definitely established by 'descent', the act of wife-giving or even feast-giving can no longer legitimately operate to define social superiority. Women, instead, begin to move in the opposite direction as tribute. There is no structural novelty here, only a change in dominance. Among *gumsa* Kachin, hypergamy does occur in secondary marriages along with the usual hypogamy. The former is permitted when there is a virtually absolute difference in rank between the wife-giver and the wife-taker. But this relation, which is secondary among the Kachin, becomes generalized during the evolution of 'Asiatic' states because *all* rank differences become absolute. Similarly, redistributive feasts lose a great deal of their former significance and no longer function to maintain chiefly rank. On the contrary, using a much smaller portion of the total surplus, they symbolize the ritual–economic power of an already established position.

Expanding potential surplus is realized in the transformation of the old aristocracy. In the Kachin Hills a chiefly lineage can indeed exploit the labour of the community, but sibling lineages are excluded from such possibilities.[11] The process of verticalization, by raising the status of aristocratic lineages, accords them a ritual importance which must appear necessary to economic success. In this way, all ritual is hierarchized and all aristocratic lineage ancestors are incorporated in a single segmentary structure headed by the deified ancestors of the chief, now a king or prince. The nobility belongs, as it were, to the imaginary, fetishized, conditions of social and economic reproduction. This is *not* a question of the ideological reflection of some more material reality, but of the very content of the principal relation of production. While tribal aristocrats are commoners in most economic respects, their increasing ritual importance entitles them to a portion of the total surplus. But these aristocratic rights depend entirely on 'genealogical' proximity to the royal line. The emergent structure, a quasi-sacred aristocracy, the conical clan-state can be found among the earliest Chinese states (Shang, Chou), which are similar to much-enlarged Kachin-type domains. These states, often considered feudal, are surely some of our best examples of the marxist definition of the 'Asiatic' social formation. There is even evidence of the development of elaborate bureaucracies in these pre-irrigation states, i.e. long before supposed necessary by proponents of the hydraulic hypothesis (Wittfogel 1957).[12] The doubling of genealogical ranking by an ordered series of administrative functions reinforces status differences with a largely imaginary division of labour, which tends to reduce competition by defining necessary functions for each segment in a larger bureaucratic entity. This is an instrumental mechanism in the process whereby the exploitation of a community by a single lineage is expanded into class exploitation. A sacred segmentary hierarchy whose function is to control the reproduction of the society through its access to the supernatural emerges as a class which is identical to the state. The two phenomena are indistinguishable in 'Asiatic' social formations.

The structural transformation outlined above presupposes only those expansionist mechanisms which are already present in the tribe. Slaves are captured as well as generated internally, and the two categories tend to be reintegrated as a lower class, one which is entirely cut off from the essential rituals of fertility and prosperity and which is, therefore, completely dependent on the aristocracy for its own well-being. This process is a necessary concomitant of verticalization where tribute and corvée are the main transfers of wealth in an imaginary division of labour between real producers and a sacred uureaucracy.

The 'Asiatic' state evolves directly out of tribal structures in the process of verticalization of the relations of production. Following this, the principal economic flows are determined by absolute segmentary position. *Gumlao, gumsa,* and 'Asiatic' state societies can be said, thus,

Figure 16 Conical Clan Structure in the 'Asiatic' State: Pre-Han China

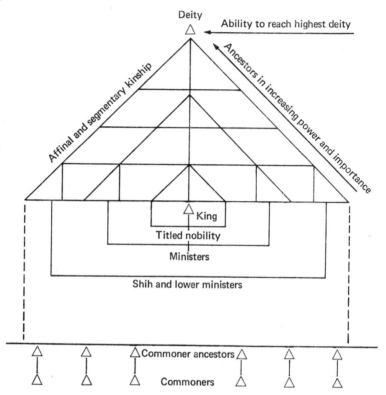

to lie on a continuum. Relative rank is first established by horizontal exchange, then converted into absolute rank through claims on the supernatural. With the continued growth of surplus and the emergence of the state, the political hierarchy which had formerly been generated by the economic flows of horizontal exchange comes, finally, to dominate that flow. The chief who becomes a sacred king naturally appropriates all of the community rituals. This is certainly the case for pre-Han China, where all shrines were housed in the royal compound. The head of state climbs a good deal further up the ancestral hierarchy—he is no longer the representative of the community to the gods, but descends from the heavens as the representative of the gods to the community (*Figure 16*).

196

CONCLUSION

Our object has been to show how a single model of social reproduction might generate a number of variants whose order of appearance is determined by the evolution or degradation of the conditions of production, and in which, at least for devolution, the transformation of these conditions might be the result of the functioning of the social system itself. Devolution and evolution appear as two modes of transformation of a single structure in expansion. The tribal system tends towards increasing verticalization in a way which demands the acceleration of surplus production. Where technological conditions permit such a development, the system evolves toward an 'Asiatic' state formation. In usual conditions of hill swiddening, however, the limits of productivity, especially of land, create an absolute barrier to the internal tendencies of the relations of production. Where ecological degradation occurs, a number of transformations follow: the segmentary hierarchy collapses and landed property appears—the latter can serve as the basis of a new 'semi-feudal' hierarchization if there is a new growth of productivity. Large exogamous acephalous clans develop where big-men compete to little avail, being eventually replaced by village councils of clan elders. Asymmetrical exchange can no longer be maintained. Reciprocity increases between exchange units, and restricted exchange, warfare, and headhunting become the dominant transactional modes.

We have tried to demonstrate how all of these variations are parts of a single system of transformations in which particular variants are 'determined in the last instance' by the transformation of the conditions of production which limit the possibilities of variation of the relations of production and of the entire social structure. The notion of determination implied by the present approach will undoubtedly be at odds with a number of other materialist models. Determination in the last instance is never a necessary and sufficient determination by which the existence of a particular social form can be explained. In order to arrive at truly deterministic statements we must consider the intersection of two forms of determination, one, dependent on the dominant relations of production, which generates structural variation, and the other, the constraints of the productive forces, which limits that variation. But even this is not enough, for structural transformations occur only within the larger process of social reproduction. We must, of course, consider the tendencies that emerge from the continual confrontation of dominant productive relations with their constraints of reproduction, but we must also include in our analysis the internal logic of the social formation as a whole, for it is this logic which determines the way economic functions may become dominated by new structures, i.e. where the entire material structure of reproduction is altered. This is what occurs in the verticalization process leading to state formation as well as in the horizontalization which leads to the possibility of pre-feudal structures and,

197

at the same level of productivity, to acephalous clan formations. These changes in mode of production cannot, I think, be understood in terms of technological constraints alone, nor in terms of the organization of work, which, as we have shown, can be seen only as the result of the imposition of the relations of production on a particular set of organizational possibilities afforded by the productive forces.

A change in dominance can be explained only by taking the whole social formation into account, for if we restrict ourselves to the infrastructural level alone, we exclude the possibility that a formerly superstructural element will become part of the relations of production, a phenomenon which characterizes the great majority of historical transformations.

We are, in effect, discussing two kinds of variation. The first occurs within a level of a social formation and is equivalent to the Lévi-Straussian notion of system of transformations where all variants can be generated by a single underlying structure. Here we refer to the internal properties of cultural systems or institutions and not to their functions in material reproduction. The second kind of variation is more difficult, since it logically includes, as a higher-order phenomenon, the intra-systemic variation of the cultural structures. This intersystemic variation occurs where infra- and superstructural functions are redistributed among new institutional or cultural forms. But the two kinds of variation are inextricably linked in a larger structure. Thus, the cultural transformation whereby a formerly affinal relation between the chiefly lineage and the highest deity becomes patrilineal, where the genealogical distance to that deity is greatly reduced, occurs simultaneously with the verticalization by which the formerly superstructural aspects of the relation between the community, its ancestors, and the higher deity become essential properties of the dominant relations of production. Change of form and change in place are thus generated as aspects of the same process. While it would be disastrous to confuse the two kinds of variation, it must be stressed that both occur simultaneously in the process of reproduction, so that in order to delineate the different modes of transformation we must ultimately discover the deeper structures that link internal structural variation to material intersystemic variation. The deeper structure which we are brought to face when we consider the process of transformation is one whose properties can be defined only with respect to time. It would seem to imply that any particular social formation is no more than a cross-section of a larger diachronic system, and that synchronic models are deducible from the properties of diachronic models, appearing as the various stages in a multilinear system of trajectories.

If we are to transcend the false determinism that claims to be able to explain a society in terms of one of its parts, systematically doing away with the problem of history, we must aim at a complete theory of structural transformation in which determination is correctly located at the juncture of intra- and intersystemic variation in the process of social reproduction.

Notes

1 Reported population densities for the three 'ecological' zones, while not highly accurate, are nevertheless quite useful for comparison:

data from *Gazetteers of*   Zones: A — 5–6/mi²
Upper Burma, Census Tables 1921,   C — 12–30/mi²
and Harvey (1933)   B — 30–45/mi²

2 We oversimplify here to some extent. In fact, the main structural difference between *gumsa* and *gumlao* is the hereditary claim to rank in the former case. The matter is discussed more fully in Friedman (1972). See also La Raw Maran (1967).

3a For an extensive critique of this position see Ekholm (1974).

3b *Mayu* rank higher than *dama*, as can be seen in the process outlined in *Figure 2*.

4 Cattle, the most important prestige item in Kachin economy, have little or no cost of production since they live by browsing in the jungle and are so tame that they can always be got when needed. The cost must certainly increase, however, when density goes up and the forest is reduced to lighter vegetation and grassland.

5 Where succession is by ultimogeniture, as among most Kachin, the yoS ranks highest within any generation, while between generations superiority is in accordance with natural seniority. In either case, the internal logic is identical, since what counts is social age, i.e. political superiority, and not real birth-order. We note, however, that among the Tsasen Kachin of Assam, where class structure was the most evolved, primogeniture replaced ultimogeniture.

6 This graph and the following analysis are to a large extent based on the very important article by I. Sachs (1965) who first attempted to deal theoretically with the problem of surplus in the context of social reproduction, thus taking the discussion much further than earlier anthropologists had done.

7 The inequations here do not capture the whole truth. It is not enough that the chief controls an increasing proportion of the total surplus. The real contradiction occurs when he begins to control an accelerating portion of a decelerating surplus (L_1 on the graph) and this is intensified to critical limits after L_2, where he begins to accumulate an increasing portion of an absolutely decreasing surplus:

$$\left. \begin{array}{c} \dfrac{d^2Sc}{dS^2} > 0 \\[2mm] \dfrac{d^2S}{dY^2} < 0 \end{array} \right\} \implies \dfrac{d^2D}{dS^2} > 0$$

8 With a new development of productivity it seems quite possible that a feudal class structure will evolve. This kind of phenomenon is represented by the Lolo of Yunan, where an endogamous land-owning aristocracy, the Black Lolo, exploit White Lolo commoners and slaves, both of whom cultivate their fields.

9 'The authority of a Sema chief is quickly sapped when he can no longer shed off his brothers and sons to found new villages with retainers of their own' (Hutton 1965: 23).

10 It is interesting to note that the title 'village founder' applies to secular chiefs among the Sema and continues to be a rank attributed to those who have given a certain number of merit feasts among the Western Angami.

11 It appears, however, that 'elS', non-reigning, lineages may sometimes be included in the chiefly upper class, specifically when they perform crucial judicial and ritual functions (La Raw Maran, personal communication). This is exactly the kind of phenomenon which we discuss here as instrumental in 'Asiatic' class formation and which gives that class the appearance of a bureaucracy necessary to the well-being of society.

12 Most bureaucratic functions were directly tied to court life and to ritual activities, not to the organization of production. Even economic officials, however, were more concerned with the collection of taxes than with the management of the technology, which was largely controlled at the village level.

Bibliography

ALLEN, B. C. 1905. *Assam District Gazetteer: Naga Hills and Manipur*, Vols. A and B. Shillong.

ALTHUSSER, L. and BALIBAR, E. 1968. *Lire le Capital*, Paris.

ANDERSON, J. 1875. Papers connected with the development of trade between British Burma and Western China and with the mission to Yunnan. *Parliamentary Papers* 56.

BARNARD, J. T. O. 1925. The History of Putao. *Journal of the Burma Research Society* 15.

BARTON, R. 1929. *Wa Diary*. Rangoon.

BENEDICT, P. 1941. *Kinship in Southeast Asia*, unpublished Ph.D. Thesis, Harvard University.

BETTELHEIM, C. 1959. Variations du taux de profit et accroissement de la productivité du travail. *Économie appliquée* 1.

BLAUT, H. M. 1960. The Nature and Effects of Shifting Africulture. In *Symposium on the Impact of Man on Humid Tropics Vegetation*, UNESCO.

BRYCE, J. A. 1893. The Chin and Kachin Tribes. *Asiatic Review* 5.

BUCHANAN, F. R. 1820. An account of Assam with some Notices concerning the neighboring territories. *Annals of Oriental Literature* 1.

BUTLER, J. (Maj.) 1847. *A Sketch of Assam with Some Account of the Hill Tribes*. London.

CAREY, B. and TUCK, H. 1896. *The Chin Hills: A History of the People, Our Dealings With Them, Their Customs and Manners*. Rangoon.

CARRAPIETT, W. J. S. 1929. *The Katchin Tribes of Burma*. Rangoon.

CORYTON, J. 1875. Trade Routes Between British Burma and Western China. *Journal of the Royal Geographical Society* 45.

DAWSON, G. W. 1912. *Burma Gazetteer: Bhamo District*. Rangoon.

EKHOLM, K. 1974. Materialismen och det vetenskapliga objektet i socialantropologi. MS.

FRIED, M. 1957. The Classification of Corporate Unilineal Descent Groups. *JRAI* **87**.

FRIEDMAN, J. 1971. Marxism, Structuralism and Vulgar Materialism. *Man* n.s. **9**, 1974.

— 1972. *System, Structure and Contradiction in the Evolution of 'Asiatic' Social Formations*. Ph. D. Columbia University. To appear London 1975.

— 1973. The Place of Fetishism and the Problem of Materialist Interpretations. *Critique of Anthropology* (1), 1974.

— 1974. *Marxism, Structuralism and Vulgar Materialism*. To appear Cambridge, 1975.

FÜRER-HAIMENDORF, C. VON. 1938. The Morung System of the Konyak Naga. *JRAI* **68**.

— 1969. *The Konyak Nagas*. New York.

FÜRER-HAIMENDORF, C. VON and MILLS, J. 1936. The Sacred Founder's Kin Among the Eastern Angami Nagas. *Anthropos* **31**.

GILHODES, C. 1911. Naissance et enfance chez les Katchins. *Anthropos* **6**.

— 1918. Mariage et condition de la femme chez les Katchins. *Anthropos* **14**.

— 1922. *The Kachins; Religion and Customs*. Calcutta.

GODELIER, M. 1966. *Rationalité et irrationalité en économie*. Paris.

— 1967. La notion de mode de production asiatique et les schémas marxistes d'évolution des sociétés. In R. Garaudy (ed.), *Sur le mode de production asiatique*. Paris.

— 1973. *Horizon, trajets marxistes en anthropologie*. Paris.

GRANET, M. 1951. *La religion des Chinois*. Paris.

— 1952. *La féodalité chinoise*. Oslo.

— 1953. *Études sociologiques sur la Chine*. Paris.

HANNAY, S. F. 1847. Sketch of the Singphos or Kakhyens of Burmah, the Position of this Tribe as Regards Bhamo and the Inland Trade of the Irrawaddy with Yunnan and their Connection with the Northeastern Frontier of Assam. Calcutta.

HANSON, O. 1906. *The Kachins*. Rangoon.

HARNER, M. 1970. Population Pressure and the Social Evolution of Agriculturists. *SWJA* **26**.

HARRIS, M. 1968. *The Rise of Anthropological Theory*. New York.

HARVEY, G. E. 1933. *Wa Précis*. Rangoon.

HEAD, W. R. 1917. *Handbook on the Haka Chin Customs*. Rangoon.

HERTZ, W. 1912. *Burma Gazetteer: Myitkyina District*. Rangoon.

HEUSCH, L. 1971. *Pourquoi l'épouser*. Paris.

HSU, CHO YUN 1965. *Ancient China in Transition*. Stanford.

HUTTON, J. H. 1921a. *The Sema Nagas*. London.

— 1921b. *The Angami Nagas*. London.

— 1949. A Brief Comparison Between the Economics of Dry and Irrigated Cultivation in the Naga Hills. *Advancement of Science* **2**.

— 1965. The Mixed Culture of the Naga Tribes. *JRAI* **95**.

IZIKOWITZ, K. G. 1951. *Lamet: Hill peasants in French Indochina*, Göteborg.

KIRCHOFF, P. 1968. The Principles of Clanship in Human Society. In M. Fried (ed.), *Readings in Anthropology* II. New York.

LA RAW MARAN 1967. Toward a Basis for Understanding the Minorities of Burma. In Kunstadter (ed.), *Southeast Asian Tribes, Minorities and Nations*. Princeton.

LEACH, E. R. 1946. *Cultural Change with Special Reference to the Hill Tribes of Burma and Assam*. Unpublished Ph.D. thesis, University of London.

— 1949. Some Aspects of Dry Rice Cultivation in North Burma and British Borneo. *Advancement of Science* **6**.

Jonathan Friedman

LEACH, E. R. 1954 (1964). *Political Systems of Highland Burma*. London; Boston.
— 1961. *Rethinking Anthropology*. London.
— 1967. The Language of Kachin Kinship. In M. Freedman (ed.), *Social Organization*. Chicago.
— 1969. Kachin and Haka Chin: A Rejoinder to Lévi-Strauss. *Man* n.s. **4**.
LEHMAN, F. K. 1963. *The Structure of Chin Society*, Urbana.
— 1969. On Chin and Kachin Marriage Regulations. *Man* n.s. **4**.
LÉVI-STRAUSS, C. 1953. *Anthropologie structurale*. Paris.
— 1967. *Les structures élémentaires de la parenté*. Paris.
— 1971. *L'Homme nu*. Paris.
LÖFFLER, L. 1960. Patrilateral Lineation in Transition. *Ethnos* **25**.
— 1964. Prescriptive Matrilateral Marriage: a Fallacy. *SWJA* **20**.
MANNIVANNA, K. 1969. Aspects socio-économiques du Laos mediéval. In Garaudy (ed.) *Sur le mode de production asiatique*.
MARX, K. 1967 (1883). *Capital*. Trans. from 3rd German edn. Moscow.
— 1968a (1905–10). *Theories of Surplus Value*. Moscow.
— 1968b (1857–8). *Fondements de la critique de l'économie politique*. Paris.
MASPERO, H. and BALAZS, E. *Histoire et Institutions de la Chine Ancienne*. Paris.
MEILLASSOUX, C. 1972. From Reproduction to Production. *Economy and Society* **1**.
MILLS, J. P. 1922. *The Lhota Nagas*. London.
— 1926. *The Ao Nagas*. London.
— 1937. *The Rengma Nagas*. London.
— 1939. The Effect of Ritual Upon Industries and Art in the Naga Hills. *Proceedings* of the International Congress of Anthropological Science, London.
NEUFVILLE, J. B. 1828. On the Geography and Population of Assam. *Asiatick Researches* **16**.
PARRY, N. E. 1932. *The Lakhers*. London.
POKORA, T. 1967. La Chine a-t-elle connu une société esclavagiste? *Recherches internationales à la lumière du marxisme*.
ROSMAN, A. and RUBEL, P. n.d. The Potlatch Model in Societies with Generalized Exchange. MS.
SACHS, I. 1965. Le concept de surplus économique. *L'Homme* **5**.
SAHLINS, M. 1972. *Stone Age Economics*. Chicago.
SCOTT, J. and HARDIMAN, J. 1900. *Gazetteer of Upper Burma and the Shan States*. Rangoon.
STAMP, L. D. 1924. Notes on the Vegetation of Burma. *Geographical Journal* **64**.
— 1967. *Asia*. London.
STEVENSON, H. N. C. 1937. Religion and Sacrifices of the Zahao Chins. *Man*.
— 1968 (1943). *The Economics of the Central Chin Tribes*. Farnborough, Hants, England.
TERRAY, E. 1969. *Le Marxisme devant les sociétés 'primitives'*. Paris.
TÖKEI, F. 1967. Le mode de production asiatique en Chine. *Recherches internationales à la lumière du marxisme*.
WEBSTER, C. and WILSON, P. 1966. *Agriculture in the Tropics*. London.
WITTFOGEL, K. 1957. *Oriental Despotism*. New Haven.

Maurice Bloch

Property and the End of Affinity

'*dès qu'on s'aperçut qu'il était utile à un seul d'avoir des provisions pour deux, l'égalité disparut, la propriété s'introduisit, le travail devint nécessaire, et les vastes forêts se changèrent en des Campagnes riantes qu'il falut arroser de la sueur des hommes, et dans lesquelles on vit bientôt l'esclavage et la misère germer et croître avec les moissons.*'

Discours sur l'Origine et les Fondemens de l'Inégalité parmi les Hommes
J.-J. ROUSSEAU

Marx's concept of mode of production has been much discussed recently in anthropology. Much of this discussion has been difficult since the concept was first elaborated with capitalism very much in mind. Marx of course discussed other modes of production than capitalism but in less detail and perhaps with less insight. Two problems seem to me to stand out in the discussions which have followed from the attempt to apply marxist concepts to pre-industrial societies. The first is what is superstructure and what is infrastructure in these societies? In particular is kinship to be treated as part of the relations of production and of reproduction, in other words as part of the infrastructure or as part of the superstructure? The second question follows from the first: if with Marx we accept that the infrastructure must be, in the last instance, the driving force of the superstructure, how does this driving force affect the societies we are considering? The relationship is for Marx and for all honest social scientists complex but, clearly, the degree of complexity is dependent on the 'distance' of the social phenomenon under examination from the material base. In this way the relationship between kinship and the material basis of society cannot be postulated until the former question concerning the status of kinship is answered. The way out of such circular problems lies in a materialist examination of history and this is what will be presented here. In doing this I attempt to show that such an approach is not a device to overcome problems arising from its own definition but a way of accounting for history, which is the task of anthropology and the other social sciences.

Before considering the relationship of kinship and the mode of pro-

203

duction we must, as Engels did, bear in mind a third element, that is the place of property in productive resources. The relationship between property, kinship, and stratification is a familiar problem in evolutionary theories of society. On the one hand we have Rousseau's amazingly bold insight that 'inequality' 'only becomes stable and legitimate as a result of the establishment of property' (1964: 193) and on the other we have the work of Morgan, which was such a seminal influence on Engels and Marx, where types of kinship system were seen as intimately associated with the type of property system and ultimately with the mode of production. Marx and Engels's views were naturally hampered by the limitations of contemporary knowledge of pre-industrial societies, and the details of their scheme seem hardly worth criticizing. More important, however, is the clear realization throughout their work that property is represented by ideology as a relationship between people and things but is in material terms a social relationship. As is the case for many other of Marx's ideas, this premise has come into social anthropology in dribs and drabs. Maine (1861) had already shown with characteristic clarity how ancient law merged property relations and the law of persons and that it was only in 'progressive' society that property relations existed as such. Following such lawyers as Hohfeld, Gluckman (1965) and Goody (1962) have also stressed that the notion of property as a relationship between a person and a thing is a contradiction in terms and that there can only be relationships between people. In this way any statement of property or of rights is a statement of what can be done by the owner to the non-owner if these rights are infringed. Furthermore, these writers, together with Goodenough, point out how, in the various pre-industrial societies with which they are concerned, property is rightly represented as a system of social relations.

Social anthropologists seem therefore to be agreed on the two following points: (1) that property relations are a type of social relations in all societies, and (2) that in pre-industrial societies property relations are rightly represented for what they are. It is strange, therefore, that a third question which seems to follow from these two observations has not been asked: What is it in the nature of the societies where property is misrepresented as a relation between people and things which we do not find in those societies which need no such misrepresentation?

The reason why such an obvious question has not been asked seems to me in part to be due to the introduction of the concept of 'rights' to replace the concept of 'property'. This substitution has characterized the treatment of the subject in the work of many social anthropologists. Criticizing notions like that of primitive communism and its contrast with private property, anthropologists stressed that really the contrast was far from absolute. What really is the case is that property is always a 'bundle of rights' and that the contrast between primitive and industrialized is one of degree not one of kind. In primitive societies rights are distributed among many different individuals and groups, in industrialized societies they are bunched together and vested in single individuals or groups. None the less, there is a continuum from one position to the other. This is a perfectly good description of the nature of the restriction of access to productive resources in these different societies but the problem lies in the fact that the concept of right is seen to be found both in the material situation *and* in the ideological system of the people studied (usually their legal system). For the concept of right to be applicable at both the material and the ideological level would imply that ideology is a true representation of the material basis of life. This we know not to be the case simply by the fact discussed above, viz. that in some societies property is represented as though it were a relationship between people and things. It is essential, therefore, that we keep the representation of property relations and their reality separate. The continuum in material terms between different property systems does not remove the question of why property is *represented* in such sharply different ways; it makes it all the more arresting.

In this paper I shall try to answer this question by considering the reconstructed historical process which explains why two closely related cultures in Madagascar, the Merina and the Zafimaniry, differ in this respect. The Merina hold a view of property like our own. They say 'this is my land, this is his land. We must marry close relatives because we must reunite our lands'. To hear them talk, land, as property, is a more active participant in their lives than people (Bloch 1971a: 108 ff.). The Zafimaniry, on the other hand, say such things as 'if he cuts the forest here, he must come and give me honey and the backside of an animal and follow my political leadership. If I cut the forest there, then I must give him honey and the backside of an animal and follow his political leadership'. For them, owned land is not a thing at all. In their ideology it is nothing other than part of the many rules which regulate interpersonal relations.

There can be no question in a discussion such as this of giving 'sufficient' ethnography to support the argument, even if such a thing were not an illusion (Terray 1973: 133) and much of the information on which this paper is based has already been published and more is in preparation, but my purpose is to give the minimum of facts necessary for the argument. I shall first discuss only the grosser features of the traditional system of the Zafimaniry and only consider the significance of changes in this traditional system at the end of the paper.[1] A few complementary facts will be presented in the appendix.

I have already referred to the two societies I am dealing with. One is the Merina of Madagascar, and the other is a smaller group called the Zafimaniry. The Malagasy are probably, culturally and ethnically, a mixture between a Malayo-Polynesian element linked with S.E. Asia, and one or perhaps several negroid elements. The mix varies in different parts. In some areas the Malayo-Polynesian element is more obvious, while in others the negroid element is more obvious.

The central plateau of Madagascar where the Merina live (over a million of them) is the area where the Malayo-Polynesian element is strongest. The political history of the Merina clearly sets them apart from any other people in Madagascar. However, the village organization of the Merina, and of the Northern Betsileo (Raharijaona 1957) [2] who are the other people on the plateau, are almost identical. They live by a similar type of agriculture dominated by irrigated rice cultivation. In the other parts of Madagascar, the negroid element in the population is more important. In spite of this ethnic fact, however, the degree of cultural and linguistic uniformity throughout the island is very great. This is especially striking in the case of the similarity between the people of the plateau and the people of the east coast forest, who seem to share a basic cultural heritage in such matters as religion, kinship, and political concepts. In spite of this, however, the natural environment and the type of agriculture could not be more different. While the plateau is largely treeless, and has rainfall for about six months of the year, the east coast is densely covered with tropical forests. The people of the plateau concentrate their agriculture on irrigated rice valleys principally in the very narrow areas left between the hills, while the east coast forest people practise on the whole what is a very orthodox type of swidden agriculture. The basic cultural similarities of the people of the forest and the people of the plateau, taken together with their very different method of getting a living, has suggested a nice test situation to several anthropologists who are interested in the effects of economy on culture. This problem is all the more interesting because we know that the irrigated rice cultivators of today were once swidden cultivators, while in some cases some of the groups of rice cultivators of the plateau were pushed back into the forest by military defeats and once back in the forest reverted to swidden agriculture. The most famous such study is that of Linton, who argued that the passage from dry rice, cultivated in swiddens, to wet rice, cultivated in terraces, was accompanied by the development of an authoritarian state from an earlier period of greater egalitarianism (Linton 1939). This Wittfogel-like thesis would be interesting if Linton had known a little bit more about Madagascar and the people he was writing about.[3] Let me just say, however, that the people who are grouped together as Tanala, people of the forest, his example of dry-rice cultivators, include the people I shall be comparing with the Merina—that is, the Zafimaniry—and that his remarks about the passage from dry- to wet-rice cultivation were intended to apply particularly to the Zafimaniry, about whom he had obtained information from an informant, in spite of the fact that the Zafimaniry do not actually cultivate dry rice in their swidden but maize, sweet potatoes, and taro. The value, however, I see in Linton's work, is that he asked the right question, and to a very large extent this is the same question that I am asking now. I am asking again: What is the effect of passing from swidden agriculture to irrigated rice agriculture? If it seems presumptuous of me to go over where Linton seems to have failed, I do have the advantage over him of possessing the results of recent work on the Zafimaniry and of having been among them and having made relatively detailed studies of both the communities. (For information on the Zafimaniry see Verin (1964) and Couland (1973).)

The problem I am dealing with is one which to a very large extent is set by Merina ethnography. The Merina in their original area are irrigated rice cultivators. They make their terraces at the bottom of valleys, but since these are few and on the whole narrow, suitable land is very scarce.[4] The crowding of their cultivation, by contrast to the surrounding wide expanse of hill land of very poor quality, is very striking. The traditional situation is for a valley to be surrounded by several villages relying for their rice on the irrigated valley bottom, which they hold at one level in common (Bloch 1971a; Raison 1972). There is another feature of irrigated rice cultivation which is very obvious and which makes the apparent shortage of land much greater. Irrigated rice cultivation is only possible after very considerable earthworks in transforming what was once a hillside into level terraces, and also in channelling the water of the streams so that it can then be controlled to obtain the appropriate level of water in the field at different times. From an economic point of view, this has another implication than increasing land scarcity. This type of agriculture, by contrast with most other types of peasant and primitive agriculture, is, in the way an economist would put it, a type of agriculture requiring a very high capital outlay, or more straightforwardly, cultivation of a particular set of rice fields is heavily dependent on labour put in by previous generations. By contrast, however, the third factor of production (I have just considered land and capital) is much less critical: this is the factor of labour. Obviously, in irrigated rice labour is also very necessary, but there are various important reasons for aguing that, for traditional Merina production, labour is not the bottleneck of production in the way that capitalized land is. The time of the year when labour is really scarce is during transplanting, and indeed people, or rather one should say women, are very pushed during the three-month season when this can be suitably done. There are, however, two reasons why this may be less significant than might at first appear. The first is that there is an alternative technique if there really are not enough women to transplant the rice seedlings. What is done then is that instead of planting the rice seedlings first and then transplanting them into their fields the rice is broadcast directly into the flooded fields. This means that the work of several weeks of a dozen women or so can be done by just one man in a day. The yield, of course, is much lower, about two-thirds for a given area, and the ratio of seed to product is also much worse, but it does mean that in the end land will never be uncultivated because of a shortage of labour.

Labour for the Merina is not an absolute bottleneck in the way that shortage of irrigated riceland is, but in the representation of the pro-

207

ductive process labour hardly features at all. The reason for this is the place of slavery in the traditional social system. From the end of the eighteenth century the Merina state relied more and more on captured slaves obtained from neighbouring people and also bought from traders. This freed the Merina men to fight as soldiers to obtain yet further slaves. Their farms back home were worked by the captured slaves. From the point of view of the Merina, their production depended exclusively on irrigated riceland, the labour input was not theirs or at least not directly, since the immediate effort was produced by slaves and women. The representation of the mode of production—the means of production and relations of production—could thus be given as land and capital (earthworks) > than labour. This is still how the Merina think of production, thus hiding the contribution of labour but replacing it by the 'fetish': ancestral land which is seen as producing as if of itself. Production is not a matter of labour in their ideology but a matter of control of land and so the social rules regulating relations between people can be represented by rules regulating the relationship of people to land (a relationship which we noted above is necessarily an illusion). This false representation of production reproduces Merina social organization.

The dominant feature of the traditional Merina kinship system is groups which I have chosen to call demes (Bloch 1971a: 46). These are best thought of as groups of contiguous villages usually co-owning one, or several, nearby rice valleys. These villages usually have an ideology of descent from a founder or perhaps several founders, but their real symbol of continuity is in a strange way looking to the future rather than to the past. These are the tombs placed in the deme territory where people will be buried.

Tombs are the symbols of the continuity of the group not only because they are the containers of the ancestors but because they are the containers of the ancestors fixed in a particular place. The basic representation of the deme is the permanent link of people to land, the land of the ancestors (*Tanindrazanu*) (Bloch 1971a: 105). The importance of the tombs is that they create the permanent relationship of people to land by placing them there. The deme is therefore represented as a group owning land. Deme membership in Merina ideology is seen as a relationship not between people but between people and land. This misrepresentation is achieved by substituting for people corpses in the tomb and so the mechanical relation of corpses being put on a piece of ground is made to hide a fluid social relationship between people.

The establishment of edges to these corporate groups is a more complicated matter because of the basic bilateral nature of demes. Traditionally, and to a large extent still today, the definition of the edges of a descent group is due to endogamy. This is expressed by the Merina themselves as being the result of the system of inheritance of these valued and highly capitalized ricelands. The Merina call marriages

within the deme and with close kinsmen (so long as these are not inces-
tuous) 'inheritance not going away', or sometimes 'closing the breach'.
The reason is simple. With a system where all children, irrespective of
sex, inherit land, every out-marriage represents a threat of potential
alienation of land to outsiders. Endogamy leads to a mix-up of rights to
land, but however tangled they do not go outside. The representation of
marriage among the Merina is thus again seen not as a relationship
between people but as a type of property manipulation dealing with
things.

We have seen so far how the representation of the productive process
land capital > labour leads to a representation of fundamental social
relations: descent and marriage in an ideology of property. However,
two further facts follow from this for the nature of Merina concepts.

First, kinship and affinity in the broadest categorical way, are merged.
Since one marries kinsmen it is not surprising to find that there is one
category that covers both kinsman and affines—the term *havana*, while
there is no term whatsoever that can be translated as affines, or kinsmen
but excluding affines. Furthermore, there is no distinction to be made
between kinsmen–affines and neighbours, since it follows from what I
have said above that neighbours are kinsmen are affines. The world in
this system is thereby divided between two basic opposed categories:
kinsmen–affines–neighbours, that is *havana*, and outsiders, called
vahiny. This very sharp distinction is all the more important in that it
will be obvious that, with such a system, there is no way of transforming
vahiny into *havana*. One cannot become neighbours with a *vahiny*, and
also you cannot marry. He is out and that is it. Now it is not surprising
that this should be so in such a system, if we bear in mind the original
reason for endogamy, which was precisely to keep outsiders out and
stop them getting claims to this highly valued land invested with the
work of one's own ancestors. The Merina categorical system is therefore one which says: outsiders keep out of my land.

Here, however, I must defend myself against a possible criticism.
When saying that there is no category of affines among the Merina, I
am in one sense going against the evidence. Merina kinship terminology
is of a simple Hawaiian type using only distinctions by sex for the grand-
parental generation, by sex and relative age for the parental generation,
by sex and relative age for Ego's generation, and usually only one term
for descending generations. These terms can all be used very freely
according to principles which have very little to do with genealogy for
anybody who is in some ways a *havana* (Bloch: 1971b). There are, however, also certain affinal terms, but these behave very differently. These
can be glossed as spouse, mother-in-law, father-in-law, brother-in-law,
sister-in-law, son-in-law, daughter-in-law. When I say that they can be
glossed by these kin-types while I would hesitate to say anything of the
sort for the kinship terms, the reason is simple. By contrast to all the
other terms which can be freely used for large numbers of people, these

terms are restricted to own spouse, own father-in-law, etc., and the specific behaviour which accompanies them is equally so restricted. Beyond these own affines, kinship terms are again used, and indeed the relationships are normally traced through kinship rather than through affinity round the back, so to speak. I feel therefore justified in saying that there is no category of affines as a group, and although an element of affinity is present in the system it is played down.

The second consequence of the role played by the representation of the ownership of land in the Merina kinship system can be seen when we look at the concepts associated with the Merina household family. The webs of claims to land that is kinship within the deme mean that the stress of any particular group on their absolute rights is extremely disruptive. The complexity of the mixture of bilateral inheritance and repeated in-marriage means that in the end everybody has a claim to everybody's land and normally some sort of agreement is reached to let the matter lie. However, in some ways the individual existence of the domestic family continually represents a potential threat to this agreement, and everybody else's domestic family is a threat to one's own. This seems to me reflected in the way the Merina seem to consider the individuality of the nuclear family as being in some ways antisocial and by extension women, as symbols of the domestic family, are also seen as antisocial. This concept manifests itself in various forms.

One of the most striking manifestations is the way children are actively discouraged, indeed almost forced, not to spend all their time with their own parents, but to sleep in the house of other relatives, and especially to eat in the house of these other relatives. Too strong an exclusive attachment of children and parents in domestic matters is strongly disapproved of. This insistence that parent–child links should not be exclusive manifests itself in an extreme form by swopping around of children in a more permanent way: fostering, a practice the frequency of which is extremely high among the Merina. The notion that the individual household is antisocial also manifests itself in various forms of 'assaults' on the domestic unit, represented by women. A kind of anti-women ideology can be seen in the way that kinsmen or kinswomen passing the house of a neighbour will snatch food in the kitchen and try to disrupt the cooking process or insult the housewife in various semi-ritual ways (Bloch 1971a: 101).

When a kinsman passes the house of a relative, he shouts out: 'What's cooking?' as if immediately demanding food. The woman at the hearth will answer: 'It is just about ready' or 'It will be ready soon.' Normally the kinsman will not stop, but just might throw in for good measure a remark like: 'I wouldn't wait for *your* cooking anyway'. Otherwise he might just go in and help himself in a way which is reminiscent of snatching. This negation of the individual household and the parent–child link reaches its clearest level of expression in the Merina circumcision ceremony, where the child is snatched from his mother and to a lesser extent from his father inside the house to be taken outside by the united men of the deme to be circumcised. In other words, the sharp division of the social world between *havana* and *vahiny*, which I referred to above, is yet further heightened by an attempt at producing an undifferentiated category of *havana* where the division of the domestic groups within the category is ignored. The *vahiny* category itself is, of course, undifferentiated by definition.

The kind of analysis produced so far stresses first of all a series of connections. These connections can be summarized in the following way:

1 Techniques $+$ environment imply for the Merina: (a) shortage of land, and (b) highly capitalized land.

$$+$$

2 Relations of production, especially slavery, imply devaluation of labour.

$$\downarrow$$

3 Taken together, (1) $+$ (2) are ideologically represented as land $+$ capital $>$ labour.

$$\downarrow$$

4 This representation (3) implies a representation of social relations in which demes are seen as groups bound by land and marriages are seen as property deals.

$$\downarrow$$

5 This implies a system of social categories (terminology) which divides sharply between insiders (*havana*) and outsiders (*vahiny*) and rules out the possibility of transforming one into the other.
∴ *Havana* $-\!/\!\!\to$ *Vahiny*.

$$\downarrow$$

6 This implies a view of the domestic unit symbolized by women as antisocial.

The similarity of these conclusions to those of Leach in *Pul Eliya* (1961) is very clear. In Ceylon, in a village based on irrigated-rice cultivation, Leach argues that kinship and property are much the same, or in other words that kinship is a way of talking about property. The difference between Leach and myself is also clear. While Leach talks of property as though it equalled the mode of production, I see it here as already part of the superstructure. For me, property in these systems is already 'talking about' production and indeed misrepresenting it. The link between property and kinship is between two aspects of the super-structure, not between the superstructure and the infrastructure.

The system of connections given above, as it stands, however, is nothing more than that. It says nothing definitely about causation, it only demonstrates 'fit'. To go and try to understand the *necessary* relations between these levels we must move to an examination of other evidence.

The analysis presented so far is satisfactory for the Merina, but here we face a major problem. The general features of the formal aspects of the kinship terminology and the social categorizing which we have examined for the Merina are not limited to the Merina at all, but seem to be very widespread throughout Madagascar; in particular it is reported in the literature for people whose mode of production is entirely different. Does that mean that the kind of connection between production and kinship outlined here is somehow illusory?—an illusion that I may say would be shared as much by myself as it is by the Merina, since it is they who stress the importance of keeping riceland within the deme through endogamous marriages. To test the hypothesis I turn my attention to another Malagasy people with similar kinship categories but practising swidden cultivation—the Zafimaniry. The reason why swidden cultivation was chosen was that in some ways the economic implications of shifting cultivation can be said to be almost the opposite of those of irrigated-rice agriculture. In swidden agriculture, almost by definition, land is not ancestral property, since there is a sense in which, in shifting cultivation, labour creates land, that is by clearing the forest. Second, although an initial capital investment can be said to be made by the original clearing it is an investment for only a very short time, completely unlike the kind of investment involved in making rice terraces, which is of value for perhaps a century or more. So, in such a system, labour is the bottleneck in the productive system, the limiting factor on the amount of production, although what particular kind of labour seems to vary from one swidden system to another. Among the Iban of Borneo (Freeman 1970) or the Majangir of Ethopia (Stauder 1971), it is clear that it is labour in weeding which is the bottleneck. Among the Zafimaniry it is weeding to a certain extent, but above all the work involved in frightening away birds when the crops are ripening (Couland 1973: 163). Putting it in a more concrete way, we can say that a newcomer household joining a village practising irrigated rice cultivation diminishes the per capita product since it will have to be given some of this land, while an outsider joining a village of swidden cultivators at least does not diminish the per capita income but may even actually increase it. This being so, we can ask the question: How can the Zafimaniry possibly hold a formally similar system of kinship categories to that of the Merina, when their production seems to imply the very opposite premises?

The technical and ecologically determined aspects of production among the Zafimaniry stress labour as the significant factor but this is strengthened because the relations of production do not require the mystification of property that we find for the Merina. The Zafimaniry, like the peoples discussed by Gluckman (1965: ch. 3), rightly represent property relations as part of social relations, so access to land is seen as the same kind of thing as relations of labour, that is a type of social relations. Second, labour is part of the social relations for the Zafimaniry because they do not rely on a class of slaves [5] as do the Merina, but do the labour themselves. Production is directly seen to be the result of interpersonal relations and so we can say that the representation of their production is the exact opposite of that of the Merina: labour > land and capital.

One qualification to this statement must be made. The Zafimaniry do not think of relations of production as 'labour', a thing separated from aspects of interpersonal relations. Marx's work would lead us to suspect this, since he shows how the notion of labour as a commodity is closely linked with the capitalist mode of production.

The Zafimaniry do not therefore consider labour as a factor in their relationships; indeed, they have no word that could possibly be translated as labour. For them, the relationship is the relationship is the relationship. Thus, when I stress how the Zafimaniry system is well adapted to the requirements of people who will do such things as frighten away parrots, one cannot separate this from the requirements of people who will also be political followers. Indeed, there is no distinction, because the relationship does not separate activities and make them into things. This does not mean that it would perhaps be worthwhile rephrasing the conclusion so far reached and to say that the Merina system is concerned with property and is antisocial in that it is concerned with keeping people away from this property, while the Zafimaniry system is concerned with people both as political and economic units and is social since it is concerned with bringing people in. This being so, we can again ask the question: how can the Zafimaniry possibly hold a similar system of kinship categories to those of the Merina, when their mode of production seems to imply the very opposite premises?

The Zafimaniry number approximately 15,000 (Couland 1973) and are settled on the edge of the plateau in an area which is at much the same altitude as the plateau itself, but forested like the east coast area of Madagascar. It is extremely mountainous country and the villages are a long way one from another, perched on hilltops or mountain tops surrounded by a sea of forest. Various attempts at political control over them have gone on from the eighteenth century onwards, but they were on the whole so inaccessible that they were never truly under anyone's political rule and this is still so today. More relevant than political overlordship is the system whereby the locality and kinship system forms links between villages. D. Couland, a geographer who had worked in the area before me, showed me what looked like a massive genealogy of the Tiv kind (Couland 1973: 118–19), which he said included all the Zafimaniry. At first I found this very puzzling, since it was most un-Malagasy. After a short period, however, I realized that this was not a genealogy of ancestors but a list of villages placed in a genealogical relationship, parent villages being villages from which children villages had split off to form new units. Sometimes these villages were associated with certain named ancestors, sometimes not; but never was it the ancestors who were stressed, it was the villages. And indeed it is quite

213

interesting that it is possible to produce a genealogy just as satisfactorily with the names of localities as it is with people. The villages are made up of houses, surprisingly solid houses for shifting cultivators, until one knows that they are like Meccano and can be unpegged and moved to another village and reassembled in a day. Generally each house contains an elementary family (Couland 1973: 78–9). The households are related in the following number of ways. A new village may be composed of almost any selection of houses from the old village from which it stems; but once there, sons should ideally build their houses in the villages of the parents with whom they have been living. If one thing is unthinkable it is uxorilocal marriage. This, however, does not mean that in time the villages become simply patrilineal descent groups, because it is acceptable for sons to go and live in their mothers' or their mothers' brothers' village. If they do so they are in no way inferior in status to people who are patrilineally linked with the previous generation in the village. The village can then be seen formally as a non-unilineal descent group, but this would be misleading because the Zafimaniry do not really stress descent to any extent. Much more relevant is the system of marriage alliances. This, however, proved quite difficult to isolate. The basis of my problem was that the Zafimaniry produced no preferential or prescribed marriage rules when asked. It was only when I had obtained a genealogy of actual marriages that I was able to see a clear pattern.[6]

The village I studied was divided into two halves, each under the leadership of different elders, and the frequency of marriages between the two halves was very high indeed. This looked at first like a moiety system, but the reason why the regular exchanges of women was not expressed by a marriage rule is also clear. The basis of the exchange was the two geographical halves of the village, but since these were not lineal groups no rules specifying certain relatives could express the exchange. The categories of the two halves of the village were, however, quite clear; after my laborious work with the genealogy people *then* agreed that they did indeed normally marry between these two halves named after topographical features. It also became clear in time that affinal terms tended to be used between these two halves, and the joking behaviour associated with affines was also characteristic of this relationship.

This moiety system defined relationships within the village, and the fact of intermarrying in this way was given me as a sign of the unity of the village. Indeed, one can read the village genealogies backwards and see that the accompanying territorial segmentation of villages is a process of segmentation linked to the process of marriage exchange. If one thinks of the primary unit as two intermarrying moieties, segmentation begins when one of the moieties begins to feel itself so large as to be able to marry within itself and thus divide itself into two moieties, at the same time diminishing the frequency of marriages with a higher-level moiety with which it had intermarried previously. We therefore get the following sort of pattern:

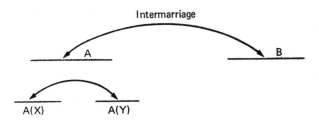

Here, however, the significance of the fact that we are not dealing with a categorical rule must again be borne in mind. This process of segmentation is painless; no rules are broken and the breach need never be final. Indeed, it will not normally be final, producing the following type of pattern:

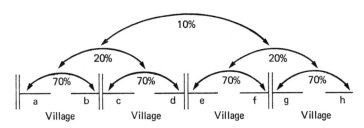

Percentages are of total marriages within one village

This diagram is a simplification of reality. An actual example is given in the appendix. It is possible that in some cases a village may consist of only one moiety, e.g. *a*, the other being a separate local unit. In other words, options and exchange of social relationships are not normally completely closed but may well be maintained. This marriage policy can, also, be projected forward. A village divided into moities between which 70 per cent of the marriages take place can begin to intermarry with another village at a rate of 20 per cent of marriages, thus at one level putting this new village in the kind of moiety relation with itself that it might have with another village with which it shares common descent.

Such a system is well adapted to the two requirements of mobility and the realization of the primacy of labour, as well adapted as the Merina system is adapted to the concept of property. It is a system where a household can maintain a large number of links with other villages, which it may then join if, for example, the forest should become exhausted in its own village. Furthermore, it is a system in which a household can form new links with other villages (usually with virgin forest) for the same purpose. This gives, for the individual household,

215

the possibility of moving from village to village and of choosing between different villages. This enables the Zafimaniry to move through the forest as it becomes exhausted, less by the movement of villages than by the flow of households through villages. Second, the system is well adapted for the double purpose of drawing people to oneself and drawing oneself to others. In other words, in transforming outsiders into kinsmen. The steps are simple. First, intermarriage with either neighbours or complete foreigners is possible. This turns them into affines, who at the next generation may either remain as affines or be transformed into kinsmen, according to where they choose to live. The contrast with the Merina system is therefore complete. The Zafimaniry system is well adapted to mobility, while the Merina system is, in fact, a denial of the possibility of movement. The Zafimaniry system opens alleys of transformation of outsiders into insiders by means of affinity, while the Merina system closes them by denying the category of affines.

Schematically we can contrast the Merina kinship category system as one that classifies the world as:

Outsiders ‖ Insiders
Vahiny ‖ *Havana* (Kinsmen–Affines–Neighbours)

where ‖ represents an unbridgeable division; whereas the Zafimaniry kinship category system can be represented as:

Outsiders⟶Neighbours⟶Affines⟶Kinsmen

where ⟶ represents a potential line of transformation.

We note, therefore, that the stress on affinity as opposed to the stress on in-marriage is a critical feature differentiating the two systems. But then it may be asked: 'What is the Zafimaniry category for affines?' The first surprise here is that the Zafimaniry kinship terms are practically identical with those of the Merina. The following differences, however, exist. First, and this is a minor one, the term for brother-in-law is different for the Merina and the Zafimaniry. For the Zafimaniry it is *vady lahy* = 'male spouse'. It is intended as an insult and is part of the joking relationship that characterizes brothers-in-law in both societies. It is not normally used by the Merina but it can be used occasionally precisely as an insult. The second difference is that the age differential comparison in the ascending generation on the patrilateral side, i.e. such terms as father's older brother, father's younger brother, does not exist, and all are equally grouped with father. The third difference is of a totally distinct kind and is much more important. It concerns the use of terms (tactical meaning) rather than their moral meaning, which is the same as for the Merina (Bloch 1971b).

The terms for affines among the Merina: mother-in-law, father-in-law, brother-in-law, sister-in-law, etc., are used only for own affines, and are not in any way extended further. Thus there is no large group of affines and they are affines only in relation to Ego. However, for the

216

Zafimaniry these terms can be extended to anybody of the appropriate sex and generation in the in-marrying moiety, so there is a large group of affines. Following from this is the fact that the term *havana*, which can include affines among the Merina, is for the Zafimaniry restricted to kinsmen; members of one's own moiety. So the world is divided not into two categories but three, between *havana*, in this case kinsmen, affines, and non-kinsmen.

Furthermore, as a result of the differentiation between a group of insiders and semi-outsiders (affines), the notion of the deme has no place. The deme as a unit gains its strength as the result of in-marriage and the following clear break between *havana* and *vahiny*. This does not exist among the Zafimaniry, and marriage with non-kinsmen is not only possible but normal. Nor is the other basis of the deme, the attachment of this exclusive group to a particular territory, present with shifting cultivation. There is thus no territorially based descent group among the Zafimaniry and, significantly, their tombs tend to be outside any specially appropriated territories under rocks deep in the forest.

The implications of the presence of a group of affines are rather more complicated than might seem at first sight because of the non-lineal nature of the moities. It means that all potential affines are also po-tential kinsmen, depending on which geographical half of the village they choose to live in, a choice made for political reasons. If the husband of Ego's sister lives with his father in the other half of the village to Ego, he will be called by the affinal term *vady lahy* (brother-in-law). If he chooses to live in the same part of the village as Ego, because his mother came from this half, he will be called by a kin term *rahalahy* (brother), and likewise with other affines. Thus a relationship by marriage is not a sufficient condition for affinity, a man must also live in the right place. Furthermore, anybody living in the part of the village where one's own moiety's affines live will be referred to by an affinal term.

This is really all that can be said about the categorical system, but it is very interesting to note that with hardly any changes in the repertory of terms (nearly all the terms are used in both systems), but with different marriage rules, a slightly different application of the term *havana*, and the extension of affinal terms from individuals to a group, a completely different kinship system from the social point of view can be produced.

Before we consider the importance of this at a more general theo-retical level, yet one final fact must be noted. I pointed out how, as a result of the stress on the unity of the deme and the importance of not distinguishing between individual rights within the group, the domestic family is devalued among the Merina. We find that this is not at all so among the Zafimaniry.[7] Indeed, the wider group is extremely vague conceptually. It can be recognized as existing, and it has a much more physical existence than it has among the Merina, but at an ideological level it is extremely weak (Couland 1973: 93). On the other hand, the primary existence of the domestic group as an ideological concept is stressed throughout Zafimaniry ideology. Of course, stressing the individuality of the domestic group among the Zafimaniry presents no threat to anyone at all, and it is also associated with the possibility of this individual domestic group moving from village to village—a necessity with the particular type of agriculture.

To conclude this brief examination of the Zafimaniry's traditional mode of production and society, we may again summarize the connections outlined above as we did for the Merina.

1 Techniques + environment imply for the Zafimaniry (a) no attachment to land and the need for mobility and (b) shortage of labour for the protection of the crop.

+

2 Relations of production not differentiated from other aspects of social life.

↓

3 Taken together, (1) + (2) result in the Zafimaniry mode of production, which is represented (accurately) as people (labour) > land + capital.

↓

4 This representation (3) implies production seen as the result of labour.

↓

5 This implies a system of social categories which enable people to draw themselves closer to others to facilitate labour cooperation. Neighbours——→affines——→kinsmen.

↓

6 This implies a stress on the domestic unit as an independent force.

The comparison of the two systems of connection described here raises several questions. I want to consider two here by way of conclusion. First, since the repertory of kinship terms of the Merina and the Zafimaniry are almost identical, does that mean that there is no connection between social systems and kinship terms and that kinship terms are therefore in no way related to the mode of production? Second, if the Merina mode of production was substituted for the Zafimaniry mode, would the social system transform itself accordingly and would the reverse process also be possible? In other words: can we move on from demonstrating 'fit' to demonstrating causality?

To talk of the adaptation of a mode of production and a conceptual system along the lines suggested so far is a way of suggesting a historical connection without history, a process which the criticisms made of such studies as those of Redfield in Yucatan should warn us against. So to complete the argument I want to consider what has happened as a result of two actually documented changes. This can be done because some Zafimaniry, as a result of increasing population pressure, have had to turn to irrigated rice agriculture, while many Merina have had to adapt to a situation where labour rather than land is at a premium, and mobility essential.

Let us first consider the Zafimaniry situation. Zafimaniry villages have, in the past and still now occasionally, been caught in the rear in a general movement through the forest from the west to the east, so being in the rearguard they have suddenly found themselves in an area where they could not expand territorially any more (Couland 1973: ch. 3 [8]). They have consequently had to return much more often to their swiddens than they would have wished, a process leading to a familiar deterioration of the soil. This ultimately brings about the kind of vegetation that we are familiar with on the plateau, a poor savannah and no forest. When this happens, the Zafimaniry have had inevitably to turn to irrigated rice cultivation in much the same way as the Merina probably did a few centuries before when the forest in their homeland ran out. What happens when this occurs? I studied one village [9] which had gone very far along this course, and although a rather superficial study it made certain things quite clear. First, inheritance was a major topic of conversation, while this is not so in those Zafimaniry villages practising swidden agriculture, and I was told of the typical Merina marriages: 'inheritance not going away'. Further evidence from this village seemed to suggest that the actual pattern of marriages was losing its moiety character and becoming more like that of the Merina, that is generalized exchange within a small endogamous group. Here, however, I have a great problem demonstrating this. I have a genealogy of the whole village linking everybody up, but it is information not obtained by myself, and as a result of the non-lineal nature of the moiety system a genealogical record is not enough to demonstrate the existence of this sort of network or the absence of the moiety system. If marriage was becoming more and more directly linked with problems of inheritance, as is suggested, it is perfectly clear that the whole system would almost automatically transform itself into a deme situation, where affinity is played down and where unbridgeable barriers are established between outsiders and insiders. The fascinating thing to me here is that this radical transformation is possible quasi-mechanically from the Zafimaniry system, without any categories or ethical principles being changed or even challenged but simply by the introduction of permanently held land invested by the labour of previous generations. This may still seem rather hypothetical but it is, I think, a fairly reasonable hypothesis. One ethnographic fact that tends to confirm that this process is happening and that the Zafimaniry are in some ways aware of it, was an event I witnessed almost the first day I arrived in the village where I was to work. I went to see an old man who wanted to make some rice fields and he had taken some of his daughter's sons—strong, strapping lads—with him. When we got to the place a long and very hard bargaining session took place over how much the youths should be paid. The Merina boy who was with me found the whole proceedings terribly

219

shocking and I must say I myself found it rather unpleasant. When we returned to the village I discussed the situation with several people, who said that the making of rice fields was an entirely different type of cultivation from shifting cultivation. For other work the youths would never ask for payments from their grandfathers, but this was special cultivation, not the cultivation of the ancestors. They would not elaborate further, but the distinction is suggestive. This is work which transforms itself into inheritance, which is a permanent asset, therefore an asset of potential inequality which, if not repaid in kind, is a token of future exclusion.

I am arguing that, theoretically at least, the adaptation of the Zafimaniry kinship system into the Merina one is an almost automatic result of the type of property introduced as a result of settled agriculture. As soon as in-marriage for purposes of keeping land within a group of close relatives takes place, given that a rule of bilateral inheritance exists, the moiety pattern produced by political marriage alliances among the Zafimaniry disappears. It is replaced by an undifferentiated single endogamous group within which marriage relations do not form any particular pattern (complex structure). This means that, simply as a result of a different marriage policy employed by the actors, demes appear. This change in marriage policy has not in any way meant a change in marriage rules. The Zafimaniry had no preferential marriage rules; their *de facto* marriage pattern was produced by the concerns of ensuring mobility and building links for cooperation. As they change their marriage policy, they are only doing what they had done before: followed their own interests, which have changed as a result of their new concern with land. By doing this, however, they do more than just create demes, i.e. in-marrying groups attached to a locality, they also reduce the application of affinal terms. Affines are no longer a group standing in relation to another group, but a few people standing in an affinal relation to Ego. The group as a whole is therefore represented as a group of kinsmen, and it is among your kinsmen that you look for a spouse. In other words, by doing nothing other than change the actors' marriage policy, the Zafimaniry kinship system can be transformed into the Merina one. No changes in marriage rules or kinship terminology need occur to wipe out affines as a significant social category and to produce a system where people are basically classed as either insiders or outsiders.

If the transformation of the Zafimaniry kinship system into that of the Merina is a simple step, we cannot assume that the new Zafimaniry system will be represented in exactly the same say, since one element of the traditional Merina mode of production is missing in the new Zafimaniry situation. This element is slavery. In the Merina case it led to the total devaluation of labour in the representation of the Merina mode of production. This one would not expect to happen in the new Zafimaniry system.

Now the next question is: What happens the other way round? Here we have rather better evidence. The Merina, after the French conquest, and as a result of the freeing of the slaves, and the pacification of their frontiers, began to pour out of their traditional territory to new empty lands. Irrigated rice cultivators arriving on new land are, however, faced with the opposite economic problem to that of irrigated rice cultivators already settled. Their greatest need suddenly is labour to make new terraces, but they have no slaves. Moreover, an automatic result of this sort of territorial movement is that, unless the whole deme moves in a body, the people spacing themselves around the new valleys will not be *havana*. However, they have come with a conceptual system which contrasts sharply *havana* and *vahiny* and excludes the possibility of transforming one into the other. Can there be a modification of this system back into a Zafimaniry system? The answer is no, and is interesting for our understanding of the dramatic effect of having represented the means of production as private property. (See Bloch 1971a for a fuller discussion.)

I have discussed elsewhere how the absolute notion of *havana* presents a most serious moral problem in these new areas, as people try to form links with non-kinsmen. They have to pretend in one context that their cooperators are kinsmen, yet as soon as their backs are turned they deny it—a situation leading to very great tension. In other words, the division of the social world into insiders and outsiders cannot be smoothly reversed by easily reintroducing a type of half-out-siders (affines). The Merina artificial kinsmen are 'half-outsiders' because of the economic requirements of the situation they find themselves in, but they cannot fit these people into their scheme without breaking the rules, that is behaving towards *vahiny* in a way which is inappropriate. This ambiguity is not just terminological but leads to further social action such as witchcraft accusations and leading a 'double' life; on one side pretending that the new locality is the total social world, and on the other that the ancestral society is the total social world. The implication of all this is that, whereas one conceptual configuration (the Zafimaniry) contains within itself the possibility of smoothly transforming itself into another, the other (the Merina) seems to hold within its very *form* obstacles to a reverse transformation. In this way one can say that it may be the source of yet further dialectical processes which it would not be too far-fetched to argue constitute present-day Merina society.

CONCLUSIONS

At the start of this paper I asked three questions: (1) Under what circum-stances is property misrepresented as a relationship between people and things? (2) Is kinship a part of the infrastructure in pre-capitalist societies? (3) How is kinship determined by the material basis of society? The material presented here gives the following answers:

221

1 The misrepresentation of property relations is due, as Rousseau saw, to inequality, the fact that those in control of the political system are not the workers; but this can be so only when the social implications of the technology of production make reasonable the representation of production as the fruit of property and not of labour. This is the traditional Merina situation.

2 The first point to notice here is that, before a connection can be established between the mode of production and the kinship system, another level (at least for the Merina case) needs to be analysed. That is the representation of the mode of production. In the Merina system, as is the case for the capitalist mode of production, the folk economics system is already part of the superstructure and stands in the kind of dialectical relation with the mode of production that superstructure does to infrastructure. In the Zafimaniry case, however, the representation of the mode of production is an accurate representation and therefore is the mode of production. Again, as for the Merina, the representation of the mode of production and the kinship system are congruent. But here this means that the mode of production, the representation of this mode of production, and the kinship system are one and the same thing. The kinship system for the Zafimaniry is the relations of production. In other words, while for the Merina the kinship system is part of the superstructure, for the Zafimaniry it is part of the infrastructure. The reason for this difference can be seen in the place of slavery in the Merina social system in the context of Merina production.

3 The conclusions given immediately above furnish the answer to the third question. Since, for the Zafimaniry, kinship is itself part of the mode of production it changes directly in reaction to changes in the mode of production. For the Merina case, changes in the mode of production affect kinship not directly but through a dialectical process. The result of a change in the mode of production on the superstructure can be understood only in terms of the form of the superstructure seen separately from the form of the infrastructure. The historical transformations of the Merina system are also determined by changes in the mode of production, but in this case only in the last instance.

Appendix

The purpose of this appendix is to give an actual example of the kinship structure of a Zafimaniry village. Examples of Merina villages are given in *Placing the Dead*.

The village studied is called Ranomena [10] and lies in the very heart of Zafimaniry country. Its population is 192, which makes it typical among Zafimaniry villages. (It is almost exactly the norm for a village, Couland 1973: 77.) The village is approximately seventy years old since it was founded from another village, Ambohimanjaka. The old Ambohimanjaka is no longer in existence, but it has two 'children' villages, Ranomena and the new Ambohimanjaka. None of the people of the founding generation who left old Ambohimanjaka are still alive, but the next generation is still partly represented.

It is a village which still has a lot (by Zafimaniry standards) of forest and has hardly turned to irrigated rice cultivation. There are, however, some more favoured villages in this respect (see Couland 1973: passim).

This is a village where the two moieties are clearly distinct, their houses being on two levels on the hill which the village crowns. These two areas and the two moieties are referred to as Ranomena High and Ranomena Low. This use of hierarchical terms to distinguish the two moieties is not typical and has no social significance. Ranomena Low consists of 74 people, while Ranomena High consists of 119. Ranomena High is showing a tendency to internal division into two sub-moieties— that is, marriages are beginning to occur within it. The two moieties are the descendants of four siblings, only one of whom is still alive. The fact that three of these siblings are women is interesting. These women went to live in their husband's village at marriage (in the case of two of them this was New Ambohimanjaka, in the third case I have no information). Their children, however, went back to live in their mother's village. This high incidence of matrilocality is to be explained by the fact that Ranomena was then a new village with abundant forest resources, while Ambohimanjaka was already much less well provided. Another element is also found in Ranomena High, that is the descendants of siblings of an in-marrying woman. This woman looked after her young siblings when they were orphaned. They then settled in the village and merged with Ranomena High. Of the 37 married couples present in the village at the time of fieldwork, 25 live in Ranomena High and 12 in Ranomena Low. Of these, 21 were couples where both the spouses came from the same village, viz. Ranomena. This means that of 58 married people in Ranomena 42 (72 per cent) had married within the village while 16 (28 per cent) had married out. Of those 21 married couples in Ranomena, 15 had one partner from Ranomena High and one partner from Ranomena Low, while in the case of 6 of these marriages both partners came from one moiety: Ranomena High. The exchange between the two moieties was symmetrical. Ranomena High received 8 women; Ranomena Low received 7. The situation can be represented diagrammatically thus:

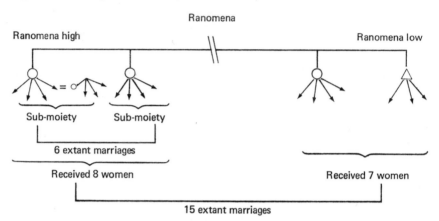

Now, if we want to turn to the nature of marriages between people from Ranomena and other villages, several facts must first be noted. These marriages were almost all contacted with three other villages: Ambohimanarivo, Ambohimanjaka, Soahanitanana. In the genealogy of villages these villages are linked in the following way:

Villages not still existing are given in italics (see Couland 1973: 118, for a slightly different genealogy).

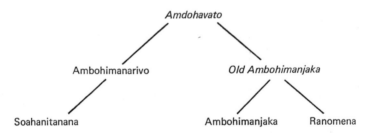

Of the four villages, Ambohimanjaka and Ambohimanarivo had less good forest for swiddens while Soahanitanana had more.

Less Forest for Swiddens		More Forest for Swiddens
Ambohimanjaka	Ranomena	Soahanitanana
Ambohimanarivo		

If we look at marriages recorded in my Ranomena genealogy between Ranomena and the other three, we get the following figures:

Ranomena 10   Ambohimanjaka (pop. 375)
Ranomena 8   Ambohimanarivo (pop. 400)
Ranomena 7   Soahanitanana (pop. 125)

The number of marriages with Ambohimanarivo and Ambohimanjaka
is easily explained as Ranomena maintaining its place in two previously existing moiety systems from which Ranomena originated. This
can be represented in the following way:

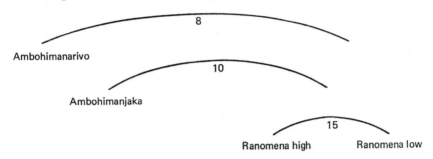

It is at first surprising to find as many as seven marriages with Soahanitanana, especially given its small size. This relatively high frequency
is all the more marked if we look at extant marriages only. This gives the
following figures.

Ranomena 6   Ambohimanjaka (pop. 375)
Ranomena 4   Ambohimanarivo (pop. 400)
Ranomena 6   Soahanitanana (pop. 125)

Another feature distinguishes the marriages between Ranomena and
Soahanitanana from the others, that is in the direction of the exchange
of women. Figures on this are very tentative since the genealogy on
which they are based was recorded in Ranomena and so, because of the
rule of uxorilocality, it probably records exactly marriages where the
women have come to live in Ranomena but does not properly record
marriages of women from Ranomena who have gone to live in other
villages, since these do not appear on the village census. None the less,
the difference between Ranomena/Soahanitanana marriage patterns
and the others is suggestive:

Extant Marriages
Ranomena   =   Ambohimanjaka
Received   Received
   4 (women)   2
Ranomena   =   Ambohimanarivo
Received   Received
   3   1
Ranomena   =   Soahanitanana
Received   Received
   3   3

225

Maurice Bloch

The figures given above suggest: (1) that more recently Ranomena has diminished the frequency of its marriages with Ambohimanjaka and Ambohimanarivo and has increased the frequency of its marriages with Soahanitanana; (2) that while Ranomena tends to receive women from Ambohimanjaka and Ambohimanarivo, it probably tends to give women to Soahanitanana. Both tendencies seem to be explicable by the fact that, because of the more favoured ecological position of Ranomena in relation to Ambohimanjaka and Ambohimanarivo, it is those villages which want to keep the link with Ranomena so that households from them will ultimately be able to move to Ranomena; and that the same relationship exists between Ranomena and Soahanitanana. However, while, for Ranomena, Ambohimanjaka and Ambohimanarivo are the past, Soahanitanana is the future, and so the Ranomena villagers are placing themselves in a moiety relationship to Soahanitanana while they are trying to extricate themselves from such a relationship with Ambohimanjaka and Ambohimanarivo. The reason for this, as people in Ranomena will admit, is the difference in amount of forest in the various villages. One question remains: Why is Soahanitanana willing to be so absorbed? The answer lies in the fact that the abundance of forest of Soahanitanana is paid for at the cost of geographical isolation. Ranomena is their nearest, indeed their only near, village. They are therefore natural and necessary allies.

Notes

1 I am not considering, for example, the growth of wage-labouring among the Zafimaniry.

2 Kottak discusses the organization of the S. Betsileo who, in terms of village organization, are much more different from the N. Betsileo than the latter are from the Merina. The Zafimaniry are closely related to the N. Betsileo (Linton 1933: 36; Verin 1964; Kottak 1971).

3 Among mis-statements made by Linton, we may note: that the Zafimaniry have extended families whereas the Betsileo do not (in fact it is the other way round); that the border Betsileo had a strong state organization (see Ratsimbazafimahefa 1971). He gives a totally erroneous kinship terminology. He makes the amazing statement that the Zafimaniry are dry-rice cultivators, which he contradicts elsewhere (Linton 1933: 46).

4 There is, of course, an exception to this in the great marshy plain that surrounds Tananarive (Isnard 1954).

5 The Zafimaniry had some slaves, but these were a small proportion of the population, quite unlike the Merina situation where more than half were slaves.

6 The discussion of kinship given here seems to contradict parts of the information given by Couland. Apart from minor but real disagreements, this discrepancy springs from the fact that I studied the ex-free Zafimaniry (nine-tenths of the population), while Couland concentrated on the ex-slaves, whose kinship system is different.

7 Women are still inferior, but for a different ideological reason.

8 The process is excellently described by Couland, but I feel he overemphasizes the present turn to riceland because of his concentration on ex-slave villages, which have the worse and more exhausted land.

9 Ambohimitombo.

10 It is referred to by Couland as Ranomena Sud.

Acknowledgements

I wish to thank the Nuffield Foundation for enabling me to carry out fieldwork in Madagascar among the Merina in 1964, 1965, and 1966, and the Social Science Research Council of Great Britain for enabling me to carry out further fieldwork in 1971 among the Merina and the Zafimaniry. I am particularly grateful to Professor P. Verin and M. D. Couland for my introduction to the Zafimaniry country and for their work, which I have relied on heavily.

I wish to thank Miss A. Akeroyd for useful comments and suggestions on an earlier draft of this paper.

References

BLOCH, M. 1971a. *Placing the Dead: Tombs, Ancestral Villages and Kinship Organisation in Madagascar*. London and New York: Seminar Press.
— 1971b. The Moral and Tactical Meaning of Kinship Terms. *Man* 6: 79–87.
COULAND, D. 1973. *Les Zafimaniry: Un groupe ethnique de Madagascar à la poursuite de la forêt*. Tananarive: Fanontam-Boky Malagasy.
ENGELS, F. 1884. *The Origin of the Family, Private Property and the State*. In *Karl Marx and Frederick Engels, Selected Works*. London: Lawrence and Wishart, 1968.
FREEMAN, D. 1970. *Report on the Iban*. London School of Economics Monographs on Social Anthropology, No. 41.
GLUCKMAN, M. 1965. *The Ideas in Barotse Jurisprudence*. New Haven and London: Yale University Press.
GOODENOUGH, W. H. 1951. *Property, Kin and Community on Truk*. Yale University Publications in Anthropology, No. 46.

GOODY, J. R. 1962. *Death, Property and the Ancestors.* Stanford, Calif.: Stanford University Press, London: Tavistock Publications.

ISNARD, H. 1954. Les Bases géographiques de la monarchie Hava. In *Eventail de l'histoire vivante: hommage à Lucien Febvre.* Paris: A. Colin.

KOTTAK, C. P. 1971. Kinship Groups and Social Calculation among the Southern Betsileo. *American Anthropologist* **73** (1): 178–93.

LEACH, E. R. 1961. *Pul Eliya, A Village in Ceylon: A Study of Land Tenure.* Cambridge University Press.

LINTON, R. 1933. *The Tanala: a Hill Tribe of Madagascar.* Chicago: Field Museum of Natural History, Publication 317.

— 1939. The Tanala of Madagascar. In A. Kardiner, *The Individual and his Society.* New York: Columbia University Press.

MAINE, H. S. 1861. *Ancient Law.* London: John Murray.

RAHARIJAONA, S. 1957. Population de la haute vallée de l'Imady, district d'Ambositra. In the Library of the Bureau pour le Développement Agricole.

RAISON, J. P. 1972. Utilisation du sol et organisation de l'espace dans l'Imerina ancienne. *Tany Malagasy* **13**.

RATSIMBAZAFIMAHEFA, P. 1971. Le Fisakana: Archéologie et couches culturelles. Musée d'Art et d'Archéologie de l'Université de Madagascar. *Travaux et Documents* **9**.

ROUSSEAU, J.-J. 1754. *Discours sur l'Origine et les Fondemens de l'Inégalité parmi les Hommes,* reprinted in J.-J. Rousseau, *Œuvres Complètes,* Vol. 3, Bibliothèque de la Pléiade, Paris: Gallimard, 1964: 171.

STAUDER, J. 1971. *The Majangir: Ecology and Society of a Southwestern Ethiopian People.* Cambridge University Press.

TERRAY, E. 1973. État, Tradition, Technologie en Afrique Noire. *Annales* **28** (5).

VERIN, P. 1964. Les Zafimaniry et leur art. Un groupe continuateur d'une tradition esthètique Malgache méconnue. *Revue de Madagascar* (27): 1–76.

Biographical Notes

BLOCH, MAURICE. Born 1939, Caen, France; educated in France and England; London School of Economics, B.A. (Hons.) anthropology; Cambridge University, Ph.D. (1968).

Fieldwork in Madagascar, 1964–6, 1971; Lecturer, University College of Swansea (University of Wales), 1968–9; Lecturer, London School of Economics, 1969– .

Author of *Placing the Dead*, 1971; and papers Malagasy on Madagascar and on anthropological theory.

FEUCHTWANG, STEPHAN. Born 1937, Germany; educated in England; Oxford University, B.A. (Hons.) Chinese; London School of Economics, M.A. anthropology. Fieldwork in Taiwan, 1966–8; Lecturer in Asian anthropology, School of Oriental and African Studies, London 1968–73. Lecturer in Sociology, The City University, 1973– .

Author of a forthcoming book on Chinese geomancy and several articles on Chinese religion.

FIRTH, SIR RAYMOND WILLIAM, Kt. 1973, F. B. A., Hon. D.Litt. (Exeter), etc. Born 1901, New Zealand. Studied at Auckland University (College), B.A., M.A.; London School of Economics, Ph.D.

Lecturer in Anthropology, University of Sydney, 1930–1; Acting Professor of Anthropology, University of Sydney, 1931–2; Lecturer in Anthropology, London School of Economics, 1933–6; Reader in Anthropology, University of London, 1936–44; Professor of Anthropology, University of London, 1944.

Author of *Primitive Economics of the New Zealand Maori*, 1929 (second edition as *Economics of the New Zealand Maori*, 1959); *We, The Tikopia*, 1936 (second edition, 1957); *Primitive Polynesian Economy*, 1939 (second Edition, 1965); *Work of the Gods in Tikopia*, 1940 (second edition, 1967); *Malay Fishermen: Their Peasant Economy*, 1946 (second edition, 1966); *Elements of Social Organization*, 1951 (third edition, 1961); *Social Change in Tikopia*, 1959; *History and Traditions of Tikopia*, 1961; *Essays on Social Organization and Values*, 1964; *Themes in Economic Anthropology*, 1967; *Tikopia Ritual and Belief*, 1967; *Rank and Religion in Tikopia*, 1980; *Symbols: Public and Private*, 1973.

229

Biographical Notes

FRIEDMAN, JONATHAN. Born 1946, New York; educated at Columbia University, B.A., 1967; École Pratique des Hautes Études, Institut d'Ethnologie, Sorbonne, Licence, 1968; Columbia University, Ph.D., 1972.

Chargé de cours, École Pratique des Hautes Études, 1972–3; Visiting Lecturer, Institute of Social Anthropology, Uppsala, Autumn 1972; Institute of Social Anthropology, Göteborg, 1973, 1974; Lecturer, University College London, 1973–4.

Author of 'Marxism, Structuralism, and Vulgar Materialism', *Man*, 1974; *System, Structure and Contradiction in the Evolution of 'Asiatic' Social Formations* (forthcoming); 'Hypothèses sur la dynamique et les transformations tribales', *L'Homme*, 1975; 'Religion as Economy and Economy as Religion' in *The Great Feast*, Festschrift for K. G. Izikowitz (forthcoming); 'Le lieu du fétichisme et le problème des interprétations matérialistes', *La Pensée*, 1975; *Marxism, Structuralism, and Vulgar Materialism* (forthcoming).

Editor, with M. J. Rowlands, of *The Evolution of Social Systems* (papers presented at the Seminar on Archaeology and Related Subjects, London, 1974) (forthcoming).

GODELIER, MAURICE. Born 1934, Cambrai, France; educated at École Normale Supérieure, Aggrégation de Philosophie.

Fieldwork in New Guinea, 1967–9. Currently Sous-Directeur d'Études, École Pratique des Hautes Études, VIième section.

Author of *Rationality and Irrationality in Economics* (French edition 1966, English translation 1973); *Horizon: trajets marxistes en anthropologie*, 1973.

Editor of *Anthropologie économique*, 1974.

KAHN, JOEL SIMMONS. Born 1946, Oshkosh, Wisconsin, USA. Studied at Princeton University; Cornell University, B.A.; London School of Economics, M. Phil., Ph.D. 1974.

Field research in Indonesia, financed by the London–Cornell Project for Southeast Asia, 1970–2; part-time Lecturer in Anthropology, Goldsmith's College, London, 1972–3; Temporary Lecturer in Anthropology, University College, London, 1973– .

TERRAY, EMMANUEL. Born 1935, Paris. Studied at the École Normale Supérieure (Rue d'Ulm) and at the University of Paris.

Chargé d'enseignement at the University of Abidjan, 1964–8; and at the University of Paris VIII, 1968– .

Author of *L'Organisation sociale des Dida*, 1969; *Le Marxisme devant les sociétés 'primitives'*, 1969 (translated as *Marxism and 'Primitive' Societies*, 1972).

230

Name Index

Abdullah, T., 156n, 157
Alavi, H., 137, 157
Alland, A., 105, 109–10, 134n, 134
Allen, B. C., 192, 200
Althusser, L., xi, xiii, 17, 25n, 68–70, 81, 90–1, 146
Althusser, L., and Balibar, E., 17, 90, 103, 134, 157, 164, 200
Anderson, J., 200
Aquinas, St Thomas, 55n
Aron, R., 54n, 55n, 56n, 57
Asad, T., 49, 53n, 57
Avineri, S., 45, 57

Bachtiar, H., 156n, 157
Bailey, F. G., 57n, 57
Balandier, G., 56n, 57
Balibar, E., xi, 17, 103, 156n, 157, 164
Banfield, E. C., and Banfield, L. F., 152–153, 157
Barnard, J. T. O., 200
Barton, R., 200
Belshaw, C. S., 55n, 57
Benda, H., and McVey, R. T., 148, 156n, 157
Benedict, P., 200
Benquey, Capt., 101, 113–17, 119–20, 124, 126, 132, 134n
Bettelheim, C., 200
Binger, L., 104, 121, 134n, 134
Birdsell, J., 8, 9, 25
Birnbaum, N., 31, 49, 52, 54n, 57
Blaut, H. M., 200
Bloch, M., xiv, 205, 207–10, 216, 221, 227
Bohannan, P., 54n, 57
Bottomore, T. B., 32, 54n, 55n, 57
Bottomore, T. B., and Rubel, M., 54n, 57
Bouglé, C., 54n
Bowdich, T., 118–19, 125, 134
Boyle, R., 29, 52, 58
Braulot, Capt., 121, 135
Brunhoff, S. de, 35, 55n, 58

Bryce, J. A., 200
Buchanan, F. R., 200
Bukharin, N., 93, 135
Burridge, K., 50–1, 57n, 58
Busia, K., 109, 135
Butler, J., 194, 200

Carey, B., and Tuck, H., 200
Carrapiett, W. J. S., 200
Clozel, F. J., 101, 115–16, 123, 126, 135
Clozel, F. J., and Villamur, R., 114–16, 120, 132, 134n, 135
Comte, A., 33
Confucius, 79
Coquery-Vidrovitch, C., 56n, 58
Coryton, J., 200
Couland, D., 207, 212–14, 217, 219, 223–224, 226n, 227
Cramer, P. J. S., 156n, 157
Cuisinier, J., 156n, 157
Cuvillier, A., 55n, 58

Davidson, D. S., 8, 25
Dawson, G. W., 200
Diamond, S., 46, 54n, 58
Draye, 193
Dumont, L., 62, 66–7, 70, 81
Dunayevskaya, R., 56n, 58
Dupuis, J., 122, 125, 135
Durkheim, E., 31–3, 53, 53n, 54n, 55n, 58, 61
Durkheim, E., and Mauss, M., 32, 54, 58

Ekholm, K., 199n, 200
Elkin, A. P., 5, 8, 13, 21, 25
Engels, F., xv, 23n, 25, 31–3, 41–2, 46, 50, 54n, 56n, 61, 85–6, 92, 95, 135, 204, 227
Espinas, A., 42
Evans–Pritchard, E. E., xiii

Fei Hsiao-t'ung, 74–5, 77, 81
Feuchtwang, S., xiii, xiv, 78–9, 81

231

Name Index

Subject Index